The Economic Analysis of Government
and Related Themes

The Economic Analysis of Government
and Related Themes

ALAN PEACOCK

Martin Robertson

First published in 1979 by Martin Robertson & Co. Ltd., 108 Cowley Road, Oxford OX4 1JF.

ISBN 0 85520 298 X

Typeset by Santype International Ltd., Salisbury
Printed and bound by Richard Clay (The Chaucer Press) Ltd., Bungay, Suffolk.

Contents

Foreword

It is somehow gratifying to be led to believe by one's publisher that one's contributions that have appeared in a wide variety of journals and in other forms have a market as a collection, that the whole is greater than its parts. I shall not question the commercial judgement of my good friend, David Martin, but I do owe an explanation to readers of what might be the benefits of this arrangement.

It is the case that this collection is brought together from widely scattered sources – journals, reviews and Festschriften. David Martin's request has been echoed by a surprising number of colleagues who have asked me to reduce the costs of search and retrieval associated with this relative inaccessibility. I have no regrets at having responded to requests to write for colleagues in many parts of the world and am grateful to them for allowing me to republish. Full acknowledgment of sources is given on p. ix.

Furthermore, gathering together this collection has given me the opportunity to make some necessary revisions and occasional extensions to the original texts. It is just possible that these have improved the final product. In addition I have used the opportunity to introduce this volume with an essay written specially for the occasion. In it I draw upon a longstanding interest in the economics of public finance and public policy generally as well as on my experience as an economist acting as a consultant in both the private and public sector. It is hoped that this introductory essay, together with the introductions to each section of the work, will aid the reader in subsequent scrutiny of each chapter.

Finally, I should mention that I have confined the selection to only certain subjects that I have written about in recent years. The bulk of the articles are contributions to contemporary debates on the economics of public policy, but I have largely excluded those concerned with the economics of fiscal policy and the economics of the arts. The former subject I hope to return to in a subsequent edition of my book with Keith Shaw, *The Economic Theory of Fiscal Policy*. The latter is adequately represented in *The Economics of the Arts* edited by Mark Blaug. I have reprinted two articles written with Charles Rowley because they fit in with the general theme of the work, and I owe a special debt to him for that stimulating experience, but have omitted the many other joint articles that have represented pleasurable collaboration with colleagues in all parts of the world.

How much I owe to this collaboration will be apparent throughout the volume, particularly that which I enjoyed during my relatively long period at the University of York (1962–78). There I was lucky enough to have experienced the excitement of starting a new Department of Economics and of founding, with Jack Wiseman of course, the Institute of Social and Economic Research. I find it easier than I had expected to acknowledge that these institutions now flourish without me. It is to my York colleagues, staff and students past and present, and to York's many visiting scholars who have stimulated us so much that this collection is dedicated.

University College at Buckingham
December 1978

Acknowledgments

The author gratefully acknowledges the help received and, where appropriate, the permission given by the following individuals and organisations in respect of previously published material:

The Editors, *Journal of Political Economy*
The Oxford University Press
The Editor, *Journal of Public Economics*
The Editor, *Scottish Journal of Political Economy*
The Institute of Economic Affairs
Croom Helm, Ltd., London
The Board of Editors, *Public Finance*
JCB Mohr (Paul Siebeck), Tübingen
Duncker and Humblot, Berlin
North Holland Publishing Company, Amsterdam
The Editors, *Finanzarchiv*
The Editor, *Lloyds Bank Review*
The Editor, *Three Banks Review*

to York Economists — everywhere

PART I

Introduction

CHAPTER 1

The Economic Analysis of Government

I. INTRODUCTION

In April 1976 the Treasury announced the setting up of a Committee on Policy Optimisation to be chaired by Professor R. J. Ball with the following terms of reference:

> To consider the present state of development of optimal control techniques as applied to macro-economic policy. To make recommendations concerning the feasibility and the value of applying these techniques within Her Majesty's Treasury.

The Committee (Ball, 1978) duly reported in March 1978 and the result, without any doubt, is one of the most useful and interesting public documents on the contribution of modern economic analysis and econometrics to the process of policy-making.

For this work the significance of the Report lies not so much in the recognition of the role of the economist in policy making – a recurring theme in later chapters – but in the fact that anyone should take seriously the analogy between control systems and the practical operation and control of the economy. The Ball Committee are very careful in their pursuit of this analogy and their examination, for example, of the difficulties in embodying political preferences into policy models is careful and circumspect. Nor do they commit themselves to any recommendation about how politicians and bureaucrats should behave rather than how they actually do. Thus, understandably, the Report falls short of a description of the complicated bargaining structure between parts of government and between government and other interest groups within which economic advice has to operate.

It is the purpose of this chapter to outline this bargaining structure and in the course of doing so to demonstrate the contribution that economic analysis can make in attempting to understand its operation. Subsequent chapters, notably chapters 6 and 16, consider parts of this structure in more detail. Apart from any intrinsic interest in the employment of economic analysis in 'unwonted places', this chapter will have achieved one of its main

3

purposes if it can show economists how they can employ the tools of their own trade to uncover the obstacles that lie in the way of their own advice being accepted by those who formulate and execute public policy.

II. THE ECONOMIST'S CONCEPTION OF THE PLACE OF GOVERNMENT IN THE ECONOMY

The normal purpose of an economic model is to explain how some part or even the whole of the economy operates and sometimes to offer guidance as to how the operation of the economy might be altered in order to meet certain objectives of policy. This latter purpose usually requires the introduction of quantification of the parameters and variables in the model – a point to which I shall return. Implicit also in this approach to economic model building is the idea that two states of world are being compared, one with a freely working economic system without government or at most a 'passive' government sector in which parameters in the model that government might control are fixed, and one with a government offered advice by economists, on the basis of the findings of the model, who are thereby placed in a position of fulfilling given policy objectives by altering parameters. Nothing in this approach necessarily requires the economist to do more than indicate what instruments of government will be appropriate for the pursuit of given policy objectives, assuming that the economist has this knowledge.

While this familiar paradigm is a useful point of departure, our approach embodies a more awkward and more ambitious task for it seeks to explain how policies are selected in the first place and how, in the course of implementation, they may be modified and extended. It has therefore to consider the political and bureaucratic process, but as economic phenomena, and therefore the motivation of politicians and bureaucrats. It has to be shown that motivation of these beings, as with households and firms, is capable of economic analysis, and this is still a matter for dispute. The task is clearly more ambitious than that found in conventional models of economic policy, where objectives of politicians are given and bureaucrats implicitly accept them. Our approach has to display the origins of these objectives and therefore to penetrate to the study of the interactions between those who formulate and execute policy and those whose actions are to be modified by policy instruments. In short, we have to justify the use of economics as a means of analysing the power structure in society from which policies emanate. It must be admitted at the outset that economics can only offer a 'technique of thinking', to use Keynes's phrase, about such matters, as will be patently clear in this and subsequent contributions in this volume.

An example that dominates a good deal of the subsequent discussion may be helpful at this stage. Modern governments in industrialised societies have in practice a wide range of instruments at their disposal for influencing the growth and structure of the economy, and this is reflected in the relative importance of the types of expenditure of the public authorities (for data see section VI). Conventional theories of economic policy have much to tell us about the way these instruments could be used, but not about how these instruments have evolved and how the choice of a particular set of instruments is made. I am not arguing that economic analysis can offer a complete or even a better explanation than other disciplines of policy evolution, but I hope to show that it does offer distinct insights.

The rest of this chapter elaborates these preliminary ideas using a simple expositional device, which is to take the conventional theory of economic policy and to show how it can be transmuted into an economic analysis of government.

III. The Conventional Theory of Economic Policy

The essence of the conventional theory of economic policy is very simple, though this is not to deny that it requires considerable sophistication and experience to understand its *modus operandi*.[1] One treats the government as one would treat a household or firm in economic analysis. The 'government', however identified, possesses a utility or welfare function containing several 'arguments' usually representing quantifiable economic objectives such as the rate of growth, rate of inflation, distribution of income, etc., which are traded off against one another. The function is maximised subject to constraints represented by the structure of the economy and the motivation of its members and by the extent of the economy's reliance on the activities of trading partners. Generally, the process of maximisation reveals that to optimise the function requires government intervention, the form of that intervention being determined by the constraints themselves, as identified by a quantitative model of the economy that, according to the analysis, best indicates the present and prospective economic situation.

Before looking more closely at the implications of the model for policy formation, it may be useful to present a very simple diagrammatic version of the model. In aggregative models of this sort, there are three, or at most four, groups of decision makers, each primarily associated with one or more major variables in the system, which the government wishes to control. In a simple Keynesian-type model of the kind used to explain fluctuations in prices, income and employment, *firms* determine the demand for physical investment and the demand for imports, *households* determine the level of consumption and *'foreigners'* determine the demand for exports. In the course of optimising the welfare function, *government* will influence the demand variables immediately controlled by the other groups and in ways that will be reflected, for example, in budget. This is so well known to be hardly worth repeating, but what is more difficult is to relate these models to the behavioural characteristics of each group of decision makers.

I shall not explore this problem but only emphasise that our model, such as it is, makes much of the fact that the motivation of the different decision makers requires careful specification.

In Figure 1.1 I identify the system of 'linkages' implied by the conventional theory of economic policy in influencing the economy to perform in an optimal fashion. Even this primitive diagram has something to tell us about the methodology of the economist who wishes to prescribe how policies may be attained.

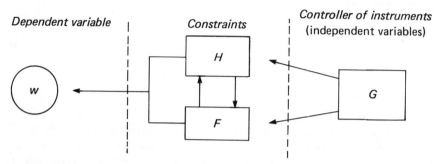

w = welfare function of 'government'
G = 'government' (collective welfare maximiser)
F = 'firms' (profit maximisers)
H = 'households' (utility maximisers)

FIGURE 1.1

First, it is assumed that the government is a unitary being with a stable welfare function that will be adhered to throughout the whole process of adjustment in maximising it. Alternatively, the adjustment process can be carried out faultlessly and instantaneously. This presupposes that it *dominates* the activities of the various organs of government both *vertically*, i.e. by layer of government, and *horizontally*, through control and coordination of policy instruments operated by individual departments of state.

Second, the government *dominates* the decision makers in the private sector, at least to the extent that by making adjustments in the opportunity sets of households and firms it can optimise its welfare function. For example, if optimising the function requires that the level of aggregate demand must be raised, the government can induce maximising firms and households to increase expenditure by the desired amount by, say, tax reductions to firms and/or increases in government transfer payments to households.

Third, recalling our interest in understanding the role of the economist himself in policy formation, it is apparent that this role is clear-cut and substantial. The economist is a specialist in denoting a *rational policy*, i.e. a policy consistent with its aims as manifested in the social welfare function. The more the claims made by the economist himself for the constrained optimisation approach to policy, the more he may be tempted therefore to dramatise his own role.

IV. Limited Explanatory Power of the Traditional Model

The theory of economic policy is first and foremost a framework for rational policy making and is not meant to offer an explanation as to how policy is in fact conducted. However, it has had more influence on the *presentation* of policy plans than is generally realised, and as such has affected the behaviour of those who are responsible for such plans.

So far as the UK is concerned, and other countries offer similar evidence, this is clearly demonstrated in the annual budget statement, which is based on a fully articulated short-term macroeconomic model in which target variables and policy variables are clearly shown. Maximisation of policy objectives traded off against one another is now fashionable jargon deployed by Cabinet ministers responsible for economic policies, by politicians interested in economic policy as well as by financial journalists and economists. The model can turn the traditional study of macroeconomics from being an arid discussion of rival theories, important though such discussion may be among pundits, into an exciting exercise in explaining the dilemma of policy choices.[2] Later chapters reflect the influence of this approach on my own thinking.

Unfortunately the world in which this kind of model might operate does not exist, and, more important in my view, it would be a world I would not like to see come into being. The latter assertion – clearly a value judgement – may be left for comment in other essays in this volume, but the former requires detailed investigation.

First, a 'government' is not a monolithic being but a collection of individuals with Cabinet status, who, while they may all trade off loyalty to one another and their party against personal ambition, have differing trade-off functions and differing perceptions as to how to maximise them. Their own welfare function, arrived at by intra-Cabinet bargaining, may not be stable.

Second, firms and households are not passive adjusters to a change in their opportunity sets forced on them by government, except perhaps in the short run. In parliamentary democracies, firms and households can adjust not only through 'investment' in ways of minimising any unfavourable effects of being subjected to state control that presuppose that such controls are imperatives. They may also enter into bargaining arrangements with government, employing the threat not only of non-cooperation but also of campaigning for removing the government itself.[3] In the language of control systems, the use of particular policy instruments has to take account of 'feedback', which in extreme cases may render it both impossible and, with a change of government, undesirable to execute the policy at all. This kind of feedback is rarely embodied in a systematic form in macro-policy models, and one can well sympathise with model builders faced with the difficult task of re-specifying the models to take such feedback into account.

Third, the problem of embodying feedback into policy models draws attention to one overriding technical difficulty, how to take account of uncertainty in making government economic decisions. Uncertainty is treated in the theory of economic policy in various ways. The effect of policy measures on the dependent variables representing arguments in the government welfare function can be viewed as 'certainty equivalents', after embodying some estimates of the degree of probability of alternative possible outcomes resulting from policy changes. Alternatively, 'important' parameters in the model may be given ranges of possible values and the model then tested for sensitivity. My purpose in mentioning these tricks of the trade is not to mount a discussion of their legitimacy but to examine the consequences of honest admission by the economist of the frailty of policies relying heavily on economic prediction. The way is open for considerable disagreement over the weight to be placed on economic advice, and with the temptation to individual politicians and administrators to select the advice that offers the most support to their particular policy hobby horses. Therefore, the picture of a 'government' following a rational mode of policy intervention buttressed by sound predictions of what that intervention will achieve, with government members and their administrative support operating the instruments assigned to their control in a coordinated and mechanical fashion, is already disappearing rapidly!

V. Revising the Policy Paradigm

What we have to capture in any model of economic policy is the important fact that the very evolution of policy instruments designed to control the actions of households and firms and to influence overseas suppliers, buyers and governments sets in motion a concomitant development of protective devices. Concentrating on the domestic economy, households and firms organise themselves into pressure groups for the particular purpose of treating with government and with the bureaucracy. As Daniel Bell (1974) has shown, the variety of such groups in pluralistic societies is astonishing:

they comprise functional economic groups (business, labor, farmers); symbolic status groups (religious, national, racial); socially disadvantaged groups (poor, aged, handicapped); culturally expressive groups (women, youth, homosexuals); civic purpose groups (civil rights organisations, consumer and environmentalist groups); economic special purpose groups (taxpayers associations, veterans lobbies); cultural special purpose groups (universities, scientific and professional associations, arts associations); functional political associations (conferences of states, or city and municipal organisations); and 57 other varieties.

An economist would note that the fortunes of these groups rise and fall, depending on the costs and benefits of political action, and their motivation, designed to maximise the difference between benefits and costs, may lead to coalitions between groups of varying stability.

The important consequence of well-organised pressure group activity is that bureaucrats lose their inscrutability as they become forced to reveal their motives and their actions. If pressures are strong enough, such that the bureaucracy faces the prospect of being under close and continuous surveillance, the bureaucrats themselves seek to organise themselves more effectively. The nature of our economic model has to be completely transformed. It can no longer maintain the characteristics of a general equilibrium model that assumes perfect competition in the factor and goods markets upon which government is superimposed. A multi-sector bargaining model is the very minimum construction necessary to convey the essential features of the environment in which economic policy has to be conducted.[4]

Figure 1.2 is an attempt to display the basic features of any such model. Instead of one dominant decision maker, the government, we identify four sets of decision makers – firms, households, government and the bureaucracy. Each attempts to maximise a welfare function subject to the constraints exercised on it by the actions of other bargaining groups.[5] Therefore, alongside the traditional factor and goods markets (and, in a fully articulated model, the capital and money markets), there will be a 'political' market in which competing political parties will attempt to achieve power (and to retain it when they do) by offering policies in exchange for votes. There will be a 'policy supply' market in which bureaucrats will offer alternative administrative packages to promote the policy aims of politicians. There will be a 'policy execution' market in which firms and households supply 'cooperation' with bureaucratic measures in return for 'services rendered', such as financial aid and government contracts.

The market structure, which is capable of endless elaboration to fit the explanatory tasks of the model, is represented by two changes in Figure 1.1. The first is the separation of government from bureaucracy and the redefinition of the motivation of policy decision makers. The second is the identification of feedback effects from the private sector to the government sector and within the government sector itself. It is recognised that the term 'feedback' implies that policy initiatives still lie with the government sector

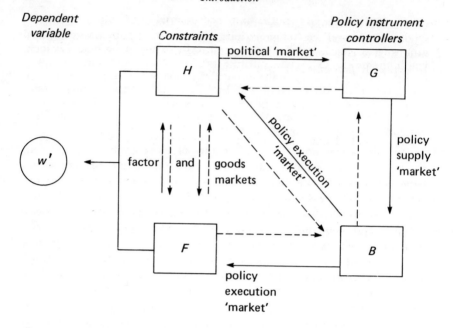

w' = policy outcome (as reflected in objectives, e.g. rate of inflation, employ-
     ment, etc.)
G = government (vote maximiser)
B = bureaucracy (output maximiser? budget maximiser?)
H = households/voters (utility maximisers)
F = firms (profit maximisers)

FIGURE 1.2   *The revised 'model'*

and that the private sector 'reacts' through its organised pressure groups. This
is no more than a convenient fiction, an artificial break in a complicated
circuit of group action and reaction in the whole system, but it is a useful
expositional device. Therefore, in Figure 1.2, the firm lines with arrows
represent the transmission of 'instructions' from one maximising group to
another, whereas the hatched lines represent 'feedback', designed to modify
and in extreme cases to nullify the impact of the instructions. An example of
the way in which the model might be used as an explanatory device is
given in the next section.

   Though the model classifies behavioural groups in an arbitrary way and
specifies only in telegraphese the type of maximising behaviour that each
group is supposed to follow, the group classification and their maximands
can easily be modified. Thus we can extend it to the case of an open economy
and make allowance where need be for the existence of different layers of
government. Trade union power may be reflected, for example, in the
alteration of the objective function of firms, by categorising them as, say,

employment maximisers. It can even be restructured to reflect the characteristics of a 'command' economy, so long as there are 'peripheral' economic
groups, such as consumers and independent producers, whose activities have
to be explicitly *forecasted* in government plans.

VI. Example: The Expanding Public Sector

The rise in government expenditure as a proportion of GNP in Western
industrial countries is one of the economic phenomena that are now producing
a concomitant growth in professional comment and discussion. Speculation on
the causes and consequences of government expenditure growth of a
recognisably professional character is at least as old as De Tocqueville and
reached an early peak in contemporary comments on Wagner's famous 'Law'
predicting the growth of government services alongside the growth of national
output. (For a summary of earlier discussion, see Peacock and Wiseman, 1979.)
Indeed, Wagner's Law, its alternative interpretations and its econometric
verification are regarded as a convenient point of departure for modern
discussion (see Peacock and Wiseman, 1961; Musgrave, 1969; Gandhi, 1978;
Brown and Jackson, 1978).

Explanations of the causes of growth have presented a challenge to the
public finance theorist. The earlier contributions concentrated on building a
kind of dynamic theory of consumer demand for public services, emphasising
complementarity between economic growth and growth of government. Such
explanations encountered considerable difficulties. Analytically, for example,
they assume that government actions reflect the explicitly stated preferences
of private consumers, and this clearly ignores important features of most
political systems as well as the well-known problem of finding methods of
inducing consumers to reveal their preferences for public services. Empirically,
such explanations have some difficulty in accounting for structural shifts in
government expenditure and thus for the *timing* of changes, as well as in
coping with changes in the relative importance of different layers of government as public spenders. Following my earlier investigations with Jack
Wiseman, more attention is now being paid to the role of *suppliers* of policies
(see Breton's (1974) use of our 'displacement effect' hypothesis), ranging
from governments 'selling policies for votes' to the role of bureaucrats as
suppliers of specific policy 'inputs' (Noll and Fiorina, 1978).

The Statistical Findings

A useful starting point for studying government expenditure growth is
G. Warren Nutter's recent study *Growth of Government in the West* (1978):

(a) He confirms the well-known observation that in Western industrial countries government spending rose quite rapidly between the 1950s and 1970s. The median increase in government current expenditure (including transfers) as a percentage of Gross National Product at factor cost rose as follows in sixteen OECD countries:

1950	25.0%
1953	27.4%
1965	33.5%
1970	36.1%
1974	39.8%

Source: Based on G. Warren Nutter (1978) Appendix B.

(b) Transfer payments rose on average at a much faster rate than expenditure on goods and services. Transfers as a percentage of GNP, taking the median, rose from 7.3 per cent in 1950 to 19 per cent in 1974, a rise of 160 per cent, whereas the median percentage of other domestic expenditures rose only 59 per cent. (Transfers are not a component of GNP, of course, which raises some conceptual problems about expressing them as a percentage of GNP that I do not consider here. For further discussion of these and related problems, see Peacock and Wiseman, 1961, chapter 1 and Nutter, 1978, pp. 1–2.)

(c) There is an inverse relation between the size of government in 1953 (as measured by G/GNP) and the growth in government over the period 1953–73, though the relation is statistically only marginally significant. In the case of EEC countries we find that the differences in size of government using this measure have perceptibly narrowed over this period.

(d) Nutter draws attention to the possibility that government spending has grown faster at local levels of government than at the central level, but provides no data. However, this is a matter that has been extensively investigated by Pommerehne (1977) who confirms that this is so for the period covering 1950 to 1970 in a cross-country comparison of Canada, France, West Germany, Switzerland, the UK and the USA.

As Oates (1978) and others have pointed out, we must be careful about placing any particular interpretation on this kind of result as a measure of the degree of centralisation of government. The spending authority may be subject to very different degrees of constraint by the central government, which cannot be reflected in simple statistical comparisons, and even within the scope of these comparisons a better measure of what Jack Wiseman and I have labelled the 'concentration effect' may be found in the proportion of *total* government expenditure that is *centrally* financed (see Peacock and Wiseman, 1961).

The 'Illusion' of Government Growth

In our earlier investigations (Peacock and Wiseman, 1961, pp. 163–6) Jack Wiseman and I drew attention to the fact that before we can make any statement about changes in the real size of government in relation to GNP, we have to express changes in both series in constant prices. There is no reason why the deflator for GNP should be the same as for government expenditure, given that the latter includes transfer expenditure as well as a different input-mix for government services compared with the aggregate input-mix for all economic activities. The result could be a divergence between G/GNP expressed in current prices and expressed in constant prices. Most studies of long-term expenditure growth have largely ignored this problem; and we concluded from our own, quite elaborate, statistical investigation for the UK, covering a period from 1890 to 1955, that the divergence between G/GNP expressed in current and then in constant prices was slight.

Whatever may have been the case in the earlier period we considered, the evidence for the last two decades indicates that the divergence is now marked. As Table 1.1 shows (supplied by Morris Beck; cf. also Beck, 1976) the constant price elasticity of government expenditure *on consumption only* with respect to GNP is much lower than the current price elasticity. In cases where the elasticity is less than unity, this obviously means that G_c/GNP

TABLE 1.1 *Elasticity of government expenditure for consumption, 1950–1974, and size of public sector: before and after adjustment for inflation*

	Current price data			Constant price data	
	Elasticity 1950–74 (1)	$G/Y(\%)$ 1950 (2)	1974 (3)	Elasticity 1950–74 (4)	$G/Y(\%)$ 1974 (5)
Austria	1.39	11.3	15.3	0.48	7.1
Canada	2.00	10.3	19.2	1.27	12.4
Denmark	2.43	10.2	23.2	1.47	13.4
Finland	1.59	11.1	17.2	0.96	10.7
France	1.02	12.9	13.0	0.52	8.6
Germany, West	1.41	14.3	19.7	0.78	12.0
Greece	1.20	11.5	13.6	0.60	8.0
Ireland	1.54	12.1	17.6	1.09	12.9
Netherlands	1.45	12.2	17.2	0.55	8.6
Sweden	1.82	13.7	23.6	1.19	15.4
Switzerland	1.08	11.2	12.0	0.67	9.0
United Kingdom	1.30	16.3	20.5	0.78	14.1
United States	1.74	12.1	19.1	1.23	13.7
MEDIAN	1.59	12.1	17.6	0.79	12.4

Legend: G = government consumption expenditure
Y = gross domestic product
Elasticity: ratio of % change in G to % change in Y
Sources: United Nations, *Yearbook of National Accounts Statistics; National Accounts of OECD Countries* (privately communicated by Professor Morris Beck, Rutgers University).

falls rather than rises (where G_c = government consumption expenditure), as happens in the case of France, West Germany and the UK. Government capital expenditure on goods and services being a relatively small component of total government expenditure, any 'real' rise in G/GNP over this period in these countries can only be brought about by a compensating increase in the real value of transfer expenditures. Such a compensating increase appears to have taken place in these countries, but the overall effect of allowing for the deflation procedure is to convey the impression that the real relative growth in government in Western countries since World War II has been comparatively modest.

It will be noted, however, that this conclusion, viz. that current price data offer the illusion of rapid growth, rests on the important assumption that we can accept social accounting conventions about the measurement of the productivity of government services. As is well known, a large proportion of government services is not priced and the unit of output, as with all personal services, is difficult to define. Statistical methods for circumventing these difficulties must of necessity be mere subterfuges.

'Self-Sustaining' Growth of the Public Sector

Now let us set the model to work.

A useful point of departure is to consider the interpretation placed on the 'illusion' of growth by the well-known public choice theorists, Buchanan and Tullock (see Buchanan and Tullock, 1977), in considering the position of the USA. They explain the disparity in growth of government expenditure and government output in terms of what they label the 'Wagner squared' hypothesis. Civil servants' wages can grow faster than in comparable occupations in the private sector, without concomitant increases in their productivity (which, significantly enough, is difficult to measure) simply because, as government agencies grow, bureaucrats become a larger proportion of the total voting constituency. In addition, as the proportion of adult population receiving transfer payments (including sickness, unemployment and pension benefits) increases, so will their interests in and influence on the amount and scope of transfer payments increase. Therefore, even if the share of population employed by government were held constant (and presumably also the share receiving transfers), this does not imply that the share of government in total *spending* should become stabilised. As they conclude: 'we infer from the record that the growth of the public sector may have, indeed, changed its form, but that the prediction of long-term developments must be viewed with considerable foreboding. The data may suggest that the public sector is "out of control" in the literal sense of the term.'

While the approach is suggestive, it leaves an unexplained element in the process of government spending growth. The benefits received by utility maximising transfer receivers and bureaucrats must be matched by the cost imposed on taxpayers, i.e. utility-maximising consumers/voters and profit-maximising producers. Moreover, the decisions that lead to the imposition of a growing tax burden to finance spending growth have to be taken by vote-maximising politicians. Buchanan and Tullock fail to explain why the resolution of forces released by the group bargaining process should produce 'self-sustaining growth', leading politicians anxious to maximise their length of life in office to press for ever-larger budgets. A more cogent explanation may lie in the 'isolation paradox' besetting the position of the voter-cum-taxpayer. There may be general support for preventing a rise in the size of the public sector relative to GNP and in eliminating 'bureaucratic waste', but only a small proportion of voters is likely to have a direct interest in forgoing the advantages they derive from improved government services, subsidies and grants in their capacities as consumers and income receivers. With the nexus severed between what the individual taxpayer contributes and what he receives by way of government services, there can be no guarantee that a willingness to go without these services will be matched by a con-comitant fall in tax burdens, once the political process gets to work on the necessary fiscal adjustments. The voter, maximising under such a degree of uncertainty, may prefer to accept an ever-growing tax burden, though up to some (obviously indefinable) limit, provided that his political representatives will facilitate access to government services from which he can benefit. Thus no single group in the bargaining chain – politicians, voters, bureaucrats, firms, etc. – has any incentive to reduce its own opportunities for 'milking' the public services.

Clearly the system must at some stage converge to an equilibrium, though it would be hazardous to specify some fixed ratio of government expenditure to GNP that would represent it, or to assume that it would be stable. It is more profitable to consider what forces would work to produce equilibrium. Breton (1978) has identified two such forces. One is obvious. At some stage it becomes impossible for politicians with bureaucratic support to avoid introducing a growing proportion of the electorate to the joys of paying taxes. The marginal cost of private goods forgone in tax payment must begin to increase and political support for further expansion of the public sector relative to GNP diminish. The second is not so obvious and possibly more questionable. Breton argues that a point comes when bureaucrats' own increasing tax burdens mean that they can no longer gain from expansion of their bureaus. This proposition clearly depends on the opportunities for tax avoidance open to particular occupational groups, and bureaucrats may be better organised than most to obtain tax concessions that transmute part of their earnings into non-taxable allowances.

The general point remains. While it is true that the analysis of public sector growth in its simplest form does at least recognise the existence of a 'political market', it is not possible to develop a satisfactory explanation of this phenomenon without using a multi-sector bargaining model. There is a parallel here with post-Keynesian developments in macroeconomic theory where the microeconomic foundations of macroeconomic models have been thoroughly explored. Our basic model has been used to explore, though without the same empirical and analytical thoroughness, the micro-foundations of one important sector of the macro-economy – the public sector.

VII. Conclusions

The tasks of a normative economic policy model of the conventional kind and those of a model of the interaction of government and other decision-making groups are essentially different. The former attempts to provide the ingredients of a consistent economic policy while the latter tries to show how governments actually behave (and not how they ought to behave) in order to conform to a given set of objectives. However, it is all too easy for the economist to assume that by using the instruments of government to correct market failure there will be no concomitant 'collective failure'. As our revised model demonstrates, this failure can take various forms. First, there is the insurmountable problem of how to forecast movements of important economic variables under alternative policy regimes, for, apart from the more obvious difficulties of economic forecasting, there is the difficulty of discerning the nature and the effects of strategic behaviour of firms and households designed to minimise the economic consequences to them of policy measures. Second, as major policy measures affect the individual fortunes of politicians and bureaucrats in markedly different ways, there can be no guarantee that agreed policy measures will be rigorously and consistently applied. No better example can be found than the failure of Western governments to control the growth of public spending, for it is manifestly not the case that this growth represents the outcome of a rational planning process derived from an economic policy model.

Though the main purpose of this chapter is to set the stage for illustration in some later chapters of the properties of the revised model, it is interesting to note in conclusion that the limitations of control systems are having their impact on the methodology of the theory of economic policy itself. Thus, James Meade in his Nobel Lecture, in confessing to having been 'full enamoured' with the control system approach, writes as follows:

> It is most desirable in a modern democratic community that the ordinary man or woman in the streets should as far as possible realise what is going on, with the responsibilities of success or failure in the different fields of endeavour being dispersed but clearly defined and allocated. To treat the whole of macro-economic control as the single subject for the mysterious art of the control engineer is likely to appear at the best magical and at the worst totally arbitrary and unacceptable to the ordinary

citizen. To put each clearly defined weapon or armoury of weapons in the charge of one particular authority or set of decision makers with the responsibility of hitting as nearly as possible one well defined target is a much more intelligible arrangement. [Meade, 1978]

Meade recognises that a return to the approach in which there is a line-up of particular targets with particular instruments requires close internal co-ordination of policy in order to achieve consistency, but he clearly believes that this is a price worth paying for public acceptability. It is a matter for con-jecture whether this approach will do much to reduce the use of strategic behaviour of pressure groups who would presumably have better information at their disposal for promoting their own ends, which need not conform with those of policy makers. The really difficult problem of achieving coordination, what Meade calls 'a convergent process of mutual accommodation', is how to strengthen the *will* to coordinate (see chapter 16 below). The economic analysis of government may only be able to explain why these problems and related problems beset policy making but at least it acknowledges their existence.

NOTES

1. For a typical example employing the techniques first fashioned by Tinbergen, Theil and Bent Hansen, see Turnovsky (1977). For a simpler application to fiscal policy, though with reservations, see Peacock and Shaw (1976).
2. See, for example, the excellent 'macroeconomics game' devised by the Esmee Fairbairn Research Centre, Heriot-Watt University, in Lumsden (1978).
3. The basic objections to treating firms and households as passive adjusters is further investigated in chapter 5 below.
4. Sir Douglas Wass (1978), Permanent Secretary, HM Treasury, has specifically pointed towards the need for policy makers to recognise changes in the economic environment that require changes in the explanations of economic behaviour, though he is more concerned with the impact on economic policy of consumer and producer reactions to inflation and of the increasing internationalisation of economic and financial activity resulting from growth of multinational companies.
5. See also my earlier contribution in the Robbins *Festschrift* (Peacock, 1972). The diagrammatic treatment embodies features found in the very interesting work by Bartlett (1973). See also the work of Frey (1978).

REFERENCES

Ball, R. J. (Chairman) (1978) *Report of the Committee on Policy Optimisation* Cmnd 7148, HMSO, London.
Bartlett, R. (1973) *Economic Foundations of Political Power* Macmillan, New York.
Beck, M. (1976) 'The expanding public sector: Some contrary evidence' *National Tax Journal* Vol. 29, March.

Bell, D. (1974) 'The public household – on "fiscal sociology and the liberal society"' *The Public Interest* No. 37, Fall.

Breton, A. (1974) *The Economic Theory of Representative Government* Macmillan, London.

Breton, A. (1978) 'Accountability, bureaucracy and representative government' in H. C. Recktenwald (ed.) *Secular Trends of the Public Sector* Proceedings of the 32nd Congress of the IIPF, Edinburgh 1976, Editions Cujas, Paris.

Brown, C. V. and Jackson, P. M. (1978) *Public Sector Economics* Martin Robertson, Oxford, chapter 5.

Buchanan, J. M. and Tullock, G. (1977) 'The expanding public sector: Wagner' *Public Choice* Vol. 15, Fall.

Frey, B. (1978) 'Keynesian thinking in politico-economic models' *Journal of Post-Keynesian Economics* Vol. 1.

Gandhi, V. D. (1978) 'Trends in public consumption and investment: A review of issues and evidence' in Recktenwald *op. cit.*

Lumsden, K. G. (1978) 'New technologies in higher education' mimeo, Heriot-Watt University, Edinburgh.

Meade, J. E. (1978) 'The meaning of "internal balance"' *Economic Journal* Vol. 88, September.

Musgrave, R. A. (1969) *Fiscal Systems* Yale University Press, New Haven, Conn.

Noll, R. G. and Fiorina, M. P. (1978) 'Voters, bureaucrats and legislators' *Journal of Public Economics* Vol. 7, No. 2, pp. 239–54.

Nutter, G. W. (1978) *Growth of Government in the West* American Enterprise Institute Studies in Economic Policy, Washington, D.C.

Oates, W. E. (1978) 'The changing structure of intergovernmental fiscal relations' in Recktenwald *op. cit.*

Peacock, A. T. (1972) 'Fiscal means and political ends' in M. Peston and B. Corry (eds) *Essays in Honour of Lord Robbins* Weidenfeld & Nicolson, London.

Peacock, A. T. and Shaw, G. K. (1976) *The Economic Theory of Fiscal Policy* revised edition, Allen & Unwin, London.

Peacock, A. T. and Wiseman, J. (1961) *The Growth of Public Expenditure in the United Kingdom 1890–1955* Princeton University Press, Princeton.

Peacock, A. T. and Wiseman, J. (1979) 'Approaches to the analysis of government expenditure growth' *Public Finance Quarterly* Vol. 7, No. 1.

Pommerehne, W. W. (1977) 'Quantitative aspects of federalism: A study of six countries' in W. E. Oates (ed.) *The Political Economy of Fiscal Federalism* D. C. Heath, Lexington, Mass.

Turnovsky, S. (1977) *Macroeconomic Analysis and Stabilization Policy* Cambridge University Press, Cambridge, chapter 14.

Wass, Sir D. (1978) 'The changing problems of economic management' *Economic Trends* HMSO, March, No. 293.

PART II

The Political Economy
of Government

INTRODUCTION

Throughout the non-communist world, there is clearly a remarkable consensus on the scope and method of positive economics, otherwise it would be difficult to account for the strong similarities in both the content and the ordering of economics courses in different countries, and also to explain why teams of economists from countries working on policy problems within international agencies and in national planning agencies can work together.

This recognition of common ground in the theory and application of economics might be assumed to satisfy economists that the hallmark of their profession is a scientific approach and that the spirit of free enquiry and the resolution of debate by appeal to fact and argument would be sufficient to create a professional ethos. Yet there is a large proportion of economists who would claim that there is an additional requirement for entry into our profession, and this consists of the acceptance of certain basic normative propositions associated with Paretian welfare economics. It might just be possible to defend such a view on the grounds that those who live in the non-communist world and accept its mores would be bound, broadly speaking, to agree on basic value judgements and that there are operational reasons, e.g. the examination of the economic implications of policy norms, that govern this extra requirement. However, even if this were true, it would hardly be necessary to regard acceptance of a consensus on values as a *sine qua non* for describing oneself as a professional economist. Moreover, as I hope to demonstrate, the Paretian welfare judgements have been used to justify a range of policies extending far beyond those that one could regard as embodying the essential elements in a non-collectivist set of values.

Perhaps more puzzling is why economists often appear to claim that Paretian welfare criteria have some kind of scientific status. Such an eminent economist as Lord Robbins comments on this view as follows:

> if [these criteria] approach within a thousand miles of practical application, [they] usually prove to involve concealed neglect of consideration involving judgments of value. I would be the last to deny the importance of the distinction between purely scientific economic analysis and normative prescription. But, for me at any rate, Welfare Economics has always seemed a draughty half-way house. Why not cross the dividing line and, like the Classical Economists before us, when we pass to prescription, use with due acknowledgment – which they did not always make – whatever ethical and political premises seem appropriate? [Robbins, 1976, p. 3]

I have no hesitation in following this advice and cheerfully cross the 'dividing line'.

Even more curious than the supposed necessity for all right-thinking economists to accept all the tenets of Paretianism is the associated belief that in doing so one will arrive at non-authoritarian solutions to problems of economic policy, for Paretianism accepts that economic policy must conform with individual preferences. Liberalism is therefore held to be synonymous with or at least embraced by Paretianism. Part II of the book seeks to destroy this position. Charles Rowley and I have examined the distinction between the two positions in a separate longer work (Rowley and Peacock, 1975), but our earlier joint articles, which he has kindly allowed me to reprint, perhaps demonstrate more forcibly our mode of entry into a con- temporary discussion of some importance (see chapter 2). The second of these articles (chapter 4) deals with a subject not dealt with in our book (see also Rowley, 1978).

The articles on welfare theory are complemented by an attempt to show how liberal principles of action would govern the operation of contemporary economic policy. I try to show how Paretian initial axioms and static frame- work, if used as a point of departure for policy discussion, would stultify analysis. I believe, for example, that the use of a Paretian frame of reference to examine the views of Adam Smith on public finance would leave their essential essence undetected (cf. chapter 3). When, as I believe, the operation of a liberal economic policy requires important changes in political and economic organisation, it is soon found that these changes run counter to much of the thinking of those Paretians who, having identified the failure of the market to deliver important goods and services, deny that the political process can be so designed as an alternative method of delivery (cf. chapters 5 and 6). There seems an obvious contradiction, to a liberal at least, between the agreed position that individual preferences should count and that the articulation of these preferences where the market fails calls for the inter- vention of some Superman. Judging by the functions assigned to him by Paretians, Superman has to be able to identify the 'true' preferences of individuals for publicly provided goods and services by sophisticated devices (cf. chapter 15 below) that obviously call for the skills of economists. However, always to the fore in liberal thinking is Juvenal's time-honoured question: *quis custodiet ipsos custodes?*

Economic policy is too important a matter to be left to economists.

REFERENCES

Robbins, Lord L. (1976) *Political Economy Past and Present* Macmillan, London.
Rowley, C. K. and Peacock, A. T. (1975) *Welfare Economics: A Liberal Restatement* Martin Robertson, London.
Rowley, C. K. (1978) 'Liberalism and collective choice: A return to reality?' *Manchester School* September.

CHAPTER 2

Pareto Optimality and the Political Economy of Liberalism[1]

(with Charles K. Rowley)

The mode in which the government can most surely demonstrate the sincerity with which it intends the greatest good of its subjects, is by doing the things which are made incumbent on it by the helplessness of the public, in such a manner as shall tend not to increase and perpetuate, but to correct, that helplessness. A good government will give all its aid in such a shape, as to encourage and nurture any rudiments it may find of a spirit of individual exertion. [John Stuart Mill *Principles of Political Economy* book 5, chap. 11, paragraph 16]

'Consensus' is the mid-twentieth-century euphemism for 'orthodoxy'. Antisocialists, too, sometimes seek 'consensus', but they should beware lest they find themselves committed to the enforcement of a moral and social orthodoxy. [H. B. Acton *The Morals of Markets* Longmans, 1971, p. 101]

I. INTRODUCTION

It has long been assumed that the value assumptions embedded in Paretian welfare economics bear a close affinity to a liberal (or Whig) outlook, especially in view of the former's acceptance of consumer sovereignty as a fundamental axiom. Indeed, those economists and other social scientists who have rejected the framework of Pareto welfare economics as a policy guide frequently have done so because of the emphasis it appears to give to liberal individualism (for example, Dobb, 1969). However, recent applications of Paretian welfare economics to problems of policy action have generated conclusions that run counter to policy recommendations commonly associated with latter-day liberal economists, especially in the field of social policy. Amartya Sen, in a recent contribution, forcibly suggested that 'in a very

23

basic sense liberal values conflict with the Pareto principle' and that 'if someone does have certain liberal values, then he may have to eschew his adherence to Pareto optimality' (1970, p. 157).[2] More specifically, economists contributing to the recent debate on the most appropriate pattern of income redistribution have demonstrated – in some cases it seems with manifest *Schadenfreude* – that Pareto criteria support redistribution in kind rather than in cash.

The purpose of this article is to explore further the nature of the relationship between liberalism and Pareto optimality, with particular attention to the debate on income redistribution. It is argued that the affinity between two sets of value judgments which underpin these separate approaches is more apparent than real and indeed that liberalism is as distinct from the Paretian approach as it is from conservatism, with which also it is only too frequently confused (see Hayek, 1960). It is shown that liberals need not suffer any discomfort if their policy recommendations are not in harmony with Paretian welfare criteria and that any alleged inconsistency in the liberal position is a myth.

II. THE PARETO PRINCIPLE

When sufficiently pressed upon the subject, few economists would deny that Paretian welfare economics, in common with all normative analysis, is characterized by a number of important value judgments, and that acceptance of the welfare implications of the Pareto principle is dependent upon the prior acceptance of those value judgments (see, especially, Nath, 1969). Many would argue, however, that the value judgments concerned – which need to be specified rigorously – are so obviously acceptable that no discussion is required concerning policy recommendations supported by the Pareto principle.[3] The truth or otherwise of this contention will be assessed following a formal specification of the value judgments at issue:

(i) The concern is to be with the welfare of all the individuals in the society rather than with some organic concept of 'the state'. In this sense, the Pareto principle defines an individualistic approach to social welfare and makes it possible to write an ordinal social welfare function of the form

$$W = W(U^1, U^2, \ldots, U^s), \qquad (1)$$

where W is social welfare and $U^1, U^2, \ldots, U^s$ are the levels of utility of each of the s individuals.

(ii) An individual should be considered the best judge of his social welfare. This is not implicit in value judgment (i), as is evident both from recent discussions of 'merit wants' and from earlier acceptance of the principle of paternalism. This value assumption (for cases where there are no interdependencies between the utility functions of the separate individuals) makes it possible to write the following ordinal utility functions for each of s individuals:

$$U^g = U^g(x_i^g, v_j^g) \; (g = 1, \ldots \ldots s), \qquad (2)$$

where x_i is the ith commodity and v_j is the jth productive service in economy.

(iii) If any change in the allocation of resources increases the social welfare of at least one person without reducing the social welfare of any other person, then this change should be treated as improving total social welfare. This value judgment – which implicitly denies the possibility of making interpersonal welfare comparisons – is frequently referred to as *the* Pareto value judgment, and it implies that W is a monotonically increasing function of any U, that is,

$$\frac{\partial W}{\partial U^g} > 0. \qquad (3)$$

It is difficult to exaggerate the significance for public policy discussion of the third value assumption of the Pareto model, for it recognizes explicitly the impossibility of comparing the economic welfare of separate individuals. Whenever a change is under consideration which improves the welfare of some at the cost of a reduction in the welfare of others, the Pareto model, necessarily, is silent.[4] For this reason, the Pareto principle offers an approach to public policy likely to find favour with those concerned to maintain the status quo. A single objection is sufficient to cloud the welfare issue and to render unambiguous public policy judgment impossible. Unanimity for public policy recommendations of any substance is rarely forthcoming in the real world.

This is equally the case in applications of the Pareto principle to political behaviour, where the only acceptable voting system is that which requires unanimous consent for any action by the government, since any other voting rule allows state intervention which is damaging to one or more members of the voting public.[5] The unanimity rule, not surprisingly, meets with considerable favour among groups concerned with preserving the status quo and is treated with suspicion by those radicals concerned with transforming society. A recent example is discussed below.

III. LIBERALIST PHILOSOPHY

The liberal principles of the classical economists were not in any narrowly professional sense economic principles.[6] Rather they were an application to economics of principles that were believed to apply over a much wider field and which, indeed, provided a foundation for the political ideals of, for example, Thomas Jefferson and his supporters. It is important to recognize that this is as true now as it was two centuries ago, and that confusion over this aspect of liberalism lies at the centre of the present challenge to liberalism which finds its foundation in the Pareto principle.

Above all else, liberalist philosophy is concerned with minimizing restrictions on individual freedom, whether imposed by private bodies or by the state *even at a cost in terms of sacrificed material welfare.*[7] The liberal values individual freedom above all other social objectives and will not easily consent to the restriction of such freedom (see Machlup, 1969, pp. 1–10). For this reason, the once widely held contention that economic freedom generated economic efficiency never really provided more than secondary support for liberalist philosophy. This largely explains why classical liberalism has not been destroyed by the mounting exceptions to the economic case for free-enterprise capitalism and why apparently well-argued cases for collectivist intervention frequently fail the liberal test. For, within limits, the liberal is prepared to trade off economic efficiency for individual freedom where such a policy conflict becomes apparent.

The major threat to individual freedom is seen to stem from concentrations of economic and political power, whether in the hands of private citizens, of bureaucrats, or of the state. The liberal is acutely aware both of the potential for abuse in a system – any system – characterized by significant discretionary power and of the difficulty of effectively eliminating discretionary power once it has been established (see Director, 1964). Because the available mechanisms for preventing emergent power and for dissipating existing power in the marketplace are better tested and more widely trusted than equivalent mechanisms within the public sector, the liberal is strongly motivated to restrict the size of the public sector and to curtail the economic importance of the state while emphasizing its fundamental importance in maintaining the rule of law.

We are now in a position to compare and to contrast liberal 'political economy' with Paretian welfare judgments. Liberals clearly have a preference for a system which encourages voluntary exchange through market processes and a belief that competitive capitalism provides the strongest safeguard for such a system. Second, they share a belief in decentralized government rooted in the democratic tradition and a profound hostility to any philosophy of government which upholds the doctrine that the state is a being independent of the individuals who compose it.

Clearly, therefore, liberalist philosophy has no quarrel with the first value assumption of the Pareto principle, which directs attention to the welfare of individuals and denies the relevance of any organic concept of the state. There is no necessary compatibility, however, between liberalism and the crucial second assumption of the Pareto principle, and indeed this is precisely where so much of the confusion has occurred. The problem arises in circumstances where individuals express a present preference for the destruction of a market or for the preservation of an existing bureaucracy under conditions where a viable market solution is available. The Pareto principle is then clear – individual preferences are the final arbiter. But the liberal must assess the situation within a wider value system which attaches positive utility to market exchange and is sceptical of the acceptance of the concept of impartial and omniscient government pervading so much of the economic theory of public policy.

This does not mean that the liberal is unwilling to place faith in the ability of individuals to conduct their own affairs. Individuals, however, learn by doing and may require initial encouragement to make use of market processes in areas where they are considered alien, and the individual who has been reared in an economic environment where individual choice is limited may be excessively prone to making comparisons between real-world market situations and unreal perfect government.

It is essential to liberalism, however, that all men should have the same share in making the law even when such a system of government results in illiberal policy actions. To quote F. A. Hayek (1960): 'Liberalism regards it as desirable that only what the majority accepts should in fact be law, but it does not believe that this is therefore necessarily good law. Its aim, indeed, is to persuade the majority to observe certain principles' (p. 103).

The liberal, therefore, will abide by the decisions arrived at by majority rule while exercising all reasonable means of persuasion available to him, short of coercion, to alter the preferences of those who would encourage illiberal policies, and, in particular, those who are concerned with extending further the scope and power of the state. In this sense, the liberal is a true radical, never constrained by the existing order and always prepared to expound forcefully on matters which run counter to the conventional wisdom. In particular, in fields of economic activity long characterized by state provision (for example, education) where the actors have not experienced market forces and vote for the status quo out of fear of the unknown, the liberal response will be one of encouraging experimentation with market processes (if necessary, initially on a pilot scale) and of stimulating the provision of information which will supply the raw material for rational debate, in the hope that as individuals gain experience and confidence in their ability to manage their own affairs they will come to recognize that they prefer such a situation (see Peacock and Wiseman, 1964; Rowley, 1969).

Much of the conservatism inherent in the Pareto principle is derived from the third value judgment, which rejects the notion that interpersonal welfare comparisons are possible. For there are few situations in which substantial shifts in the pattern of resource allocation harm nobody while some benefit. Adherence to the Pareto principle, therefore, emasculates radical reaction to the status quo. By contrast, liberalist philosophy was never self-crippled by this kind of restrictive value judgment, and liberals for the most part are strongly committed to a more equal distribution of wealth than that which exists, even in countries such as the United Kingdom which operate progressive taxation policies.[8] This does not mean that liberals are egalitarians, since differentially high rewards for skill, effort, and enterprise have always featured importantly in liberal philosophy, both as an aid to efficiency and on grounds of equity. Policies designed to improve equality of opportunity via the market mechanism, coupled with cash transfers for those who fall below minimum standards of well-being, are central to liberal thinking (see Friedman, 1962).

Liberals are unwilling to pursue income redistribution objectives which involve the suppression or the destruction of markets, preferring always to pursue the distribution objective separately while emphasizing the rule of competitive markets in attaining individual freedom. Indeed, it is in evaluating recent contributions to the debate on income redistribution from a liberal viewpoint that the deep-rooted differences between those who adhere to the Pareto principle and those who ascribe to liberalist ethics are most sharply focused.

IV. THE DEBATE ON INCOME REDISTRIBUTION

The General Case for Income Redistribution

If we consider first of all the general case for income redistribution, we encounter an important example of the conservative attitude which is inherent in the application of Pareto principles. In such circumstances, a Pareto-preferred redistribution of income of whatever kind can only occur where interdependencies exist as between the utility functions of separate individuals. A typical example is that by H. M. Hochman and J. D. Rodgers (1969), who analysed Pareto-optimal income redistribution between Mutt (the rich member of a two-person economy) and Jeff (his poorer counterpart) where their respective utility functions took the form

$$U_M^o = f_M(Y_M^o, Y_J^o), \tag{4}$$

and

$$U_J^o = f_J(Y_M^o, Y_J^o), \tag{5}$$

where U_M^o and Y_M^o were the initial values of Mutt's utility index and income, respectively, prior to any redistribution, and U_J^o and Y_J^o were the corresponding values for Jeff.

Given certain restrictions on the utility functions – specifically that $\partial U_M/\partial Y_M$, $\partial U_J/\partial Y_J > 0$ and that $\partial U_J/\partial Y_M \leqq 0$ at Y_M^o, Y_J^o (or if $\partial U_J/\partial Y_M > 0$ then $\partial U_J/\partial Y_J > \partial U_J/\partial Y_M$) – it follows that all transfers are entirely a matter of Mutt's volition, and that the process of determining a Pareto-optimal redistributive transfer can concentrate on Mutt's preferences alone. Since transfers large enough to reverse the initial distributional ordering are not allowed, it follows in the two-person case that the transfer cannot be greater than $(Y_M^o - Y_J^o/2)$.

The degree of income redistribution which is Pareto optimal in the context of the Hochman–Rodgers model is a function of the initial distribution of real income and Mutt's marginal rate of substitution between the utility derived from income retention and that derived from income redistribution. It is important to note that so-called Pareto-optimal redistribution constitutes a secondary redistribution which still depends on the *initial* distribution of real income. Within the Hochman–Rodgers model, such secondary redistribution is limited to cash giving by the rich to the poor. The model precludes all discussion of *primary* redistribution and of *secondary* redistribution in kind.[9] Nevertheless, in the Hochman–Rodgers world, income transfers are possible which make everyone better off. Given the two-person economy postulated in their model, Hochman and Rodgers present no convincing case why Pareto-optimal redistribution should not take place through private charity. Thus, although they claim to justify a system of state intervention through fiscal instruments, their argument is less than convincing. Once the model is extended to an N-person economy,[10] however, a case for state intervention is easily established, as long as each rich person cares about his own welfare and the welfare of the poor, but not about the welfare of other rich people.

In a society of N persons, of which $k < N$ are poor, suppose that the government were to raise £1 each from the rich (that is, £$N-k$) to be distributed equally among the poor. The utility gain of R_i would be

$$\left(\frac{N}{k} - 1\right) \sum_{j=1}^{k} \frac{\partial UR_i}{\partial Y_j},$$

while his utility loss is $\partial UR_i/\partial UR_y$, so that the net gain from the tax and redistribution is

$$\left(\frac{N}{k} - 1\right) \sum_{j=1}^{k} \frac{\partial UR_i}{\partial Y_j} - \frac{\partial UR_i}{\partial YR_i}.$$

If instead, R_i had given through charity and the £1 had been distributed in the same way, the gain would have been

$$\frac{1}{k} \sum_{j=1}^{k} \frac{\partial UR_i}{\partial Y_j} - \frac{\partial UR_i}{\partial YR_i},$$

which is clearly smaller as long as $N > (k + 1)$ that is, as long as there is more than one rich person. The reason for the possibility of gains through collective action is clear, namely the free-rider argument which renders the level of voluntary transfers suboptimal. In such circumstances, a large government poverty programme may be Pareto optimal even though private charity programmes for the poor do not receive any contributions.[11] Alternatives to state intervention would include charity contracts among the rich. But transaction-cost considerations usually preclude such arrangements, at least in their more extensive forms. Utility functions of the kind under consideration would suggest that a progressive income tax might prove successful in achieving a Pareto-optimal income redistribution.

Liberals do not necessarily agree about the 'correct' primary income distribution and 'Virginian-blend' economists[12] will find the Hochman–Rodgers approach attractive. However, the liberal need not rely upon interdependent utility functions to generate a case for redistribution of income and/or wealth. The straightforward case for cash transfers or for even more radical measures to redistribute wealth will rest on his particular view of the interpersonal and intertemporal distribution of property rights. Again it must be emphasized that the liberal is neither indifferent to the means adopted in persuading others that his view may be worth acting upon nor to the *method* by which income and wealth is redistributed. In particular, liberals and socialists may share a common view about the need for a redistribution of wealth, but liberals would be unwilling to support methods of redistribution which result in a transfer of capital to the state rather than between individuals.

Income Redistribution in Cash and in 'Kind'

The arguments used by liberal economists to promote cash transfers rather than the provision of goods as a means of income support to lower income groups are well known. In simple microeconomic terms, support may be found for cash transfers in the case illustrating the reverse of the argument indicating the excess burden of indirect taxes (cf. Peacock and Berry, 1951; and Olsen, 1971). In the usual diagram depicting individual consumer equilibrium, it can be demonstrated that, in the absence of rationing, an income subsidy places the individual consumer on a higher indifference curve than an equal amount of money used to subsidize the price of a good. The liberal argument is couched, however, in much wider terms. Generalized purchasing power, as well as offering greater freedom of choice, places the responsibility of choice more firmly in the hands of the individual. Markets need not be distorted or destroyed in order to redistribute income effectively, provided that goods can be privately produced.

These arguments, if they accord with the value assumptions of liberalist philosophy, have been shown to be in conflict with the Pareto principle in two recent contributions to the economic theory of income redistribution. The first, by Lucien Foldes (1967),[13] suggested that once uncertainty as to individual utility functions is recognized, the optimum method of redistribution is by goods rather than by generalized purchasing power, at least on the assumption that goods which are transferred may be resold, even in terms of the Pareto principle. Foldes is forthright in his view that liberalist philosophy is weakened by this contribution: 'The result that the greatest social welfare can generally be attained by redistributing all goods is an interesting example of the failure of welfare economics to support the conclusions of the classical liberal theory of economic policy. It seems that the welfare argument for redistributing only money is at its most effective only when one abstracts from that aspect of the problem – the government's ignorance of the individual's business – which liberal writers are most anxious to emphasise' (p. 32).

Foldes based his criticisms of the liberal solution upon two principal arguments. The first objective is based on the absence of a one-to-one correspondence between a pre-trade and a post-trade allocation of goods in situations where perfect competition is absent. In such circumstances, the distribution of gains from trade is not uniquely settled by the distribution of initial endowments, and if the government wishes to obtain a specific post-trade distribution it will be unable to guarantee this result by any initial set of transfers in the numeraire commodity. By contrast, redistribution of goods could achieve the government's distribution objective.

The second objective pressed by Foldes postulates that the government may be ignorant of individual utility functions. In such circumstances, it would be pure accident if transfers made in some numeraire commodity resulted in the achievement of the redistributive objective of the government (cf. Buchanan, 1968). However, if redistribution takes the form of provision of goods, trade between individuals in accordance with their own objective functions will ensure that a position on a contract locus will be attained. The government, being uncertain which is the relevant contract locus, can specify its redistributional objectives in terms of unique points on alternative contract curves. Foldes is then able to show, with clever use of geometry, that in a two-good, two-person model with two alternative contract curves, only redistribution in kind without trading constraints will guarantee the attainment of a redistribution objective which accords both with government policy and is preferred by both individuals.

In one sense, there is no fundamental conflict between Foldes and the liberals, simply because he has no intention of destroying markets in the redistributed commodities. Indeed, for this reason it may be argued that he has entirely misconceived the nature of the debate on redistribution in cash or in kind which is centrally concerned with whether or not markets should be encouraged or destroyed. Foldes appears to have underestimated the extent to which the goods most frequently under consideration in the redistribution debate cannot be traded at all (namely, education and health), in which case a genuine incompatibility would arise between his and the liberal solution.

In another sense, however, there is a genuine conflict, for implicit in Foldes's analysis is a 'nirvana' view of government which is only too common in this type of contribution. Redistribution in kind presupposes an extensive state apparatus designed to facilitate handling the commodities in question and requiring even public production as well as public distribution of the affected commodities. In two-party, majority-voting systems riddled with pressure groups and sometimes beset by inefficiency and even corruption, the potential for resource misallocation within the public sector is considerable.[14] For this reason alone, liberalist philosophy parts company with the approach advocated by Foldes by reference to Pareto criteria.[15]

The liberal, therefore, when confronted by a dilemma such as that posed by Foldes, would turn his back on the short-term implications of the Pareto principle and would seek out alternative market solutions. For example, as James Buchanan (1968) has emphasized,[16] since the principal problems arose in consequence of uncertainty, it might well be possible to allow trade itself to provide information which could then be utilized to modify the initial set of transfers in the numeraire commodity. In this manner, ignorance about individual-preference functions would soon be dispelled and the problem outlined by Foldes would disappear.

The liberal is sufficiently aware of the working of the political process, however, to expect that 'middle voter' fears concerning the market mechanism will be reflected in state income-redistribution policies. His task and indeed his challenge is that of persuading the middle voter of the advantages of numeraire redistribution and of countering the distorting influences of pressure groups who stand to benefit from redistribution in kind.[17]

The second Pareto-sponsored attack on liberalist philosophy has been mounted recently within the context of interdependent preference functions. In circumstances where interdependence arises via the concern of the rich over the generalized poverty of the poor, Pareto-optimal redistribution in cash is the unequivocal outcome, be it via private charity or the fiscal intervention of central government. But interdependence does not always assume this dimension. For example, interest in the consumption of others may be derived from the externalities accruing from the consumption of a particular commodity, with utility functions taking the form

$$U^A = U^A (X_1^A, X_2^A, \ldots, X_n^A, X_1^B), \tag{6}$$

and

$$U^B = U^B(X_1^B, X_2^B, \ldots, X_n^B), \tag{7}$$

where X_1 is the commodity whose consumption by B provides external benefits to A.

More specifically, Lindsay (1969) has recently argued, with particular reference to medicare consumption, that a more equal consumption is desired among individuals demonstrating the same 'medical need'. This suggested a utility function of the form

$$U^J = U^J(X_1^J, X_2^J, \ldots, X_n^J, e_i),\tag{8}$$

where

$$e_i = -\sum_{i=1}^{s} (\overline{X}1 - X1^i).$$

In such circumstances, Lindsay justified the public provision of medicare, partly by reference to the costs of administering either a suitable subsidy or rationing system and partly by reference to the practical problem of defining clinically identical states and of identifying individuals in such states. He urged that a single-course programme such as that found in Britain's National Health Service might well be the most appropriate second-best instrument for optimizing medicare provision given the equality of consumption constraint, and, indeed, suggested that such utility functions provided a possible theoretical foundation which might justify the institutional characteristics and structure of the British National Health Service.

If this, indeed, were the logical consequence of utility functions such as those specified by Lindsay there would be a clear conflict between liberalist philosophy and the dictates of the Pareto principle, for the public provision of medicare, associated with the destruction of market transactions, squares ill with liberalist philosophy. In practice, however, Lindsay himself has to recognize the limitations of the political process as a device for obtaining the requisite degree of equality in medicare consumption,[18] and the conflict therefore may be less real than at first sight would appear to be the case. In any event, the liberal is already aware of the need to educate the voting public as to the viable market alternatives to the public provision of medicare. As Lindsay (1969) correctly emphasizes, the politicians have clearly taken their view of the middle voter preferences and have acted accordingly: 'This may well be one of those situations in which the politician's sensitive ear may read the preferences of his constituents better than the econometrician with his computer. In any case, the politician has made his reading and acted accordingly. He apparently feels that the provision of medical care is indeed a special case calling for unique treatment by governments' (p. 362).

V. Conclusions

Professor Sen is right. Those with liberal values may have to eschew adherence to Pareto optimality, especially where the issues of market destruction and of the extension of the public sector are at stake. Nowhere is the policy conflict more apparent, perhaps, than in the debate over the most appropriate pattern of income redistribution, as is evident from the foregoing discussion.

Having said this, it is clearly erroneous to draw the conclusion that liberal economists must be reduced to a state of embarrassment because their policy conclusions do not conform to the Pareto principle. The Pareto principle itself can never be more than a useful starting point for analysis of economic policy, and it is only with the increasing professionalization of economics that it has been awarded such pre-eminence in the literature of welfare economics. In contrast, the liberal economist has always recognized that when he makes policy recommendations he is responsible for them in the round and that such recommendations are derived from a social and political philosophy embracing far more elements than arrangements which are designed solely to promote economic efficiency.

Almost two centuries ago, Adam Smith drily observed that 'there is much ruin in a Nation'. Those who still find much to be commended in his attempts to delineate the proper functions of the state must see themselves as engaged in the difficult task of trying to prevent such ruin as is likely by the power of reason and persuasion. On these matters, the Pareto principle has nothing to say, for it imprisons its adherents in a methodological straitjacket.

NOTES

1. Reproduced with minor amendments from *Journal of Political Economy* Vol. 80, No. 3, May/June 1972.
2. Using modern set theoretic techniques, Sen (1970) demonstrated that with particular configurations of individual preferences there is no social decision function which satisfies the necessary conditions for a Pareto optimum and Sen's specified condition of 'minimal liberalism'. The Pareto liberal is therefore viewed as facing an inconsistency of choice. Sen's condition of 'minimal liberalism' is merely that 'for each individual i, there is at least one pair of alternatives, say (x, y), such that if this individual prefers x to y, then society should prefer x to y, and if this individual prefers y to x, then society should prefer y to x' (p. 153). The problem of inconsistent choice arises in societies in which individuals do not respect each other's personal choices, that is, where interdependencies exist between the utility functions of separate individuals. This was the point of departure for the present article.
3. Perhaps the most consistent advocate of this approach is J. M. Buchanan (1959, p. 125): 'This Pareto rule is itself an ethical proposition, a value statement, but it is one which requires a minimum of premises and one which should command wide assent.'
4. It might be argued that the compensation principle moderates this implication of the Pareto principle. In theory, perhaps it does, but the practical problems of applying the compensation principle are immense. Moreover, it is doubtful whether anything short of actual compensation would suffice in practice, despite the emphasis in the theoretical literature upon potential compensation. For example: 'Now it is clear that Pareto's criterion cannot in all cases give us unambiguous results, and if, indeed, as Professor Samuelson has suggested, we should require perfection in our recommendations, this criterion can never give us any results' (Baumol, 1967, p. 171).

5. Buchanan argued that Wicksellian unanimity requirements may be moderated to exclude 'unreasonable' members of the group (1959, p. 135). This is a highly dubious position for a 'Paretian Liberal' to adopt. For who is to decide which members should be excluded?

6. See Robbins (1952) and also Hicks (1959). 'The liberal, or noninterference, principles of the classical (Smithian or Ricardian) economists were not, in the first place, economic principles; they were an application to economics of principles that were thought to apply over a much wider field. The contention that economic freedom made for economic efficiency was no more than a secondary support' (Hicks, 1959, p. viii).

7. As Hicks wrote: 'I have accordingly no intention, in abandoning Economic Welfarism, of falling into the "fiat libertas, ruat caelum" which some latter-day liberals seem to see as the only alternative. What I do maintain is that the liberal goods are goods – that they are values which, however, must be weighed up against other values. The freedom and the justice that are possible of attainment are not the same in all societies, at all times, and in all places; they are themselves conditioned by external environment, and (in the short period at least) by what has occurred in the past. Yet we can recognize these limitations and still feel that these ends are worthier ends than those which are represented in a production index' (1959, p. xiv).

8. There is, of course, room for considerable differences of views as between individual liberals concerning 'optimal' income distribution.

9. Primary income redistribution is a function of society's view of equity. Conflicting views within society about equity have to be resolved, for example, by the political process, or, in extreme cases, by revolution. Secondary redistribution is a necessary consequence of the acceptance of the Paretian efficiency criteria, once it is established that interdependencies exist between the utility functions of separate individuals. In contrast to the resolution of the problem of equity, it involves voluntary giving rather than compulsory taking. It can therefore be put into effect through the voluntary exchange system, except in circumstances of market failure where political intervention may again be required (cf. Musgrave, 1970).

10. See Goldfarb (1970, pp. 994–6), where the following analysis is rigorously developed.

11. Goldfarb suggests that taxes will be the more preferred to charity as a means of Pareto-preferred income redistribution the greater the gap between the N and K (that is, the greater the proportion of rich to total population).

12. That is, including Hochman and Rodgers (1969), Buchanan (1959, 1968), and Tullock (1970), together with a growing number of economists who are content to analyse the case for income redistribution within a Pareto framework.

13. Foldes assumes that the government maximizes a social welfare function of the form $w(x, y) = \phi[U_A(x, y) \, U_B(1 - x, 1 - y)]$ where (x, y) denotes a final distribution between individuals A and B.

14. And thus for Pareto-preferred solutions which favour a cash rather than an in kind redistribution of income even where the nirvana approach would reverse the solution.

15. The liberal need not depart from Pareto criteria insofar as a realistic analysis of political behaviour suggests that 'in kind' solutions involve resource misallocation which conventional analysis would ignore. On the other hand, the liberal by inclination will assume a more suspicious view of the state than would a conservative or a socialist reared in the cult of omniscient and impartial government. Moreover, even where a realistic analysis of political behaviour would still place in kind redistribution in a Pareto-preferred position, the liberal would wish to trade off the loss of individual freedom against the conventional welfare benefits of state expansion.

16. Buchanan nevertheless demonstrated his essentially conservative stance on the issue of income redistribution very clearly in this comment: 'In my view, a consistent methodological position does not allow the introduction of non-individualistic norms in *either* allocation *or* distribution. It will be objected that my approach amounts to an "opting out" of the discussion of many interesting and highly important issues of applied economic policy. So it does, but I can see no personal excuse for joining other economists in an attempt to hoodwink the public into thinking that we make more sense out of these issues than analysis allows' (p. 188).

17. Once again, the liberal would take issue with the conservatism of 'Virginian-blend' liberals on the implications of two-party, majority-vote systems. For example, Buchanan (1968) would merely seem to endorse solutions thrown up by such a system. 'My position carries with it some of the same implications for economists as that expressed by Foldes. The externalities

model could readily be extended to cover the illustrative examples he cites. Economists should devote more attention to redistribution in specific non-numeraire goods. The contrast in method should, however, be stressed. While Foldes is saying that distribution in kind may be an efficient means of achieving externally derived policy objectives, I advance the refutable hypothesis that distribution in kind is the predictable outcome of the political process' (p. 190).

18. See Lindsay (1969, p. 362): 'Such an examination might reveal factors not considered here which act to thwart the egalitarian aims of the Health Service. For example, to a certain extent medical care is clearly rationed among individuals on the basis of the opportunity cost of the time spent "waiting" for service rather than on the basis of the doctor's evaluations of the relative "medical needs" of competing patients' (p. 362). For a realistic assessment of the economics of medicare provision by the state in two-party, majority-vote systems see Buchanan (1965).

REFERENCES

Baumol, W. J. (1967) *Welfare Economics and the Theory of the State* 2nd edition, Bell, London.

Buchanan, J. M. (1959) 'Positive economics, welfare economics, and political economy' *Journal of Law and Economics* Vol. 2, October, pp. 124–38.

Buchanan, J. M. (1965) *The Inconsistencies of the National Health Service* Occasional Paper No. 7, Institute of Economic Affairs, London.

Buchanan, J. M. (1968) 'What kind of redistribution do we want?' *Economica* Vol. 35, No. 138, May, pp. 185–90.

Director, A. (1964) 'The parity of the economic market place' *Journal of Law and Economics* Vol. 7, October, pp. 1–11.

Dobb, M. (1969) *Welfare Economics and the Economics of Socialism* Cambridge University Press, Cambridge.

Foldes, L. (1967) 'Income redistribution in money and in kind' *Economica* Vol. 34, No. 133, February, pp. 30–41.

Friedman, M. (1962) *Capitalism and Freedom* University of Chicago Press, Chicago.

Goldfarb, R. S. (1970) 'Pareto optimal redistribution: Comment' *American Economic Review* Vol. 60, No. 5, December, pp. 994–6.

Hayek, F. A. (1960) *The Constitution of Liberty* Routledge & Kegan Paul, London.

Hicks, J. R. (1959) *Essays in World Economics* Clarendon, Oxford.

Hochman, H. M. and Rodgers, J. R. (1969) 'Pareto optimal redistribution' *American Economic Review* Vol. 59, No. 4, September, pp. 542–57.

Lindsay, C. M. (1969) 'Medical care and the economics of sharing' *Economica* Vol. 36, No. 144, November, pp. 351–62.

Machlup, F. (1969) 'Liberalism and the choice of freedom' in E. Streissler (ed.) *Roads to Freedom: Essays in Honour of Friedrich von Hayek* Routledge & Kegan Paul, London.

Musgrave, R. A. (1970) 'Pareto optimal redistribution: Comment' *American Economic Review* Vol. 60, No. 5, December, pp. 991–3.

Nath, S. K. (1969) *A Reappraisal of Welfare Economics* Routledge & Kegan Paul, London.

Olsen, E. O. (1971) 'Some theorems in the theory of efficient transfers' *Journal of Political Economy* Vol. 79, No. 1, January/February, pp. 166–76.

Peacock, A. T. and Berry, D. (1951) 'A note on the theory of income redistribution' *Economica* Vol. 18, No. 79, February, pp. 83–90.

Peacock, A. T. and Wiseman, J. (1964) *Education for Democrats* Hobart Paper No. 25, Institute of Economic Affairs, London.

Robbins, L. C. (1952) *The Theory of Economic Policy in English Classical Political Economy* Macmillan, London.

Rowley, C. K. (1969) 'The political economy of British education' *Scottish Journal of Political Economy* Vol. 16, No. 2, June, pp. 152–76.

Sen, A. (1970) 'The impossibility of a Paretian liberal' *Journal of Political Economy* Vol. 78, No. 1, January/February, pp. 152–7.

Tullock, G. (1970) *Private Wants, Public Means* Basic Books, New York.

CHAPTER 3

The Treatment of
the Principles of Public Finance
in *The Wealth of Nations*[1]

I

One of the direct consequences of the dominance of positive economics in contemporary economic training and research has been a sharp increase in the opportunity cost of including the history of economic thought as part of the equipment of the 'compleat economist'. In the specialized area of public finance, decline in scholarly interest in the work of past masters was arrested, it is true, by the inspiration derived from the pioneer work of Wicksell, Lindahl, and some Italian writers which led to the development of the modern theory of public goods,[2] but this may only be the exception, although an outstanding one, which proves the rule. The scant references to the work of the classical economists in textbooks and treatises have now a ritualistic air about them, and the days when it was felt necessary to devote a chapter to discussion of the Smithian 'canons of taxation' have gone.

If professional judgement of public financiers avers that Adam Smith requires no more than a passing mention, what purpose is served by an exegesis and commentary on the relevant sections of *The Wealth of Nations*? No *vade mecum* is needed for those simply interested in intellectual history, for there are his views set out, crystal clear, in Book v of his masterpiece. From time to time, the economics profession renews its interest in the history of economic thought because of some remarkable discovery, such as the Overstone papers, or some extraordinary feat of literary detection, such as the identification by Professor Fetter of the authorship of articles on economics in the various nineteenth-century reviews. I have no such major discoveries to report and my incursions into scholarly sleuthing[3] produced no results of any consequence.

Perhaps sufficient reason for reappraisal is to be found in the shortcomings of 'positive economics' itself as a framework for the discussion of the public finances. The analytical skills which positive economics develops, important though they are, do not train us to identify problems of interest and significance in economic policy. Nor do they necessarily help to develop the talent for devising workable economic institutions and instruments (such as new forms of taxation and methods of expenditure control) adapted to policy requirements.

   The Wealth of Nations is a compelling advertisement for an approach to public finance which avoids the arid scholasticism often associated with the analytical refinements of positive economics and a narrow outlook which can even on occasion lead to methodological error. I hope to show in this contribution that Adam Smith treated issues in public finance which receive close attention in the current literature with a good deal more sophistication than is often found today. Inevitably, the development of this thesis calls for a selective treatment of his views,[4] and those who would do full justice to them will find no substitute for reading Smith's pithy prose for themselves.

II

An important aspect of the modern theory of public finance is its domination by Paretian welfare economics, particularly in the theory of public (social) goods. The familiar Paretian analysis indicates that, in the absence of externalities, but in the presence of competition in both the product and factor markets, an economic equilibrium can be reached which is compatible with individual consumer choice. It is easy to draw the conclusion from this analysis that the fulfilment of the Paretian assumptions, particularly the belief in the sanctity of individual choice and maintenance of competition, would create an economy fully acceptable to liberal economists in the Smithian tradition.[5] The formal model has been developed in recent years to take account of the problem that some goods have the character of 'publicness'.[6] To maximize the welfare of an individualistic society, subject to this further condition, requires that the vertical sum of the indifference curves of each member of society is tangential to the transformation function representing the alternative production opportunities of private and public goods. To achieve Pareto optimality, all individuals would have to agree on the division of the cost of public goods which each would have to bear, and also on the amount of each public good which is to be provided. Thus arises the familiar dilemma that, as public goods can be equally enjoyed by all, there is no way in which the market can force individuals to reveal their preferences for such goods. The problem posed by this situation is to find some alternative decision-making process which individuals will all accept and which at the same time allows the Paretian optimum to be achieved.

It would take us far away from our subject to do justice to all faceı the mammoth literature on 'Pareto-relevant' decision-making process However, those who have followed the Wicksellian tradition have tried ı devise voting systems which simulate, if they do not replicate, a perfect market. Broadly speaking, these have diverged markedly from straight 'one man one vote' systems, but have required some initial distribution of voting power, coupled with freedom to trade votes, including the payment of compensation (bribery) between voters in order to obtain majority support for particular decisions about the amount and the financing of public goods, all in the interests, it must be noted, of preserving the Paretian rule.[7]

Even with the elaborate seventeenth-century discussion of the idea of a 'social contract' before him, Smith can hardly be criticized for not deriving the proper functions of government from the tastes and preferences of individual consumers, when in his day the very notion of the basic Paretian precondition for efficient operation of the economy – perfect competition – was suspect.[8]

For Smith the important preoccupation was to devise a system of public finance and other measures of public policy which did not destroy markets, either by intervention in the private economy or through the economic operations in the public economy, for the destruction of markets was incompatible with the pursuit of Smith's ultimate aim – the preservation of 'natural liberty'. Thus in a famous passage which heralds the introduction of his system of public finance, Smith writes:

> All systems either of preference or restraint, therefore, being thus completely taken away, the obvious and simple system of natural liberty establishes itself of its own accord. Every man, as long as he does not violate the laws of justice, is left perfectly free to pursue his own interest his own way, and to bring both his industry and capital into competition with those of any other man, or order of men. The sovereign is completely discharged from a duty in the attempting to perform which he must always be exposed to innumerable delusions, and for the proper performance of which no human wisdom or knowledge could ever be sufficient; the duty of superintending the industry of private people, and of directing it towards the employments most suitable to the interests of the society . . .

and he adds:

> According to the system of natural liberty, the sovereign has only three duties to attend to; three duties of great importance, indeed, but plain and intelligible to common understandings: first, the duty of protecting the society from the violence and invasion of other independent societies; secondly, the duty of protecting, as far as possible, every member of society from the injustice or oppression of every other member of it, or the duty of establishing an exact administration of justice; and thirdly, the duty of erecting and maintaining certain public works and certain public institutions, which it can never be for the interest of any individual, or small number of individuals, to erect and maintain, because the profit could never repay the expense of any individual or small number of individuals, though it may frequently do much more than repay it to a great society.[9]

Smith may avoid the important question, who shall decide the amount and form of government expenditure on goods and services, for there is no discussion in his work of voting systems or principles of Parliamentary control over expenditures.[10] At the same time, his range of interests extends to questions which are hardly touched on in books on public finance, even those in which the theory of public goods is regarded as no more than a point of departure for discussion of practical issues. Thus the 'polar case' of indivisibility is seen by Smith as the exception rather than the rule, and he seeks other, equally cogent, reasons for market failure as the basis for public provision of goods. He does not fall into the trap of assuming that 'publicness' of goods makes the case for public production, as distinct from public *finance* of goods and service by the state. Finally, he is conscious of the need to ensure that in cases where public production is inevitable, some attempt must be made to simulate market conditions in order to prevent inefficiency.

We can illustrate Smith's eclectic approach by looking at each of the 'three duties' which are laid out in the quotation above. Smith accepts that defence is a pure public good in the Samuelsonian sense, but this fact does not rule out the possibility that defence can be provided by voluntary action or imply that it necessarily requires public organization of the production of defence. Smith lays considerable emphasis on the 'state of society' as the important determinant of the form of defence provision. Thus during the second 'stage' of economic development, represented by pastoral communities,[11] the common pastimes, such as wrestling, cudgel playing, etc., develop complementary skills for conduct of warfare. Furthermore,

> when a Tartar or Arab actually goes to war, he is maintained by his own herds and flocks which he carries with him, in the same manner as in peace. His chief or sovereign . . . is at no sort of expense in preparing him for the field; and when he is in it, the chance of plunder is the only pay which he either expects or requires. [WN v.i.a.4]

With the development of technical changes in weapons, not only does defence production become more capital intensive, but specialized skills have to be developed which are no longer complementary with alternative occupations. But, during the very period when improvements in agriculture and manufacture – the third stage – are taking place, resulting in economic progress which excites the jealousy of neighbours and provokes invasion, the 'natural habits of the people render them altogether incapable of defending themselves' (WN v.i.a.15) because of the high opportunity cost of voluntary engagement in learning the new arts of war. It is at this stage that the state has to choose between enforcing military exercise through the creation of a militia or taxing the community in order to finance a standing army. Adam Smith arrives at the conclusion that the second alternative of 'public production of defence' is to be preferred, not because defence is a public good, but because, following the principle of division of labour, a standing army is more efficient. Furthermore, contrary to the contemporary republican belief that a standing army is a danger to liberty, Smith argues that the 'degree of liberty which approaches licentiousness can be tolerated only in countries where the sovereign is secured by a well-regulated standing army' (WN v.i.a.41),[12] that is to say the important public good 'liberty' can only be secured when an army firmly under government control has no rival domestic producers to contend with. As a tailpiece to his discussion, he predicts that defence becomes progressively more expensive as society advances in civilization. Technically more effective weapons not only escalate the cost of war and training costs in peace,[13] but, more important still, require the development of more expensive fortification of towns to counteract the employment of those same weapons by actual or potential enemies.

The mode of discharge of the 'second duty', the administration of justice, likewise cannot be explained solely by the necessity of making it equally available to all. The prima facie case for public production of justice rests on the poor quality of private production. Resolution of disputes over property rights can sometimes be decided by private arbitration, but to make the administration of all justice depend on private enterprise could lead to abuse. For, as Smith puts it:

> The person who applied for justice with a large present in his hand was likely to get something more than justice, while he who applied for it with a small one, was likely to get something less. Justice might be too frequently delayed, in order that this present might be repeated. The amercement, besides, of the person complained of, might frequently suggest a very strong reason for finding him in the wrong, even when he had not really been so. [WN v.i.b.14]

However, if 'quality control' is made possible only by making it impossible to buy justice, there remains for Smith, as for several important eighteenth-century liberal thinkers, one significant difficulty in turning production over to the state, how to prevent justice from being 'sacrificed to what is vulgarly called politics', for

> The persons entrusted with the great interests of the state may, even without any corrupt views, sometimes imagine it necessary to sacrifice to those interests the rights of a private man. But upon the impartial administration of justice depend the liberty of every individual, the sense which he has of his own security. In order to make every individual perfectly secure in the possession of every right which belongs to him, it is not only necessary that the judicial should be separated from the executive power, but that it should be rendered as much as possible independent of that power. [WN v.i.b.25]

Such a view is hardly exceptional in eighteenth-century liberal writing, but what is interesting are the institutional methods which Smith considered might give it practical expression. Thus courts might be financed largely by fees without danger of corruption, with judges paid by piece-work – and in arrear to make them diligent![14] But, as Smith realizes, defining the 'piece' is not easy, and instances how judges in some countries, whose emoluments were regulated by the number of pages they had occasion to write in court, easily found it possible to 'multiply words beyond all necessity'. He wonders whether freedom from executive power could be ensured by payment out of, say, the income of landed property managed by the courts themselves, but concludes that: 'The necessary instability of such a fund seems, however, to render it an improper one for the maintenance of an institution which ought to last for ever' (WN v.i.b.23).

If Smith's discussion of ear-marking sources for revenue for judicial services outside the control of the executive and legislature is tentative, he is unwilling to go any further than to admit that defraying the expenses of justice out of general taxation would involve no 'impropriety' (in WN v.i.c).

The discussion of the 'third' duty – the provision of certain public works and institutions – is often instanced as giving the lie to the charge that Smith was a proponent of *laissez-faire*.[15] The charge, of course, is false, but it must be noted that he is unimpressed by the view that such services as the transport system (and particularly canals), health, education, might be run by government departments, and is very careful in his examination of the nature and amount of general revenue which should be assigned to the support of the organizations which operate them. The only public service of a mercantile character which Smith believes can be successfully run by a government department is the Post Office because 'there is no mystery in the business. The returns are not only certain, but immediate.'[16]

In the important case of transport systems, for example, Smith anticipates modern discussion. The State has to provide finance for the building of roads and must supervise financial methods for their maintenance and improvement, because of the external benefits which would not otherwise be captured if roads were left to individual enterprise. This familiar argument is supplemented by the observation that roads break down local monopolies, in itself a further benefit to the economy, and hence their development will require state encouragement in order to overcome the opposition of interest groups.[17]

In the search for principles of operation for common transport policies, the EEC Commission (1971) have suggested that transport systems should be operated independently of the government budget, but subject to pricing rules based on the marginal cost principle which, broadly speaking, would require transport authorities to charge vehicles differentially according to their use of the system, taking account of the social costs, e.g. congestion costs, which they impose on others. These ground rules may take a lot of swallowing by UK government officials, but find more than an echo in *The Wealth of Nations*, Book v. Smith rejects the proposition that revenue from tolls should be made to operate 'as a very great resource which might at some time or other be applied to the exigencies of the state', for 'the turnpike tolls being continually augmented in this manner, instead of facilitating the inland commerce of the country, as at present, would soon become a very great incumbrance upon it' (WN v.i.d.12). The national system should be operated by trustees, whereas local street paving and lighting should be conducted by local public authorities and financed by local taxes because the benefits of such services are specific to inhabitants of the locality. The trustees should be instructed to charge vehicles exactly in proportion to the wear and tear they inflict on the system. It is at this juncture that Smith makes specific mention of tax shifting. The tax or toll is 'advanced' by the carrier, though the consumer bears the tax in full. But the *net* benefit to the consumer, it is argued, is positive for the provision of roads lowers the 'expense of carriage' so that the price of the goods bought, even after allowing for the toll, is lower than it would otherwise be. Even if such a result rests on special assumptions which are not explored by Smith, the argument shows a ready appreciation of a cost–benefit approach (WN v.i.b.4).

The problem of maintaining incentives in non-market-oriented activities which are provided directly by the state or supported by public funds is one of the dominating themes of that part of the 'third duty' which is concerned with 'public institutions', now termed the problem of avoiding '*X*-inefficiency'. Smith is primarily interested in the case where, following the usual arguments for under-provision of a service through the market, the state supports, say, educational and religious institutions by some form of endowment or ear-marked revenue such as income from state properties or the yield of a particular tax. We have already reviewed his suggestions for regulating the payment to judges, and his views on the economics of education are treated elsewhere by Mark Blaug (1976). Here we only review Smith's treatment of a familiar dilemma in public expenditure control. If the state allocates funds to higher and secondary education establishments which represent the bulk of their income, the 'discipline of colleges and universities is in general contrived, not for the benefit of the students, but for the interest, or more properly speaking, for the ease of the masters' (WN v.i.f.15). But unless the state combines such a system of public finance with detailed control and supervision of the institutions concerned, ignorant administrators with wide discretion may at best exercise ineffective control and, at worst, act in an arbitrary and capricious manner. Nothing is more likely to degrade the teaching profession, whose attention will be directed towards toadying to the government authorities. Smith never resolves the dilemma, although he is aware that he is making a powerful case for an education system financed by fees. There is much to admire here in the vigour of the prose, the wealth of illustration from both ancient and contemporary history, and the deft touches of satire, but not much practical guidance, other than for the public finance of education to be so arranged that no teacher is paid wholly from the public purse (WN v.i.f.55).

III

Having established that the optimal allocation of resources would require both some forms of public production on a limited scale, varying with the stage of development of society, and also state subsidies to private or quasi-public institutions, Smith has to consider the implications of transferring resources to the state to give effect to his public expenditure proposals. He dismisses the possibility of financing these proposals by the patrimony of the state or by state trading mainly on the grounds of their insufficiency, and turns to examine taxes.

Smith adopts a simple expository procedure in examining the tax system. First of all certain normative 'maxims' (Smith does not call them 'canons') are stated: the famous maxims of equality, certainty, convenience, and economy. Taxes are then classified into those which are *intended* to be borne by the three sources of 'private revenue', wages, profit, and rent, and those which 'fall indifferently' upon any of these three sources of private revenue. Ignoring some classificatory peculiarities of Smith, these two broad categories cover respectively taxes on incomes and taxes on expenditure. Examples of each kind of taxation are culled from the experience of several European countries as well as Britain[18] and appraised in the light of the maxims, having regard to the problem of tax shifting which complicates the appraisal procedure. What is noticeably missing from his exposition is any attempt to weight the importance of each maxim, so that no final conclusion is drawn either about the relative merits of different forms of taxation or about the 'package of taxes' which would best accord with Smith's own normative propositions. But the exposition is full of practical suggestions on the operation of particular taxes which were deservedly influential in his own time[19] We now examine the 'maxims' more closely, and consider one important example of their application before considering a more fundamental criticism of Smith's approach.

IV

The maxim of 'equality' entails the acceptance of income as the relevant measure of tax to be paid by individuals, who in relation to the services of government are like 'joint tenants of a great estate, who are all obliged to contribute in proportion to their respective interests in the estate' (WN v.ii.b.3). That Smith meant that taxes should as far as possible be proportional to income is clear enough, but this technical examination of taxes leads him to conclude that any tax falling on subsistence wages must of necessity be shifted, so that there are good practical reasons for having an exemption limit.[20] Taking all taxes into consideration, we can define Smith's optimal tax schedule (after allowing for taxes paid and with shifting taken into account) as one in which the marginal tax rate remains constant, but the average rate would rise with income in consequence of the exemption limit: in short, a mildly progressive tax structure. Proportionality has to be modified on practical rather than on equity grounds.[21]

The remaining maxims amount to principles designed to minimize the real costs of raising revenue to the taxpayer. He must suffer as little as possible the 'psychic' costs of not knowing what he is to pay and how the amount is calculated which would have the side-effect of turning the tax system into a sordid bargain between the collector and the payer, encouraging evasion and violating the principle of 'equal treatment of equals'. Convenience of payment reduces the real costs of collection which would otherwise fall on the taxpayer. Economy in collection reduces the real costs of transferring resources for public use. Heavy administrative expenses of collection, being associated with inquisitorial examination of taxpayers, e.g. in detecting smuggling, imposes a double burden on the community, the extra costs of administration and the 'vexation' of inquiry which 'is not strictly speaking an expense, [but] is certainly equivalent to the expense at which every man would be willing to redeem himself from it' (WN v.ii.b.6).

Smith's maxims are not original, and were anticipated in earlier literature, notably by the cameralists, but Smith himself did not claim that they were:

> The evident justice and utility of the foregoing maxims have recommended them more or less to the attention of all nations. All nations have endeavoured, to the best of their judgment, to render their taxes as equal as they could contrive: as certain, as convenient to the contributor, both in the time and in the mode of payment, and in proportion to the revenue which they brought to the prince, as little burdensome to the people. [WN v.ii.b.7]

But Smith's own analysis of European tax practice presents ample evidence to contradict this last sentence!

V

The application of Smith's maxims can be best understood by taking an example, and I propose to consider his extensive discussion of 'taxes on consumable commodities' (in WN v.ii.k).

For Smith the first maxim leads him to support taxes on 'luxuries', which might be defined negatively as taxes which do not impinge on subsistence which, by reducing the supply of labour, will, in the long run, raise labour's supply price, i.e. the tax will be shifted to other classes. Immediately this maxim calls for a whole range of reforms. In principle, taxes on fuel (e.g. coal), light (e.g. candles), on health (e.g. soap), on basic foodstuffs (e.g. corn), and clothing (e.g. leather) should certainly be reduced, although abolition might produce revenue difficulties. Simultaneously, subject to revenue constraints, taxes on consumable commodities should be reviewed in order to devise a system which would directly hit those of 'middling or more than middling fortune'.

Smith's reforms are not merely couched in general terms, and several taxes are examined in considerable detail, notably the taxes on beer and spirits which formed the bulk of the taxes on expenditure in his time.[22] His reform proposals in this case offer an insight into his method of tax analysis. Malt was an important input for spirits, and also for heavy beers. It was taxed as an input, and beers and spirits were separately taxed through the breweries and distilleries respectively. However, home brewing and distilling were common among richer country families who were exempt from the tax on 'output', and relatively lightly taxed on the 'input' of malt. An important administrative problem to be reckoned with was that opportunities for defrauding the revenue were greater in the brewery or distillery than in the malt-house. Smith puts forward the obvious solution, which is to increase the tax on malt and reduce the tax on brewed beer. This would benefit the poor at the expense of the rich in two ways: first of all, by lowering the price of beer with a low malt content and, secondly, by the differential increase in the price of distilled liquors bought by the rich and in the cost of home-brewed beer with a high malt content enjoyed by the country gentry. Furthermore, the alteration of the point of tax would ease the problem of evasion. Smith, however, realizes that his conclusion must take account of possible revenue loss and that what we now term the elasticity assumptions are crucial to the analysis. He circumvents this problem by recommending that the increased tax on malt should be accompanied by adjustments in the taxes on spirits and beer which would maintain the price of spirits and reduce that of beer. By assuming that all taxes are passed on to the consumer in full and that the price elasticity of demand for beer is greater than unity, he is able to conclude that revenue would in fact increase.[23] He goes further and considers how far the demand for barley, used along with malt in distilling, would be affected by tax changes, but having shown that the demand for malt would not be reduced by the tax changes, he concludes that the demand for barley would be unaffected so long as there was competition in barley production. (It does not occur to him that distillers might ever dare to alter the factor mix by substituting barley for malt!)[24] In short, although the analysis is incomplete (no clear statement is made about production functions) and several assumptions are used without evidence, Smith shows his capacity for analytical rigour as well as for practical insight.

Public financiers have often speculated on the possibility of devising a system of taxes on expenditure which would be both equitable and efficient, having regard to the administrative defects of direct taxes on income (see Buchanan and Forte, 1964). Smith also gives this idea a good run for its money. With taxes geared to hit the consumption of the rich, equity is achieved, and such taxes, too, are certain in their assessment, and convenient to the taxpayer who pays as he purchases. 'Upon the whole such taxes, therefore, are, perhaps, as agreeable to the three first of the four general maxims concerning taxes, as any other' (WN v.ii.k.60). But they are expensive to administer, encouraging smuggling for example, and vexatious to those who have to face 'the frequent visits and odious examination of the taxgatherers' (WN v.ii.k.65). Much that has been written about the 'case' for taxes on expenditure is an amplification of Smith's analysis. The rock on which reform schemes have usually foundered is that of the difficulty of adapting the system so that it can take account of the characteristics of the taxpayer, other than his income level, which are relevant to equity, such as his number of dependants and the structure of his inter-temporal preference system. The definition of the tax-paying unit – whether the individual or the household – is not considered by Smith, but he makes an interesting passing reference to the inter-temporal equity problem. Thus a man of 'great fortune' in his minority consumes little, so pays little by way of taxation on expenditure, and if in later years he is parsimonious he can continue to avoid taxation. Even if he is not parsimonious, he can avoid taxation designed to finance the protection of his property by living abroad – like the Irish absentee landlords. Smith concludes that no system of taxes on luxuries will meet his first maxim, and that being so, the system must be supplemented, for example by a land-tax which would hit the rich (WN v.ii.k.58).

VI

The method which Smith adopts in formulating principles of economic policy conforms with an honourable tradition. Explicit normative judgements are made and translated into economic objectives which conform with his ultimate aim: the establishment of the system of natural liberty. Given his analysis of the economy, the instruments of policy are then identified and their tasks defined. However, it has been claimed by Stigler that this method of analysis cannot be legitimately employed by Smith. If the pursuit of self-interest – 'the natural effort of every individual to better his condition' – is the best way of achieving wealth and prosperity, why should self-interest not be allowed to dominate their political as well as their economic actions? Commenting on Smith's famous maxims of taxation, he argues:

A Chancellor of the Exchequer would have found these rules most peculiar. If adopted, they would obtain for him at least the temporary admiration of the professors of moral philosophy but this is a slender and notably fickle constituency on which to build a party. The two basic canons of taxation are surely rather different:

1. The revenue system must not imperil the political support for the regime.
2. The revenue system must yield revenue.

Smith's maxims touch on aspects of a revenue system which are relevant to its productivity and acceptability, not always in the direction he wished, but they form a wholly inadequate basis for judging individual taxes.[25]

One can agree with Stigler that once having accepted the economic sophistication of Smithian man, there is no reason to doubt his political sophistication. Even then, Smith is quite clearly of the opinion that taxation brings with it the right of representation, and, in contrast to that formidable gentleman, Dr Johnson, supported representation of the American colonies in the British legislature.[26] Did Smith not also say that taxation was the badge of freedom and not of servitude? But it is one thing to be employing one's commercial or political talents to promote self-interest in a society which has accepted the necessity for competition as a way of channelling self-interest towards the goals of society and another to do so under conditions where entrenched monopoly privileges abound. Thus, to re-emphasize a point made earlier, while Smith might be criticized for neglecting to discuss the implication of his system of political economy for political organization, so that individual preferences could be reflected in the amount and composition of public goods and in the structure of taxation, such concerns pale into insignificance alongside his need to persuade his fellow men that sectional commercial interests buttressed by legislation which prevented competition and created inefficient state enterprises and departments were inimical to economic and social progress.[27]

The technique of moral suasion through the exposure of ignorance and prejudice seems justified in such circumstances as Smith faced, yet Stigler contends that at best 'this is an extraordinary slow and uncertain method of changing policy; at worst it may lead to policies which endanger society'. History hardly bears out Stigler's prediction, for successive Chancellors found nothing 'peculiar' about Smith's maxims and espoused them with almost indecent haste. But the creation of a political analogue to the market system – Parliamentary democracy – did not result in such a ready acceptance of Smith's principles of public expenditure. This is a problem which still engages the energies of those, including Professor Stigler and myself, who owe so much to the man from Kirkaldy.

NOTES

1. Reproduced with minor amendments from Wilson and Skinner (1976).
2. See the frequent references in public finance literature to their work which is translated in Musgrave and Peacock (1958).
3. According to Rae (1895), Smith's period of office as a Commissioner of Customs and Excise from 1781 until his death was characterized by punctilious devotion to duty (p. 330), but he did not appear to have developed further his ideas on public finance. A check on the records of the Customs and Excise Department and of Register House, Edinburgh, confirms this view.
4. Clearly this contribution is incomplete, for it covers Smith's views on the effects of public finance on the allocation and distribution of resources but says little about growth and development. I believe it impossible to provide an adequate treatment of Smith's position without reference to the alternative forms of government intervention affecting development which Smith examines, e.g. usury laws, labour legislation, debt, and monetary policy. In any case, the subject is fully covered in the admirable work by S. Hollander (1973).
5. That this is a false conclusion is shown in Peacock and Rowley (1972), reprinted in this volume as chapter 2.
6. That is to say, goods which, using fashionable terminology, are non-excludable and non-rival. Once provided to one person they are provided to all and consumption by one person does not prevent equal consumption by others. For a useful summary of public goods theory, see Peston (1972), chapter 2.
7. For a perceptive analysis of these problems, see Winch (1969).
8. Interestingly enough, David Hume's discussion of the origin of government closes with a passage which is reminiscent of modern explanations of the need for political action to cope with the problem of indivisible services: 'Two neighbours may agree to drain a meadow which they possess in common, because it is easy for them to know each other's mind; and each must perceive that the immediate consequence of his failing in his part is the abandoning of the whole project. But it is very difficult, and indeed impossible, that a thousand persons should agree in any such action; it being difficult for them to concert in so complicated a design, and still more difficult for them to execute it; while each seeks a pretext to free himself of the trouble and expense, and would lay the whole burden on others. Political society easily remedies both these inconveniences.' See David Hume *Treatise on Human Nature* (1740) iii.ii.7.
9. Adam Smith *The Wealth of Nations* iv.ix.51. All references are to the (fifth) Cannan edition, reprinted by Methuen and Co., 1961.
10. This point is considered further in section vi below.
11. For a detailed analysis of Smith as a student of the stages of the development of society, see Meek (1972).
12. For a fuller analysis of the distinction between 'publicness' of goods and 'public provision of goods', with particular reference to defence, see Forte (1967).
13. 'The powder, which is spent in a modern review, is lost irrecoverably, and occasions a very considerable expense. The javelins and arrows which were thrown or shot in an ancient one, could easily be picked up again, and were besides of very little value' (WN v.i.a.43).
14. 'By not being paid to the judges until the process was determined, [fees] might be some incitement to the diligence of the court in examining and deciding it. In courts which consisted of a considerable number of judges, by proportioning the share of each judge to the hours and days which he had employed in examining the process . . . public services are never better performed than when their reward comes only in consequence of their being performed' (WN v.i.b.20). Smith observes immediately after this quotation that a system of this sort operated in the France of his day.
15. See the notable attack on those who have so labelled Smith and his followers, by Robbins (1952), Lecture 1.
16. There is some doubt in Smith's exposition about the exact role of the state in the production of primary education and of certain recreational facilities, but I am inclined to agree with Stigler that the Post Office is the only case where government *management* is specifically mentioned. See Stigler (1976).
17. 'Though they introduce some rival commodities into the old market, they open up many new ones to its produce. Monopoly, besides, is a great enemy to good management, which

can never be universally established but in consequence of that free and universal competition which forces everybody to have recourse to it for the sake of self-defence' (WN i.xi.b.5).

18. Smith's main source of information was a remarkable book written by one Moreau de Beaumont called *Memoires concernant les droits et impositions en Europe* prepared for a commission on tax reform in France and published only for official use in 1768–9 in four volumes. The first volume gives an account of European tax systems and the remaining volumes review the French system in detail. According to Rae (1895, p. 344), Smith obtained his copy from Turgot and believed that there were only four copies available in Britain in his day. I have been able to track down only one copy publicly available which is in the British Museum.

19. For evidence see Rae (1895) Chs. 18, 20, and Dowell (1884) particularly vol. 2.

20. 'The middling and superior ranks of people, if they understood their own interest, ought always to oppose all taxes upon the necessaries of life, as well as all direct taxes upon the wages of labour' (WN v.ii.k.9).

21. I do not deny, of course, that Smith elsewhere seems to support progressive taxation on grounds of fairness, but in no more than a passing reference which is hardly a strong plea for soaking the rich: 'It is not *very unreasonable* [italics mine] that the rich should contribute to the public expence, not only in proportion to their revenue, but something more than in that proportion' (WN v.ii.e.6). E. Seligman makes the point in 'Progressive Taxation in Theory and Practice' (1908).

22. For relevant data, see Eckstein (1967).

23. 'According to this policy, the abatement of taxes upon the distillery ought not to be so great as to reduce, in any respect, the price of those liquors. Spirituous liquors might remain as dear as ever; while at the same time the wholesome and invigorating liquors of beer and ale might be considerable reduced in price. The people might thus be in part relieved from one of the burdens of which they at present complain the most; while at the same time the revenue might be considerably augmented' (WN v.ii.k.50).

24. Lord North followed Smith's advice in 1780 by increasing the malt duty with a rebate to brewers for sale so that the pot of beer would 'reach the lip of the consumer untaxed'. See Dowell (1884).

25. Stigler (1976) p. 243. I need hardly add that Professor Stigler is still one of Smith's most faithful admirers.

26. Johnson's pamphlet *Taxation no Tyranny* appeared in 1775, the year before the publication of *The Wealth of Nations*. On the American question, see Stevens (1976) p. 202.

27. Professor Stigler himself has presented a persuasive case for preserving lower layers of government as a means of fostering competition in the provision of public services (1957, pp. 213–19). His fiscal prescriptions are put forward with Smithian fervour, and with an equal disregard for the need to seek the blessing of political support.

REFERENCES

Blaug, M. (1976) 'The economics of education in English classical political economy: A re-examination' in Wilson and Skinner.

Buchanan, J. M. and Forte, F. (1964) 'Fiscal choice through time: A case for indirect taxation' *National Tax Journal* Vol. 17.

Dowell, S. (1884) *History of Taxation and Taxes in England* 3rd edition (reprinted 1965 by Frank Cass, London).

Eckstein, G. (1967) 'Adam Smiths Finanzwissenschaft' photocopy, Diplom-Arbeit, University of Nürnberg-Erlangen.

EEC Commission (1971) *Draft Decision on Common System of Charging for Transport Infrastructure* EEC, Brussels.

Forte, F. (1967) 'Should public goods be public?' *Papers on Non-Market Decision Making* No. 8.

Hollander, S. (1973) *The Economics of Adam Smith* Heinemann, London.

Meek, R. L. (1972) 'Smith, Turgot and the four stages theory' *History of Political Economy* Vol. 3.

Musgrave, R. A. and Peacock, A. T. (1958) *Classics in the Theory of Public Finance* Macmillan, London.

Peacock, A. T. and Rowley, C. K. (1972) 'Pareto optimality and the political economy of liberalism' *Journal of Political Economy* Vol. 80, No. 3, May/June.

Peston, M. (1972) *Public Goods and the Public Sector* Macmillan, London.

Rae, J. (1895) *Life of Adam Smith* Augustus Kelly, New York.

Robbins, L. C. (1952) *The Theory of Economic Policy in English Classical Political Economy* Macmillan, London.

Seligman, E. (1908) 'Progressive taxation in theory and practice' *American Economic Association Quarterly* third series, Vol. 9.

Smith, A. (1961) *The Wealth of Nations* Cannan edition, Methuen, London.

Stevens, D. (1976) 'Adam Smith and the colonial disturbances' in Wilson and Skinner.

Stigler, G. (1957) 'Federal expenditure policy for economic growth and stability' in E. S. Phelps (ed.) *Private Wants and Public Needs* W. W. Norton, New York.

Stigler, G. (1976) 'Smith's travels on the ship of state' in Wilson and Skinner.

Wilson, T. and Skinner, A. (1976) *Essays on Adam Smith* Oxford University Press, London.

Winch, D. M. (1969) 'Pareto, public goods and politics' *Canadian Journal of Economics* Vol. 2.

CHAPTER 4

Welfare Economics and the Public Regulation of Natural Monopoly[1]

(with Charles K. Rowley)

I. INTRODUCTION

A familiar way of introducing the economics student to the problems posed by market failure and to the need for public regulation of industry is by reference to the case of so-called 'natural monopoly'. (See, for example, Millward, 1971.) This case purports to demonstrate that in an industry characterised by a falling long-run marginal cost curve throughout the relevant output range only one firm can 'survive' and that this firm, in the absence of state intervention, will exploit its monopoly position, thereby creating welfare losses as price diverges from marginal cost in contravention of the famous marginal rule but in pursuit of maximum profits. Public regulation or outright nationalisation of industries with 'natural monopoly' characteristics is the conventional textbook solution to market failure of this kind.

There is a formidable literature, concerned with the difficulties encountered in applying the marginal rule to the regulated industries, which already throws doubt on the conventional wisdom of public utility pricing (Turvey, 1968, 1969; Williamson, 1966; Wiseman, 1957; Stigler and Friedland, 1962). Problems such as the identification of demand and costs under uncertainty conditions, the choice of the planning period upon which cost measurements will be based, the treatment of second-best considerations and the handling of the conflicts, which inevitably arise when state intervention results in significant income redistribution, for the most part have been thoroughly examined in the regulation literature. As yet, these problems have not been deemed by many economists to be sufficiently serious to call into question the regulatory solution to the natural monopoly situation. We shall not discuss them further in this paper.

Our doubts about the nature of and the necessity for regulation originate in another set of propositions which so far have attracted only limited attention in the regulation literature. We shall argue in this paper that (a) following the pioneering work of Demsetz (1964), the textbook prediction that a falling marginal cost for an industry leads to monopoly is a doubtful one; (b) it is no longer possible to discuss the public regulation of natural monopoly without taking into account the possibility of a shift in the marginal cost curve, through *X*-inefficiency (Comanor and Leibenstein, 1969; Crew and Rowley, 1971a; Crew et al., 1971; Crew and Rowley, 1972; Leibenstein, 1966; Kafoglis, 1969); and (c) the conventional identification of the consumers' interest with Paretian welfare economics leads to ambiguous and arbitrary results (cf. Peacock and Rowley, 1972; chapter 2 in this volume).

II. THE 'NATURAL MONOPOLY' CONTROVERSY: DEMSETZ V. TELSER

Fig. 4.1 portrays a natural monopoly as conventionally depicted in the textbook literature and this provides a useful starting point for our analysis.

Economists would normally argue (albeit on the basis of profit maximisation assumptions which now look a trifle battered) that, in the absence of

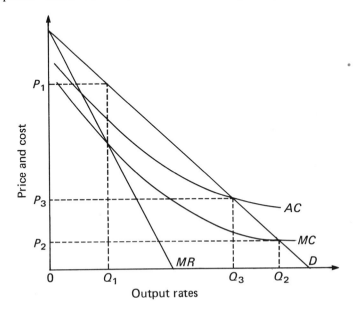

FIGURE 4.1

regulation, the long-run price and output solution would be at P_1 and Q_1 respectively. This solution would fail to satisfy the conditions for a Pareto optimum. Regulation would then be justified to attain the optimum solution, with price at P_2 and output at Q_2, and resulting losses would be financed by lump-sum transfers,[2] if sufficient consumers' surplus could not be tapped by resort to multi-part tariff pricing techniques. The public enterprise solution at first sight appears appetising in circumstances of natural monopoly since deficits are more easily handled within the public sector than between the private and the public sector.

In 1968, however, Demsetz challenged the conventional viewpoint on the natural monopoly issue by questioning the logic by which monopoly in the market-place was deduced from the presence of decreasing cost conditions in production, and by arguing that this deduction was based largely on an incorrect understanding of the concept of competition or rivalry. Where the market could support only a single producer as a consequence of scale economies in production, rival *potential* producers could offer to enter into contracts (which would be renewable periodically) with potential buyers (or their representatives) and in this bidding competition the rival who offered buyers the most favourable terms would obtain the production contract. There was no clear or necessary reason for bidding rivals to share in the production of the goods and, therefore, there was no clear reason for competition in bidding to result in an increase in per-unit production costs.

Demsetz could see no reason why the bidding outcome should be the monopoly price. Scale economies in production would imply that the bids submitted would offer increasing quantities at lower per-unit costs. They would imply nothing whatever about how competitive these prices would be. Demsetz concluded, indeed, that if the number of bidders was large, or if, for other reasons, collusion among them was impracticable, the contracted price could be very close to per-unit production costs. On this basis, Demsetz challenged a basic tenet of the regulation literature, namely that regulatory intervention was justifiable in the case of natural monopolies:

> At this juncture, it should be emphasised that I have argued, not that regulatory commissions are undesirable, but that economic theory does not at present provide a justification for commissions insofar as they are based on the belief that observed concentration and monopoly price bear any necessary relationship. [Demsetz, 1968, p. 61].

Telser (1969) clearly demonstrated in a critique of Demsetz that insofar as the bidding solution was effective in pushing price into equality with per-unit production cost the solution would be equivalent not to perfect competition but rather to Chamberlin's tangency solution of monopolistic competition, which is generally inefficient in the sense that marginal cost is not equated with price.[3] Demsetz (1971) acknowledged in his reply to Telser that the bidding solution would be at price P_3 and at output Q_3 in Fig. 4.1 and that this would not satisfy the necessary conditions for a Pareto optimum (i.e. price at P_2 and output at Q_2 even though price would be lower and output higher than in the pure monopoly solution.[4] The welfare implications of the Demsetz solution are considered further in a later section of this paper, in the light of a fundamental reappraisal of the Pareto principle. What is relevant to mention here is that Telser (1971), as a supporter of the conventional position, was bound to conclude in favour of regulation designed to achieve marginal cost pricing even though he might accede that the Demsetz prediction was correct for the bidding alternative.[5]

III. The Relevance of X-Inefficiency

The policy choice at issue in the Demsetz/Telser controversy lies between a bidding approach designed to achieve an average cost pricing solution whilst retaining private single firm production on the one hand and outright regulation (or public enterprise) designed to achieve the marginal cost pricing solution required by the Pareto principle on the other. Both parties assume, more or less explicitly, that the production function relevant in the decreasing cost case is determined quite independently from the media of regulatory intervention. There are good reasons for questioning this assumption by reference to X-inefficiency considerations.

Leibenstein (1966), in introducing the X-inefficiency concept into the economics literature, showed that firms producing in the absence of strong competitive pressures would lack sufficient incentive to maintain full internal efficiency and instead would allow their unit costs to rise, perhaps substantially, above the level that would obtain in competitive conditions. Subsequently, Comanor and Leibenstein (1969) demonstrated that market-power-induced X-inefficiency reinforced the conventional welfare economics case against monopoly by imposing welfare losses additional to those represented by the familiar Marshallian triangle. To the extent that scale economies in the case of decreasing cost industries are dissipated in X-inefficiency the cost saving case in favour of the natural monopoly solution is correspondingly eroded if not entirely destroyed.

It might be thought that the regulatory authorities (in the Telser case) could be alerted to the possibility of X-inefficiency and could take appropriate action to obtain an X-efficient marginal cost pricing solution.[6] For the most part, this is the conventional wisdom of regulation policy. Such a view, however, is derived from a quite unrealistic assessment of the regulatory process, for the regulatory authorities in the real world are not omniscient and indeed are dependent largely upon cost information presented to them by the regulated organisations (Rowley, 1971). In such circumstances, the natural monopolist would have every incentive and considerable opportunity to take out in *X*-inefficiency much of the surplus which the regulatory authorities are expected to eliminate in the pursuit of Pareto optimality.[7] The marginal cost pricing solution imposed by regulation, therefore, is likely in practice to be based upon an *X*-inefficient cost platform. The relevant welfare comparisons generated by the Demsetz/Telser controversy would seem for this reason to be better represented in Fig. 4.2 than in Fig. 4.1.

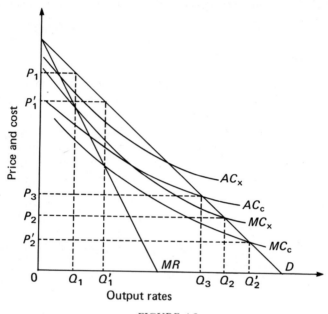

FIGURE 4.2

In Fig. 4.2 the demand curve *D*, and the marginal revenue curve *MR* are as in Fig. 4.1. The long-run average cost curve AC_c and the corresponding marginal cost curve MC_c are also as in Fig. 4.1. However, on the assumption that *X*-inefficiency strikes at marginal cost under natural monopoly conditions, AC_x represents the long-run average cost curve and MC_x the corresponding marginal cost curve in the absence of competition. How does this affect the predictions which are central to the Demsetz/Telser controversy?

Firstly, the unregulated natural monopoly solution, at price P_1 and output Q_1, will differ from that depicted in Fig. 4.1 and reflected as P_1' and Q_1' in Fig. 4.2 on account of *X*-inefficiency. But this is not strictly relevant to the controversy, which does not extend to the laissez-faire alternative to state intervention. Secondly, Telser's regulatory outcome would be at price P_2 and output Q_2 (based upon the *X*-inefficient cost platform MC_x) and not at price P_2' and outcome Q_2' as Telser predicted.

Thirdly, on the assumption that the bidding outcome is strictly competitive, the Demsetz solution at price P_3 and output Q_3 would correspond exactly with his predictions, since *X*-inefficiency would be avoided.[8]

IV. SOME SOCIAL WELFARE IMPLICATIONS

It is our intention in this section to review the public policy implications of the natural monopoly problem as outlined in section III above, by reference to (i) the Pareto principle, (ii) the 'Harberger' social welfare function and (iii) a modified social welfare function which incorporates liberalist arguments.

The Pareto Principle

The Pareto principle is so widely and so automatically applied in the economic theory of public policy that there is a tendency to ignore the important value premises which underpin it (Peacock and Rowley, 1972; chapter 2 in this volume). Since we shall challenge the desirability of its hold over the economics profession later in this paper[9] it is essential that we now outline the value premises at issue before proceeding to an evaluation of the Telser/Demsetz debate within the framework provided by the Paretian principle. There are in fact three closely related principal value assumptions which must be accepted before the implications of Pareto welfare economics can be supported. They are:

(a) The concern is to be with the welfare of all members of society, rather than with some organic concept of the state. This approach to social welfare makes it possible to write an ordinal social welfare function of the form,

$$W = W(U^1, U^2, \ldots, U^s), \tag{1}$$

where W is social welfare and U^1, U^2, ... U^s are levels of utility of each of the s members of society.

(b) Each member of society is considered to be the best judge of his own welfare. This value assumption (ignoring interdependences between the utility functions of separate members of society) makes it possible to write ordinal utility functions for each of s members of society of the form:

$$U^g = U^g(x_i^g, v_j^g) \qquad (g = 1, 2, \ldots, s), \tag{2}$$

where x_i is the ith commodity and v_j is the jth productive service in the economy.

(c) If any change in the allocation of resources increases the social welfare of at least one member of society without reducing the social welfare of any other member then this change should be treated as improving total social welfare. This value judgement – which precludes any possibility of making interpersonal welfare comparisons – implies that W is a monotonically increasing function of any U, viz.

$$\partial W / \partial U^g > 0. \tag{3}$$

In essence, therefore, the Pareto principle emphasises the relevance of individual sovereignity as a social objective, whilst presenting an extremely restrictive approach to public policy formation. An objection by a single individual is sufficient to cloud the welfare issue and even with moderately successful systems of compensation unanimity is rarely forthcoming in the real world for public policy recommendations of any substance.

The necessary conditions for a Pareto optimum are well known and they will not be reiterated here. The Telser/Demsetz debate is usefully re-examined by reference to the Pareto criteria in the light of X-inefficiency considerations as outlined in section III of this paper, and on the assumption that the compensation principle is applicable to the natural monopoly problem.

It is now apparent that the Paretian welfare implications are obscure both for the Telser and for the Demsetz solution, the former because it fails to satisfy the marginal conditions necessary for efficiency in exchange and the latter because it fails to satisfy the marginal conditions necessary for efficiency in production. At the level of generality of the Demsetz/Telser debate, it is impossible to formulate the most appropriate second-best solution (if indeed such a solution even exists). Certainly, an approach based upon a straightforward comparison between the prices and outputs of the two solutions ($P_2 < P_3$ and $Q_2 < Q_3$ in Fig. 4.2) would be naive if not entirely irresponsible. The economist restricted by the Pareto prescriptions would have to sit on the public policy fence unless he were able to devise a proposal which would guarantee technical efficiency in the marginal cost pricing solution. Telser is therefore not in a position to arrive at a definite conclusion.[10]

The Harberger Social Welfare Function

The social welfare function utilised in this section is not in fact due to Harberger (1971) but was employed extensively in the cost–benefit analysis field long before Harberger's interpretative article was published (e.g. Williamson, 1966, 1968; Crew and Rowley, 1970, 1971a). Nevertheless, Harberger's article provides the best-argued case for the retention and further adoption of this approach in applied welfare economics. Essentially, the welfare function in question adopts the Pareto principle but suppresses the Pareto restriction on making interpersonal utility comparisons, by treating the distributional consequences of any change in resource allocation as neutral to social welfare. It takes the form:

$$\text{maximise} \qquad W = TR + S - (TC - R), \qquad (4)$$

where W = net economic benefit, TR = total revenue, S = consumers' surplus, TC = total cost, and R = inframarginal rent.

As Harberger has recently emphasised (Harberger, 1971), there are three important postulates which underpin this social welfare function, namely:

(1) the competitive demand price for a given unit measures the value of that unit to the demander; (2) the competitive supply price for a given unit measures the value of that unit to the supplier; (3) when evaluating the net benefits or costs of a given action the costs and benefits accruing to each member of the relevant group should normally be added without regard to the individuals to whom they accrue.

Harberger claimed that these postulates were both simple and robust and that they were well-suited for the handling of partial equilibrium problems of the kind here under consideration. It is worthwhile re-examining the Demsetz/Telser debate within the formal framework of this approach, whilst reserving our own position concerning the underlying value premises involved. An adjusted version of Williamson's well-known trade-off diagram (Williamson, 1968) will be employed and is set out in Fig. 4.3.

In Fig. 4.3, the market demand curve for the product under consideration is represented by D and the corresponding marginal revenue curve by MR. The industry is characterised by decreasing cost conditions and, in the absence of state intervention, the natural monopolist would attain the lowest available short-run cost curve, represented by AC_1 and would produce at price $0P_1$ and at output $0Q_1$. In terms of the Harberger social welfare function, this

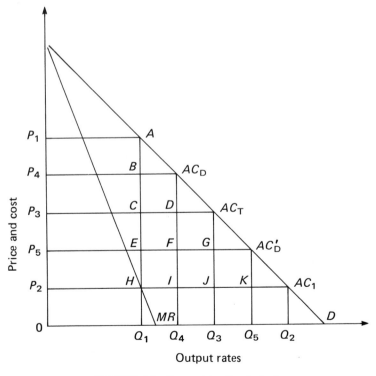

FIGURE 4.3   *Some social welfare trade-offs*

solution is inferior to the optimum which is provided at price $0P_2$ and output $0Q_2$. The loss of welfare is entirely at the expense of consumers and is reflected approximately by the triangle $AHAC_1$. The additional transfer from consumers to the producer, reflected by the area P_1AHP_2 is treated as neutral from the social welfare viewpoint. The unambiguous net gain from a switch from the natural monopoly to the marginal cost pricing solution unfortunately is unattainable (by assumption) in this instance, since X-inefficiency is supposed to be inevitable in the regulatory solution.

Rather, the Telser-type solution, modified to take account of X-inefficiency, is given in Fig. 4.3 by the intersection of the relevant cost curve AC_T with the market demand curve, i.e. at price $0P_3$ and at output $0Q_3$. On the assumption that there is no element of producers' surplus in the X-inefficiency arising in the Telser solution,[11] the loss of welfare by comparison with the optimum solution is reflected in the triangle AC_TJAC_1. This loss is un-ambiguous. By contrast, the issue is much less clear-cut when comparing the Telser with the natural monopoly solution. For, although the loss of consumers' surplus is less in the Telser solution ($AC_TJAC_1 < AHAC_1$) there is no producers' surplus in the Telser solution to balance against the area P_1AHP_2 in the natural monopoly solution. Whether in practice the net loss of con-sumers' surplus is sufficient to outweigh the gain of producers' surplus in the latter solution is an empirical issue. There is reason to doubt that this will be the general case.

These results must now be compared with the competitive bidding solution proposed by Demsetz for the natural monopoly problem. A crucial issue in this case is whether the average cost pricing solution offered by competitive bidding involves a sacrifice to scale economies sufficient to outweigh the X-inefficiency evident in the Telser solution. Since this is an empirical issue which cannot be resolved by *a priori* reasoning both solutions are outlined in Fig. 4.3. The first, in which the loss of scale economies exceeds regulatory X-inefficiency, involves the successful bidder in operating on a short-run cost curve denoted by AC_D, with price at $0P_4$ and output at $0Q_4$. By contrast with the optimum solution there is a clear loss of welfare reflected by the triangle $AC_D IAC_1$. By contrast with the Telser solution there is also a clear loss of welfare since the triangle $AC_D IAC_1$ exceeds the triangle AC_TJAC_1. By contrast with the natural monopoly solution, there is some ambiguity since the loss of consumers' surplus is less ($AC_D IAC_1 < AHAC_1$) but there is no producers' surplus to offset against the area P_1AHP_2. The second competitive bidding solution, in which X-inefficiency exceeds the loss of scale economies, involves the successful bidder in operating on the short-run cost curve AC_D', at price $0P_5$ and at output $0Q_5$. By contrast with the optimum solution, there is a clear loss of welfare reflected by the triangle $AC_D'KAC_1$. By contrast with the Telser solution there is now a clear gain of welfare since the triangle $AC_D'KAC_1$ is smaller than the triangle AC_TJAC_1. By contrast with the natural monopoly solution, there is some ambiguity since the loss of consumers' surplus is less $(AC'_D KAC_1 < AHAC_1)$, but there is no producers' surplus to offset against the area $P_1 AHP_2$.

The Harberger social welfare function is thus seen to offer a useful analytical framework (to those who accept its value premises) for a comparative institutions approach to the natural monopoly problem. Of the policy alternatives examined the ideal solution (by assumption) is unattainable, the choice between the Telser and the Demsetz solutions is seen to rest on the empirical issue whether X-inefficiency from regulation outweighs or is outweighed by the loss of scale economies in the average cost pricing solution, whilst the choice between the natural monopoly and the dominant alternative solution is yet more complex, resting upon a sophisticated comparison between net losses of consumers' surplus and gains from producers' surplus. To those who accept the Harberger social welfare function the signposts are clear if the road is somewhat winding and uneven. However, we would wish to take issue with the Harberger social welfare function itself by challenging certain of the basic premises of the Pareto principle and modifying the welfare calculus to take account of liberalist philosophy, arguably with significant consequences for the natural monopoly problem.

The 'Liberalist' Approach

There is yet a third approach to the problem of evaluating policy in the natural monopoly case, which may be called the 'liberalist' approach. Despite its support for individual sovereignty, there are circumstances, more limited as we have demonstrated than has been generally supposed, where Paretian welfare economics prescribes nationalisation of industries with natural monopoly characteristics. Liberals would argue that individual sovereignty is not to be identified with individual liberty and a major threat to such liberty is seen by them to be the concentration of economic and political power, whether in the hands of private parties or of the state. Since the machinery available for preventing emergent power and/or for dissipating existing power in the private sector is better tested than equivalent mechanisms in the public sector, the liberal has a strong preference, *ceteris paribus*, for the private rather than for the public production of goods and services. In particular, the liberal holds that competitive capitalism provides the strongest long-term safeguard for the maintenance or the restoration of individual liberty, and, further, that government intervention to prevent the concentration of power is best directed towards removing inequalities in the distribution of income and wealth.

It is impossible to summarise the tenets of an important and still influential philosophical tradition in a few sentences, but it needs to be stressed that there are differences between it and the Paretian view which are crucial in discussion of the natural monopoly problem, and which are not immediately apparent (cf. Peacock and Rowley, 1972; chapter 2 in this volume). The first Paretian value assumption is common to both, but the second and third are not. This may seem paradoxical in view of the emphasis in the latter two assumptions on the requirement that the individual is the best judge of his own welfare. Certainly to the liberal, individual preferences are the final arbiter, but there is no guarantee that individuals will necessarily associate their immediate economic requirements with the preservation of freedom in the longer term. The liberal will wish to assess the situation within a wider system of values, trading off, if need be, individual sovereignty (in the Paretian sense) against freedom from discretionary power. The paradox is resolved by recognising that in cases where the democratic political process (which does not in any case conform to the unanimity requirements of the Pareto principle) results in a nationalisation measure, the liberal does not have to like the result. The fact that he does not believe that people *always* act in their own best interests, does not lead him to wish to 'force them to be free'. Rather, will he try to persuade them to *change their preference schedules,* but within the democratic framework which liberalism itself has helped to build.

The liberal, in making his own evaluation of the natural monopoly problem, might well retain the Harberger social welfare function in a form modified to take account of the freedom issue. We are here concerned to recommend such an approach, recognising that there can be no single formula which would satisfy all liberals but believing that our proposal can be adapted flexibly to incorporate most liberal positions. In principle, the approach is simple. The benefits arising from large-scale production, as measured by reference to the Harberger social welfare function, should be discounted by a factor which increases monotonically (linearly, exponentially, or otherwise) as the degree of associated market power (appropriately defined) itself increases. There is sufficient flexibility in the choice both of the initial discount factor and of its rate (or rates) of increase to satisfy a wide range of liberal viewpoints. For instance, in the polar cases, a factor of zero would imply that no weight at all was given to freedom whereas a factor approaching the limit of infinity would imply that no weight at all was given to welfare benefits that involved increases in market power.

The thorny problems remain of defining market power and of devising an effective index to measure changes in such market power. On this, we can offer no easy solution. On the assumption that the market itself has been appropriately defined (and this is clearly necessary at the outset of any serious cost–benefit analysis) we would claim that an index of market power should incorporate some assessment of the likelihood of effective price leadership or collusion as well as single firm dominance. Following Stigler's path-breaking contribution to the theory of oligopoly (Stigler, 1964), the concentration index, now widely regarded as the most appropriate barometer of these various avenues upon which market power might emerge is the Herfindahl index:

$$H = \sum_{i=1}^{i=n} s_i^2, \tag{5}$$

where s_i is the market share of the ith firm in an industry comprising n firms. The Herfindahl index is a measure of relative concentration which is highly sensitive to changes in market structure. For example, industries characterised by natural monopoly conditions would have a maximum value of unity in terms of the Herfindahl index, whereas the perfectly competitive industry would have a value approaching the limit of zero. If this measure were to be adopted, the discount factor could be made to vary positively (in some chosen association) with the Herfindahl index.

V. Some Public Policy Implications

The comparative institutions approach to the natural monopoly problem takes on a different emphasis once the liberalist modifications are attached to the Harberger social welfare function. Those solutions which involve significant market power are valued less highly in the social welfare analysis, as the appropriate discount factor is applied to estimated benefits. In particular, the unregulated natural monopoly solution fares less well and this is significant since there would seem to be some case in favour of this solution by reference to the unmodified social welfare function.

The Telser solution also preserves monopoly in production, albeit of a regulated kind. The liberal would scarcely view regulation as an adequate safeguard for individual liberty and indeed would expect the existence of regulation to deter even such innovative competition as might otherwise erode the power of unregulated natural monopoly. For this reason (and *a fortiori* where public enterprise is involved) the liberal might well wish to apply a higher discount rate to welfare benefits estimated in the Telser than to those estimated in the unregulated natural monopoly case.

But what about the Demsetz competitive bidding solution? This raises less tractable considerations. At one extreme, the existence of single firm production (with a Herfindahl index of one) would seem to place the Demsetz solution on a par with that of Telser from the freedom viewpoint and to require a similar discount factor. At the other extreme, perfect competition in the bidding process might be taken to imply zero market power (with a low- or zero-valued Herfindahl index) and a very low discount factor. A realistic assessment evidently lies between these two extremes and the precise view adopted must depend upon a closer insight into the nature of the bidding process than so far has been provided in the Telser/Demsetz debate.

It must be conceded that there are major obstacles to be overcome in practice before a bidding solution such as that proposed by Demsetz could eliminate all discretionary power in production by forcing a competitive solution. Demsetz himself has recognised (i) that the inputs required for a successful bidder to enter into production must be available to the many potential bidders at prices determined in open markets; and (ii) that the costs of collusion on the part of rival bidders must be prohibitively high. Whilst the latter condition might be satisfied by appropriate institutional, i.e., antitrust, provisions, the former condition raises more intractable problems.

At the outset of the bidding process, rival bidders could certainly submit tenders to a central agency and the bidders judged to have submitted the most competitive tender (evaluated inevitably from a multi-dimensional viewpoint) could presumably gain access to the required factor inputs at something approaching a competitive price, though problems would even then exist in the case of factor inputs with low supply elasticities. But what of subsequent biddings when contract renewals fell due? The bidder who was initially successful, as a sitting tenant, would have substantial advantages, e.g. with respect to market goodwill built up over the initial contract period, to market information and to its property rights in specialist factor inputs. Furthermore, the costs of transferring production rights to a new producer would also tell in favour of the existing producer. It is true that counter-vailing regulatory measures could be devised to neutralise these advantages, but only at a cost which might well prove substantial in terms of the production costs under consideration. In such circumstances, the existing producer would have substantial discretionary power which might well be dissipated in X-inefficiency, since rival bidders could not possibly obtain the sort of insight into the nature of the production function that would be readily discernible in a competitive market, rather than in high profits which might well induce low-priced rival bids.

Moreover, it would be not at all easy to ensure that the successful bidder's contractual commitments in fact were honoured. Contract periods could not be very short without the transaction costs of the whole operation becoming intolerable and yet a lengthy contract period would make escalator clauses for factor input price changes inevitable. Such clauses, in association with inevitable loopholes available to the producer via quality variation and the like, would offer perhaps significant scope for discretionary behaviour however efficient the bidding process. Moreover, there would be a natural reluctance to allow the producer to bankrupt himself in trying to honour impossible contracts and this alone might encourage the submission of un-realistic bids in the knowledge that contracts subsequently might be re-negotiated in a less competitive atmosphere. For reasons such as these the bidding solution must be viewed with some scepticism both as a general solution to the natural monopoly problem and as a safeguard against the emergence of market power.

There is, however, an alternative possibility to any of those so far examined in this paper. In many decreasing cost situations the scale economies at issue are large but not momentous, especially when oligopolistic rather than monopolistic competition is the alternative scale consideration. In such circumstances, the application of the liberal discount factor to the benefits from market power might throw up a competitive solution (the degree of competition dependent upon the scale economies at risk and the discount factor applied) as a most-favoured public policy solution. Competition in production simultaneously widens the freedom of choice of individuals (workers who can switch jobs between independent employers and customers who can shop around between independent suppliers) whilst substantially reducing discretionary power within the affected markets. It is true that an imposed system of competition in production might not prove highly stable given the scale economy incentives to market concentration. It is equally true that oligopolistic competition lends itself to price leadership, collusion and conscious parallelism in price behaviour. For this reason, the competitive solution could not possibly be a proposal for *laissez faire* (Crew and Rowley, 1971a,b). Antitrust measures would be required both to enforce competition in the market place and to prevent concentration of such magnitude as might endanger competition. Decreasing cost industries might well be subjected to especially vigilant antitrust treatment and market structure would be a matter for ongoing concern and perhaps for periodic regulatory adjustment. Within a comparative institutions framework such as that outlined in this paper, and viewed from the liberal standpoint, the competitive solution might well prove a frequent choice in preference to the natural monopoly, the Telser and the Demsetz alternatives in the face of decreasing cost conditions.

NOTES

1. Reproduced with minor amendments from *Journal of Public Economics* Vol. 1, No. 1, 1972.
2. If lump-sum transfers were possible, they would be used in preference to multi-part tariffs unless the latter were entirely non-distortionary. If non-distortionary taxation were out of the question (and recent developments in the theory of the firm suggest that even lump-sum taxes may affect resource allocation) then the excess burden involved in raising revenue would be an argument against marginal cost pricing in decreasing cost conditions.
3. Telser (1969) pp. 938–9: 'In a recent article, Demsetz (1968) leaves readers with the impression that he is content with a situation in which the firm is prevented from obtaining a monopoly return and he does not raise the question of efficiency. Hence, he implies that direct regulation of an industry subject to decreasing average cost is unnecessary if it is prevented from obtaining a monopoly return and that there are no natural monopolies. This misses the point. The controversy concerns regulation to secure efficiency and to promote public welfare. It does not concern the rate of return.'

4. Demsetz (1971) p. 357: 'Indeed, in the usual sense in which monopoly is understood, the acceptance of my conclusion does imply that economies of scale, per se, do not give rise to monopoly power. They may give rise to inefficiency because of the difficulty of devising suitable contracts . . . but *not* because of an absence of competition.'

5. Telser (1971): 'I see no reason to embrace Q_2, which Demsetz pronounces as his original contribution, merely because according to some vaguely described bidding process it yields no profit to the winning supplier. Marginal cost pricing is emphasised by most economists who study this subject. . .'

6. For example, an omniscient regulator, aware of the minimum cost function available to the regulated firm, could police out X-inefficiency by setting detailed price and output targets and relating the lump-sum subsidy to this solution. Alternatively, regulatory lag has been put forward as an incentive to efficiency in the regulated sector. These possibilities are excluded from our analysis.

7. It may be relevant to distinguish X-inefficiency from the input inefficiency of fair-rate-of-return regulation first noted by Averch and Johnson (1962) though there are evident similarities.

8. The empirical testing of the X-inefficiency hypothesis is still in its infancy. Preliminary results (Leibenstein, 1966; Rowley, 1971; Crew and Rowley, 1971a) are not unfavourable.

9. Following the approach adopted in a critique of the widespread application of Pareto prescriptions to the issue of income redistribution (Peacock and Rowley, 1972; chapter 2 in this volume).

10. Demsetz explicitly rejected the Pareto criteria in his analysis of the natural monopoly problem:

    'My purpose has been to question the conventional economic arguments for the existing legislation and regulation. An expanded role for government can be defended on the empirical grounds of a documented general superiority of public administration or by a philosophical preference for mild socialism. But I do not see how a defense can be based on the formal arguments considered here: these arguments do not allow us to deduce from their assumptions either the monopoly problem or the administrative superiority of regulation' (1968, p. 65).

    'Clearly, marginal cost pricing was of secondary importance to a main objective of my paper, which was to demonstrate that the theory of natural monopoly – and, more generally, the asserted inverse relationship between industry concentration and competition – errs in neglecting an important role played by rivalry in the mitigation of monopoly power' (1971, p. 356).

11. Those who are sceptical of this assumption may treat the AC_T curve in Fig. 4.3 as being net of 'producers-surplus-X-inefficiency', retaining only that element of X-inefficiency which falls outside the scope of the W-function.

REFERENCES

Averch, H. and Johnson, L. (1962) 'Behaviour of the firm under regulatory constraint' *American Economic Review* Vol. 52, December.

Comanor, W. S. and Leibenstein, H. (1969) 'Allocative efficiency, X-efficiency and the measurement of welfare losses' *Economica* Vol. 36, No. 1, August.

Crew, M. A., Jones-Lee, M. and Rowley, C. K. (1971) 'X-theory versus management discretion theory' *The Southern Economic Journal* Vol. 38, No. 2.

Crew, M. A. and Rowley, C. K. (1970) 'Antitrust policy: economics versus management science' *Moorgate and Wall Street* Autumn.

Crew, M. A. and Rowley, C. K. (1971a) 'On allocative efficiency, X-efficiency and the measurement of welfare loss' *Economica* Vol. 38, May.

Crew, M. A. and Rowley, C. K. (1971b) 'Antitrust policy, the application of rules' *Moorgate and Wall Street*, Autumn.

Demsetz, H. (1964) 'The exchange and enforcement of property rights' *Journal of Law and Economics* Vol. 7, October.

Demsetz, H. (1968) 'Why regulate utilities?' *Journal of Law and Economics* Vol. 11, April.

Demsetz, H. (1971) 'On the regulation of industry: a reply' *Journal of Political Economy* Vol. 79, March/April.

Harberger, A. C. (1971) 'Three basic postulates for applied welfare economics' *Journal of Economic Literature* Vol. 9, No. 3.

Leibenstein, H. (1966) 'Allocative efficiency vs X-efficiency' *American Economic Review* Vol. 56, June.

Kafoglis, M. (1969) 'Output of the restrained firm' *American Economic Review* Vol. 59, September.

Millward, R. (1971) *Public Expenditure Economics* McGraw-Hill, New York.

Peacock, A. T. and Rowley, C. K. (1972) 'Pareto optimality and the political economy of liberalism' *Journal of Political Economy* Vol. 80, No. 3, May/June.

Rowley, C. K. (1971) *Steel and Public Policy* McGraw-Hill, New York.

Stigler, G. J. (1964) 'A theory of oligopoly' *Journal of Political Economy* Vol. 72, February/March.

Stigler, G. J. and Friedland, C. (1962) 'What can regulators regulate? – the case of electricity' *Journal of Law and Economics* Vol. 5.

Telser, L. (1969) 'On the regulation of industry: a note' *Journal of Political Economy* Vol. 77, November/December.

Telser, L. (1971) 'On the regulation of industry: a correction' *Journal of Political Economy* Vol. 79, July/August.

Turvey, R. (1968) 'Peak-load pricing' *Journal of Political Economy* Vol. 76, March/April.

Turvey, R. (1969) 'Marginal cost' *Economic Journal* Vol. 79, June.

Williamson, O. E. (1966) 'Peak-load pricing and optimal capacity' *American Economic Review* Vol. 56, September.

Williamson, O. E. (1968) 'Economies as an antitrust defense' *American Economic Review* Vol. 58, March.

Wiseman, J. (1957) 'Public utility prices: an empty box' *Oxford Economic Papers* Vol. 9, February.

CHAPTER 5

The Political Economy of the 'Dispersive Revolution'[1]

I

This paper with its somewhat mysterious title offers a review of how economic analysis might be used to organise our thoughts about one of the most intriguing aspects of modern society – the demand by the individual for more participation in industrial and political decision-making. Sir Henry Phelps Brown (1975) has coined the term 'dispersive revolution' for this development. The subject if properly treated calls for a depth of knowledge of society's problems which I cannot claim to possess and which economists might wisely avoid, but curiosity, stimulated by some official involvement with industrial policy and earlier by membership of the Kilbrandon Commission, has got the better of me.

By making reference to welfare and policy questions as well as to analytical issues the paper is best described as an exercise in political economy. Anyone who has examined the literature on the subject will realise that here is a vast and soggy area of debate so in the hope of retaining your interest I shall be selective. In particular, I shall attempt neither to devise measures for nor indeed to measure the extent of the demand for participation but assume that available evidence is conclusive enough to suggest that this demand is sufficient to foreshadow change in our political and economic institutions.[2]

II

The dimensions of the subject can be introduced by considering the conventional presentation of the behaviour of our old friend 'economic man', a term only used here as convenient shorthand for reasons which should become clear. In textbook parlance he is depicted as maximising his utility function in which the arguments are goods and the constraint is his income and many variations, including dating of variables, are possible on the basic model. When for convenience in welfare economics we use this formulation we reduce his functions to that of a consumer only, but if we assume that his utility is a function of his relations with the public sector through the taxes he pays and the benefits he receives from public expenditure and of his relations with his job through his supply of factor services and their price, we have to take account of a much greater range of variables. Sticking to a simple formulation of 'individual maximisation' (as distinct from consumer maximisation) we can describe the process of maximisation in the following way:

$$\text{Max } U^i = U^i(x^i, q_k, a^i)$$

Subject to

$$p_k^c \cdot x^i + T_k = Y^i = \phi \,(a^i) = p_k^a \cdot a^i$$

where $x^i =$ a vector of 'private' goods

$q_k =$ a vector of 'public' goods

$a^i =$ a vector of factor inputs

$p_k^c =$ a vector of product prices for private goods

$p_k^a =$ a vector of factor prices

$T_k =$ net tax liability (tax obligations *less* transfers)

$Y =$ personal income

k subscript denotes an exogenously determined variable.

I shall not dwell at length on analysing the steps leading to a solution. The individual is assumed to possess the usual twice-differentiable utility function in which the vectors of private and public goods and factor supplies are arguments, and the appropriate signs are registered at each stage of differentiation. He endeavours to maximise this function subject to a budget constraint. Assuming the budget constraint is exactly satisfied, the solution is obtained by solving for the vector of private goods consumption in terms of their prices, disposable income (implying a predetermined set of factor prices, quantities of factor inputs and tax liability) and predetermined levels of public goods available for consumption.

As stated, the characteristic of this formalised view of the individual maximiser is the number of constraints on his activities. The individual can adjust his bundle of consumption goods, but his utility depends crucially on exogenous influences, for factor and product prices are assumed to be beyond his control, as are his tax obligations and the vector of public goods available to him. Such a model is far from being a caricature of what may be found in advanced textbooks in which the individual is subject to various 'experiments' by the alteration of the constraints, leading to the examination of his role in a society of individuals, each with the same form of a utility function, and of how the welfare of all can be maximised which usually means meeting the Paretian welfare conditions. The classic extension of this analysis which emphasises the constrained maximisation approach is found in the Samuelsonian analysis of market failure in the provision of public goods in which it falls to an 'ethical observer' or 'impartial referee' to apply the Paretian rules using what information is available or assumed about individual welfare functions in order to produce the optimal division of community income between public and private goods (cf. Samuelson, 1958, and the doubts raised by Rowley and Peacock, 1975). Society seems to consist of individuals who in Henry Thoreau's famous words lead lives of 'quiet desperation'!

I cannot believe that this kind of formulation of the choice process in which human beings react like Pavlovian dogs to external stimuli can be anything more than a didactic device and to base judgments on it about society's welfare seems to be dangerous. The individual who did find himself in the situation which I have described would at the very least weigh the costs and benefits of trying to remove the constraints on his behaviour either alone or in concert with others.[3] Once we consider the individual in this light as viewing these possibilities but operating under conditions of uncertainty and not as an isolated passive adjuster to a certain and clearly hostile economic environment, we see more clearly the incentive he has to improve and expand his choices by investment in information about alternative opportunities. There is encouraging evidence that the simple constructs of microeconomic behaviour are undergoing a necessary and radical revision in the light of the kind of dissatisfaction I have expressed. Thus Buchanan has summed up the matter by arguing that a more useful paradigm of choice is to be found in regarding the individual not as a constrained maximiser but as a bargainer: 'Eugen v. Bohm-Bawerk's horse traders are the basic examples, not the housewife who shops for groceries in the supermarket. . . . The unifying principle becomes *gain-from-trade*, not maximisation' (Buchanan, 1975).

We can view the demand for greater control by the individual over his political environment and his work situation (including his submission to the educational process!) as striking evidence in favour of this 'break out' theory of individual economic behaviour, which suggests that he has a strong incentive to seek information on alternative political and economic systems. Our model as presented does at least indicate the areas of investigation we might pursue even though we are not bound to believe that the only significant vector of endogenously determined variables is that of 'private goods' (x^i). Thus how does the individual view the benefits and costs of trying to influence the price and quantity of factor inputs in order to improve his welfare? If the individual considers that there is little relationship between the 'mix' of public goods provided for him and which he cannot directly influence and the tax obligations he faces, what can he do in order to reduce the degree of dispersion between his optimal mix of public goods and the actual mix and between his optimal 'tax-price' and the actual tax he has to pay?

But immediately we consider the individual as acting in this kind of way, we postulate a process of social interaction and therefore bargaining, 'threat' and other forms of behaviour which cannot be tackled without utilising some such tool as Buchanan's 'contractarian paradigm'.

III

The manifestation of the dispersive revolution of direct concern to members of this Society is probably the demand for devolution of government, a phenomenon found not only in this country but also in a number of major countries with centralised government. What can a political economist say about this development?

The first area he might wish to explore is whether an economic explanation can be offered for this demand. We need some kind of a positive theory of the demand for decentralisation based on an interpretation of individual and group preference structures. The dominant approach in the theory of public finance, which derives the structure of government from the 'gains from trade' between individuals, has devoted a good deal of attention to this question. It attempts to demonstrate how rational individuals placed in a position of being able to contract with one another might determine the extent to which they are willing to use the political mechanism, with the inevitable necessity of coercion as a means of financing, and providing those public goods which the market is unable to provide, though this may mean that 'tax-prices' facing individuals do not generate exactly the quantity of public goods they would individually prefer. This analysis has recently been extended (see Buchanan, 1974) in order to explain how such individuals would decide how to allocate tax and expenditure functions between central and 'state' governments, the principal though not the sole factor governing this decision being the extent to which coercion through the political mech-anism might be reduced by having a choice of political jurisdictions in which to live and work. The view taken of the opportunity costs of decentralised government clearly depends on what other functions freely contracting in-dividuals would assign to government, such as the desire to transfer income between themselves and between generations and to maintain full employment of resources and the view they take of the relative efficiency of the private sector, the state or local units and the central government in achieving these aims. Buchanan and others have argued that it is too readily assumed that all these aims require centralised action, resting their case partly on a different view than, say, Musgrave, on how the economy works and on the logic of choice.

From what I have said already about a contractarian view it will be clear that I have considerable sympathy with this approach, but much though it may accord with the way in which one would want to think that rational individuals would take the measure of their political institutions, it clearly does not accord with the way they actually do. I need only point to the evidence submitted to the Commission on the Constitution and the Report of that body itself to indicate how widespread is the view that any bargains designed to alter the functions of different layers of government are not viewed as being between private individuals and groups who mandate some of their number to carry out their decisions but between, on the one hand, entrenched political parties advised when in power by strong and dedicated bureaucracy and, on the other hand, a wide range of dissentient groups of varying size and efficiency with widely differing views about how the world looks to them and what it is feasible for government to perform. David Hume's (1777) words are still regrettably true:

> Were you to preach in most parts of the world, that political connexions are founded on voluntary consent or a mutual promise, the magistrate would soon imprison you, as seditious, for loosening the ties of obedience, if your friends did not shut you up as delirious, for advancing such absurdities.

Any predictions derived from our basic model about the demand for political participation are better derived from an examination of the realities of the distribution of political power rather than based on an appeal to some principle of legitimacy in its exercise.

Jack Wiseman and myself tried to evolve an alternative approach arising out of our study of the growth in public expenditure in the UK (Peacock and Wiseman, 1961) in which the explanation of the expenditure growth and its division between layers of government assumes a confrontation between governments with coercive powers on the one hand and citizens on the other whose ability and willingness to influence governments would depend on a whole range of factors varying through time. We did not produce a fully worked out economic model of political behaviour and missed an important trick in not realising that the coincidence of views which produced highly centralised government in the UK – the so-called 'concentration effect' – might in the longer run provoke a reaction to the control over our daily lives which widely accepted policies have produced, and to the growing remoteness of government about which the Kilbrandon Commission offered abundant evidence.

Following the very interesting approach developed by Breton and others (Breton, 1974; Breton and Scott, 1978), we can use our model of individual maximisation to show why we should expect such a reaction and with it the demand for political decentralisation. The degree of frustration which individuals will feel with government provision of goods and services – we ignore other ways in which individuals' activities are affected by government, e.g. by regulation – will be a function of the divergence between their tax obligations and the amount and form of services which enter into their utility functions. The greater this divergence, the greater is the incentive to the individuals to incur the costs of influencing the behaviour of government directly through political action or indirectly, e.g. by tax avoidance or evasion, in order to reduce this divergence.

Breton's citizens are highly sophisticated beings possessing ample opportunity for political action, including in particular the opportunity of voting with their feet by moving from one jurisdiction to another within a federal system as a method of reducing the degree of frustration. His politicians have sensitive antennae which seek out information on just how far they have to adjust their policies to maximise their period of office in the face of political competition. They don't seem likely to be able to fool any of the people any of the time. Yet the very contrast between the political market-place he describes and what we perceive in this country illustrates the insights afforded by his approach. In essence, Breton and Scott are saying that the variance in the distribution of preferences of citizens for different types of services and their methods of finance will increase as the degree of centralisation increases. By any standards we live in a highly centralised state. Whatever the spending responsibilities of local government, standards of service are strongly influenced by central government through both legislative provisions and control over finance. Local governments are 'creatures of the centre' in a more fundamental sense for they have no separate constitutional existence, their powers being determined by a central Parliament. Action designed to influence the amount and composition of government services must be concentrated on the political signalling system which could influence central government decisions. Again in contrast to Canada and the USA this part of the signalling system is highly restricted, for policies are decided upon and implemented by a Government formed by a majority party in a Parliament which itself is elected by a system of simple majority voting. It is also restricted by complete immunity of the higher civil service from direct electoral pressures. It is no surprise therefore that pressure group action designed to exercise continuing influence over politicians and bureaucrats has become of growing importance in the UK, a development which has achieved official recognition in the elaborate consultations with bodies such as the TUC and CBI in the field of economic policy.

In the positive economic theory of democracy it is normally assumed that bargainers work within the constitutional rules but the demand for greater political participation suggests that the deviation of individual and group preferences from those reflected in the existing amount and pattern of government expenditure and its finance has become so marked that it can only be given effect through a change in the signalling system itself. What is interesting about the British case is that the nature of the change which has the most support should take the form of demand for devolution rather than electoral reform at the centre, demand for referenda, or the reconstruction of the Second Chamber.

It would be fanciful to say that the extension of the theory of individual behaviour to the demand for political change, as I have depicted it, would offer either a clear prediction of the form of devolved government or a way of judging whether it was in some meaningful sense optimal. I claim no more for it than it helps us to ask the right kind of questions about such matters and it may be worth illustrating this with reference to the present debate in this country.

It is of some interest in view of the approach that I have adopted that the abortive Devolution Act of 1978 put a good deal of emphasis on the importance of more freedom for Scotland and Wales in the allocation of its expenditures or, in terms of our model, on the closer matching of public goods allocation to Scots and Welsh utility functions. However, while a constrained maximisation approach would suggest that Scots or Welsh alone or in concert could now move to higher utility functions, our emphasis on bargaining fits much better with at least the utterances of those likely to be most affected by this change. It is clearly not sufficient to many of them to enjoin their representatives to maximise subject to no control over the amount and composition of revenue. Indeed, even if the proposed system were enacted as it stands and Scotland had no effective control over revenue, that is to say were not even considered as trustworthy as local authorities, the creation of a separate legislature with even limited power is the creation of a power base from which to argue with the central government about the size of funds available for Assembly use and about the allocation of central government purchases and subsidies within the devolved region. But all this so far assumes that the bargaining process is confined to Celts and Whitehall with the English depicted as the traditional and constrained maximisers content to see a relative erosion in their political rights. I cannot believe that this represents a state of political equilibrium and can best develop this point by breaking into a verse which I once circulated in Whitehall in a purely unofficial capacity:

DEFECTION ON THE DEVOLUTION OF OUR TIME

Alas! your proposal's clearly meant
To maim our Memorandum of Dissent
Which makes the cause none should oppose –
What suits the Thistle likewise suits the Rose.

E'en if the Dales seem now content
With centralised Imperial Government
The moment Scotia makes her Laws
Will be the sign for rioting in Hawes!

So when Northumbria's hordes advance
With clenchèd fists and Solemn Remonstrance
Haunted be in your Affliction
By Peacock's pellucid Prediction.

MORAL
Time still remains to repel Revolution
By Uniformity in Devolution.[4]

IV

The other important area of investigation of individual welfare which our simple model points towards is that of the influence of the individual's work situation. The constraints on his actions in determining his optimum position crucially depend on what control, if any, he can exercise alone or in concert with others over the price of factor inputs (p_k^a) and the work/leisure combination (a^i). There are other elements in the work situation affecting individual utility which are not explicitly depicted in our model, notably the authority relationship between worker and employer, which have played a major part in the modern development of sociological thinking based on the younger Marx's analysis of worker alienation (Marx, 1844).

Workers in Western societies are not forced to make particular employment contracts and, subject to employment conditions, have alternative opportunities, but even those who argue thus are forced to recognise the hierarchical relationship at operation in the work place and what Adam Smith called the 'torpor of mind' induced by specialised repetitive work which cannot be ignored in any analysis of the individual's reaction to his work environment. A stark contrast can be drawn between the hierarchical order at the work place and the democratic order to which at least lip-service is paid in our society.

Economists like angels have feared to tread in this field though this is not to say that sociologists have necessarily been fools for rushing into it. Yet there are two very important points which have been made by economists which put a gloss on some of the more strident utterances of Marxist sociologists and which demonstrate the virility of our general approach.

Firstly, both West and East European economists, for example Dolan (1971) and Sik (1973), have pointed out that if alienation is a function of hierarchical organisation, then it cannot be explained simply by property relations, for collective ownership of the means of production is not synonymous with democratisation at the shop floor level. Sik goes further and argues that a centrally planned system not only perpetuates hierarchies in firms but also creates another source of alienation if there are no markets – the gulf between the structure of production and the structure of needs. Recognition of the technological basis of alienation, in the name of economic efficiency, have forced radical economists and sociologists to argue the case for a 'Utopian' solution based on a rejection of modern technology and the return to a peasant-type culture where the less comfortable material conditions are secondary to the release from industrial bondage. Communes based on this philosophy abound in Western societies prompting no doubt the acid remark of Ota Sik (1974): 'romantic "back to nature" and "down with technology" ideologies . . . can probably only develop amongst the over-satiated children of the Western bourgeoisie'. In short, it would be hazardous to predict that the workers of Dundee on the look-out for ways to move to a preferred position could be persuaded to rush towards the Braes of Angus in the hope of founding a bucolic paradise, even assuming there were room for them all.

Secondly, analogous with the political decision-making process already considered, it would be surprising even when workers are contracted to firms organised in a hierarchical fashion if their actions were so rigidly constrained that their effort on the job had to be treated by them purely as an exogenous variable. If work conditions do matter to individuals and they trade off work against leisure, then they have an incentive to weigh the costs of lessening the pressure on them to produce, e.g. loss of remuneration, sacking, their felt obligations to workmates, etc., against the benefits of greater leisure on or off the job. It has been persuasively argued by Leibenstein (1976) and others that individuals have much more freedom of choice in interpreting their production role than is often realised. Indeed, a careful interpretation of the theory of the firm alone would reveal this phenomenon, particularly when it is recognised that team production imposes high costs on management in identifying individual marginal products and corporate enterprise structure with diffused ownership may not induce management to maximise the difference between revenue and cost (see Alchian and Demsetz, 1972). I shall recall both these points shortly.

While it seems possible to indicate why the individual viewing the constraints on his behaviour might finish up being rather enthusiastic for devolved government in this country, it is impossible to be sure what changes in the organisation of production are likely to evolve in Western society, other than some form of worker participation. Rather than discuss all possible varieties, I propose to concentrate only on one, the workers' co-operative or labour-managed firm, as it has excited a good deal of interest among economists.

V

'The form of association . . . which if mankind continue to improve must be expected in the end to predominate is not that which can exist between capitalist as chief and work-people without a voice in the management, but the association of the labourers themselves on terms of equality, collectively owning the capital with which they carry on their operations, and working under managers, elected and removable by themselves.'

These are the words not of Anthony Wedgwood Benn or Marshall Tito but John Stuart Mill (1871). Mill paints an attractive picture of a society in which the patrician system would disappear in both government and in the economy, in which the market would still offer the incentive for firms to be efficient and he saw the seeds of its foundation in the growing number of co-operatives in the France and Britain of his day, some of which he describes in enthusiastic detail.

I cannot attempt to record the intellectual history of Mill's vision since his day except to note that his general position has recently received vigorous support from economists and for a variety of different reasons. Without leaving Scotland we find Simpson (1975) arguing that '. . . we should not shrink from treating institutions as instrument variables. Thus, it may be that some form of worker responsibility is an essential ingredient of any framework for sustained growth in this period of history, and that institutional forms of productive organisations must be altered accordingly. Such changes would be at the same time seen to be consistent with a successful anti-inflationary policy . . . The important thing I want to emphasise is the classical principle of institutions as endogenous variables in the growth process, as opposed to the neo-classical view that they are exogenous.'[5] Whatever one may think of the claimed advantages of 'employee sovereignty' Simpson is surely right to stress that there is nothing immutable about the way production is organised, and his view fits well with my general thesis that individuals in seeking to improve their own welfare are not constrained by acceptance of any particular form of political or economic organisation. At the same time, it may be noted that a commitment to the view that the market is an effective instrument of allocation of goods and factor services – the classical view – does not necessarily entail a commitment to capitalist organisation of production, which was essentially Mill's point.

The burgeoning literature on labour-managed firms has been mainly concerned with the problem of allocation of resources. A labour-managed firm (LMF) is normally assumed to maximise income per worker rather than sales or profits. In the short run with capital stock fixed, this assumption means that the LMF equates marginal product with average net income and not the wage. Under conditions of perfect competition with given factor and product prices a firm 'transformed' into an LMF from a 'capitalist' one will produce less output and employ fewer workers. Subjecting the LMF to changes in output and factor prices produces 'perverse' effects. Thus an increase in demand leading to a rise in price will *lower* and not raise output, which has unfortunate implications at first sight for both allocation and stabilisation. In the longer run this means that an increase in demand which promotes a change in the size of the industry must take the form of an expansion in the number of firms. The size of firms in an LMF industry will therefore tend to be smaller in the long run. How price, output and employment will change will depend on the shape of the long-run industry cost curve.

There are many games that one can play with this kind of analysis such as changing the market form, the objective function, introducing taxes and subsidies, incorporating attitudes to risk; and so on. (For bibliography see Furubotn, 1976.) However, my only purpose in mentioning this approach is to demonstrate how the bias in the study of the welfare effects of the analysis is towards the effects on individuals as consumers. While it is conceivable that these effects might induce individuals to be wary of supporting policy action designed to facilitate the introduction of LMFs, one has to take into account the welfare effects produced by the change in the *organisation* of firms which may run counter to those induced by the change in the objective function. In other words, as Vanek (1970) has argued, it is simplest to collapse all the changes produced in the change-over to an LMF from capitalist organisation into a change in the firm's objective function. Its supporters have placed particular weight on increased worker satisfaction through greater participation in decision-making and have argued that this alone will improve performance on the job. It is this aspect of the case for LMFs which is of most relevance to my argument.

Returning to our utility function, then, the individual worker now with a say in how things are run is involved in a trade-off between an interest in maximising the return per head of the firm and a desire to minimise the disutility of work. There is not a great deal of controversy about the shape of the individual utility function though some writers would stress the interdependence between workers' utility functions. This would mean that an individual's utility depends on the spill-over effects on others of his work-effort and this factor would be of more importance in an LMF where now his productivity affects only his co-workers who are also the managers and owners (or have the usufruct) of the capital stock. The important area of uncertainty and therefore of controversy lies in the organisation of production. In relatively large-scale organisations with diverse technical demands for skills and aptitudes of workers it is inconceivable that production management could be carried out by referring every production decision to a democratic voting procedure. As we know in universities the price of democracy is interminable meetings and a low rate of decision through-put! Provided there is competition between firms, technical conditions dictate the necessity of a centralised, hierarchical organisation, though workers may view the organisation constraints as less binding if they have a say in the form and in the choice of personnel.[6]

Faced with a choice of being employed by a firm organised on traditional capitalist lines and a firm in all essential respects similar except that it is worker-controlled, we cannot be certain that a worker or groups of organised labour for that matter would unequivocally opt for the latter. Even if monitoring of performance is conducted by managers who are employed by the work force, there are costs as well as benefits attached to having that responsibility, particularly if workers have to take investment as well as production decisions. It is no accident that workers' co-operatives as the main extant variant of LMFs have succeeded, in the sense of surviving and expanding, in small undertakings in which workers are bound by a common interest in their skills, the dispersion of earnings between them is small, the educational attainment of members fosters understanding and appreciation of management skills and responsibilities, and communication is easy. Examples are found (ignoring professional partnerships) in printing, shoe production, construction and orchestras.

VI

I have tried in this lecture to examine the interpretative value of the utility-maximising model of individual behaviour applied to little explored areas. There are obvious extensions of the analysis, notably the delineation of the circumstances in which individuals will have an incentive to combine to take group action, which have not been considered. The lecture would fail in one of its main objects if you have not drawn the inference that my interest in the topic arises from a strong commitment to the view that society should so order its affairs that the individual so far as possible should be left to plot his own course as reflected in freedom of choice over the resources which he commands. It must be added quickly that the economic analysis has not been consciously distorted in order to convince you, if indeed that were possible, that the millennium is at hand. On the contrary, what seems likely to happen in this country in both political decentralisation and industrial democracy may not even be a move to a preferred position for those who share my view, and certainly would fall far short of the optimum.

It seems fitting to conclude by saying a word or two about this matter. One of the most striking things about the Kilbrandon Commission and the subsequent discussion of its proposals is that decentralisation of government is largely thought of in terms of the amount of the *existing* functions of government which might be devolved. The possibility was not considered that some of these functions might be carried out in different ways, e.g. the substitution of income subsidies for price subsidies, or might be returned to the private sector. I do not say that there is any more than a strong presumption that voter alienation, as measured by the disparity between T_k and the form and distribution of values within the vector q_k, could be the result of the growth of government intervention in this country, but anyone sharing my view would be bound to question whether the simple transfer of functions with or without the right to alter the size and composition of the devolved budget by independent taxing and borrowing powers would produce less coercion and less discrimination in the exercise of government.[7] A minimum condition for producing this state of affairs would require much greater opportunity for political participation than so far envisaged in official documents. Alongside the periodic election of Assembly members and the opportunity for non-elected experts to take part in Assembly policy-making, here are a few random suggestions for improvement:

(a) referenda and official opinion polls might be used as a matter of course to decide or to sound views on specific policy issues;

(b) members of the public might as a matter of right be able to ballot for time (strictly limited!) to address the regional Assembly and the Assemblies might choose to invite distinguished outsiders to address them as well as to give evidence to their specialist committees;

(c) members of the Assembly should have their attendance officially recorded;

(d) the venue of the Assembly and/or its committees might from time to time be outside the regional capital;

(e) members might issue an annual written official report to be available for consultation by their constituents;

(f) an official handbook should be available which explains to the ordinary citizen the mode of access to political participation.

These are all debatable suggestions and involve a trade-off problem between the utility of speed in political decision-making and that of fuller participation in how these decisions should be arrived at.

The growth in size of government is again a crucial factor in the extension of workers' participation of a responsible kind in which a market economy is allowed to operate. Any form of workers' participation resting on a stake in the organisation through capital-sharing could hardly be instituted in nationalised industries or in government departments. John Stuart Mill's attractive vision of 'the futurity of the working classes' rests on the assumption of greater equalisation of the capital stock *between individuals* and not on a redistribution from the private to the public sector of the kind we have experienced in the UK. I am not suggesting that industrial organisation should be forced into the mould of labour-managed firms for individual trade-offs between type and amount of work and leisure will differ and therefore their choice of work situation will differ. However, the prospect of their introduction on anything like the scale which would fairly test their ability to reduce worker alienation and to survive in the market depends on a very radical change in our political and economic structure. I would prefer to keep Mill's vision in mind as a long-term goal and to oppose attempts at workers' participation which rest on the extension of workers' control through unions fortified by the closed shop. This seems merely to impose more and not less constraints on the individual as worker and does not begin to answer the question of allying power with responsibility in management of industrial undertakings.

I suspect that several of you will already feel that I have exceeded my brief as an economist. I make no apology for that. The narrowess of the view taken of the individual as a resource-user which has dominated analytical economics has done something more than make us neglect important areas of application of our central paradigm. It has fostered a view of human action which is both unscientific and, to other social scientists, morally objectionable. It has reduced the credibility of economics even though influential criticism in the social sciences appears to be based on the naïve view that the idea of economic man means that economists are only concerned with materialistic ends. Ralf Dahrendorf recently pointed out that it was ironic that the man who did most to convince of the need for a *wertfrei* science, Max Weber, united 'the rigour of value-free science and the passion of a moral position'.[8] The logic of the distinction between scientific statements and value judgments is not in question. What we have to ask ourselves is why we wish to make scientific statements at all. If it is not ultimately for the purpose of expanding the individual's range of choice and thereby to enrich his life, then economics is no more than a Glass Bead game[9] in which we admire one another's skills. 'The passion of a moral position' may lead one to make analytical mistakes – there are always plenty of economists around to point these out – but it directs our energies to the study of issues which those most affected by them consider important, and there can be no better example of this than the 'dispersive revolution'.

NOTES

1. Eleventh Annual Scottish Economic Society Lecture delivered in the University of Dundee on 5 May 1976. Reproduced with minor amendments from *Scottish Journal of Political Economy* Vol. 23, No. 3, November 1976.
2. For evidence on the demand for devolved government in a number of countries, see Oates (1977). For a summary of various types of workers' participation and their prevalence, see Schregle (1976).
3. The parallel here with developments in modern psychology is quite striking. Liam Hudson presents a strong criticism of the self-image of the psychologist as the 'impersonal measurer' granted a 'God-like exemption from the frailties observed in others'. He expresses very well my general point in showing the dangers of such approaches as that of encouraging us 'to see the individual as passive – either as the victim of events that lie outside himself, or as a mere knot of sensations . . . we strip the individual of his special status as an *agent*: someone who makes sense of himself and the world around him, and then acts in the light of the sense he makes.' (See Hudson, 1975, Chapter 1, p. 10).
4. An official who had better remain anonymous replied as follows:

    Perk up, pale Peacock, ease your Cassandra frown,
    The dreadful hordes will stay away from Town.
    The fact is every northern Union
    Well knows which side its bread is buttered on.

If squires for autonomy worked up a rage
Working class interest would hoot them off stage.
Scotia is different: it dreams of the Oil;
The Geordie relies on his (subsidised) toil.

All-England will get him a juicier share
Of unctuous lucre that Scotia can spare
Than would Dissenters' regional assembly
Competing for benefits pumped from the sea.

MORAL
What e'er devolutions come north of the Tweed
Unions back Union for Northumbria's need.

To which my rejoinder was:

Foolhardy they who purvey political prognoses
Only the Gods know who will have the bloody noses.

5. A similar argument is found in Jay (1976) who regards employee sovereignty as essential, for working people 'need somehow to be "disalienated" enough to become infected with the entrepreneurial realities which confront their present employers, so that they will accept a non-inflationary market-determined environment as settling the level of rewards which can be afforded'.

6. McManus (1975) records a splendid story told to him by Steve Cheung: 'On the Yangtse River in China, there is a section of fast water over which boats are pulled upstream by a team of coolies prodded by an overseer using a whip. On one such passage an American lady, horrified at the sight of the overseer whipping the men as they strained at their harness, demanded that something be done about the brutality. She was quickly informed by the captain that nothing could be done: "Those men own the right to draw boats over this stretch of water and they have hired the overseer and given him his duties".' This is the best practical example I can give students of what economists could mean by the term 'an ethical observer' (p. 341).

7. For more detailed technical argument see Rowley and Peacock (1975), Chapter 6.

8. Dahrendorf's position on the state of his own discipline, sociology, is worth close examination by economists. To offer only the flavour of his argument: 'The sociologist does not endanger the purity of his scientific activity by preferring to work with testable theories that recognise the individual's rights and the richness of his life. It is methodically quite above suspicion for a social scientist to keep an eye out for ways of making his own findings further individual freedom and self-fulfilment' (Dahrendorf, 1968, p. 68).

9. I refer of course to the allegorical novel *Das Glaspernspiel* (The Glass Bead Game) by Hermann Hesse, in which a highly developed mathematical system covering all branches of learning is gradually built up out of a simple glass bead frame resembling an abacus until only an élite of privileged scholars understand its workings and significance. In his famous letter of resignation to the Glass Bead Order, the *Magister Ludi*, troubled by the corruption of élitism, remarks: 'if we examine our real feelings most of us would have to admit that we don't regard the welfare of the world, the preservation of intellectual honesty and purity outside as well as inside our tidy Province, as the chief thing. In fact, it is not at all important to us' (Hesse, 1972).

REFERENCES

Alchian, A. and Demsetz, H. (1972) 'Production, information costs and economic organisation' *American Economic Review* Vol. 62, December.

Breton, A. (1974) *The Economic Theory of Representative Government* Macmillan, London.

Breton, A. and Scott, A. A. (1978) *The Economic Constitution of Federal States* University of Toronto Press, Toronto.

Buchanan, J. M. (1974) 'Who should distribute what in a federal system' in H. H. Hochman and G. E. Peterson (eds) *Redistribution through Public Choice* Columbia University Press, New York.

Buchanan, J. M. (1975) 'A contractual paradigm for applying economic theory' *American Economic Review* Vol. 65, May, pp. 225–30.

Dahrendorf, R. (1968) *Homo Sociologicus* Routledge & Kegan Paul, London.

Dolan, E. G. (1971) 'Alienation, freedom and economic organisation' *Journal of Political Economy* Vol. 79, September/October.

Furubotn, E. G. (1976) 'The long-run analysis of the labor-managed firm: An alternative interpretation' *American Economic Review* Vol. 66, March.

Hesse, H. (1972) *The Glass Bead Game (Magister Ludi)* Penguin, Harmondsworth, Middx.

Hudson, L. (1975) *Human Beings: The Psychology of Human Experience* Anchor Press/Doubleday, New York.

Hume, D. (1777) 'Of the original contract' *Hume's Theory of Politics.* (Watkins edition, Nelson, Edinburgh, 1951).

Jay, P. (1976) *A General Theory of Employment, Inflation and Politics* Occasional Paper No. 46, Institute of Economic Affairs, London.

Leibenstein, H. (1976) 'Aspects of the X-efficiency theory of the firm' *Economics and Management Science* Vol. 5, Autumn.

Marx, K. (1844) 'Alienated labour' in D. McLennan *Karl Marx Early Texts* Basil Blackwell, Oxford, 1971.

McManus, J. C. (1975) 'The cost of alternative economic organisations' *Canadian Journal of Economics* Vol. 8, August.

Mill, J. S. (1871) *Principles of Political Economy* Book IV, Chapter VII (University of Toronto Press edition, 1965).

Oates, W. (1977) *The Political Economy of Fiscal Federalism* Proceedings of the ISPE Conference on Fiscal Federalism, Berlin, 1976, D. C. Heath, Lexington, Mass.

Peacock, A. T. and Wiseman, J. (1961) *The Growth of Public Expenditure in the United Kingdom, 1890–1955* Princeton University Press, Princeton, chapter 2.

Phelps Brown, E. H. (1975) 'The dispersive revolution' in *Crisis '75* Occasional Paper Special No. 43, Institute of Economic Affairs, London.

Rowley, C. K. and Peacock, A. T. (1975) *Welfare Economics, A Liberal Restatement* Martin Robertson, London.

Samuelson, P. (1958) 'Aspects of public expenditure theories' *Review of Economics and Statistics* Vol. 40, November.

Schregle, J. (1976) 'Workers' participation in decisions within undertakings' *International Labour Review* Vol. 113, No. 1, January/February.

Sik, O. (1973) 'The 1973 Ernest Bader Common-Ownership Lecture' mimeo.

Sik, O. (1974) 'The shortcomings of the Soviet economy as seen in communist ideologies' *Government and Opposition* Vol. 9, No. 3, Summer.

Simpson, D. (1975) 'Economic growth in Scotland: Theory and experience' in K. J. W. Alexander (ed.) *Political Economy of Change* Blackwell, Oxford.

Vanek, J. (1970) *The General Theory of Labor-Managed Economies* Cornell University Press, Ithaca, N.Y.

CHAPTER 6

The Credibility of Liberal Economics[1]

I. THE TASK

In 1836 at the close of an article in the *London Review* on 'Whether Political Economy is Useful', the protagonist of political economy, 'Mr B', whom James Mill uses to expound his views to 'Mr A', concludes with the resounding words:

> The people, therefore, in the legislature, void of knowledge, who say they distrust and despise political economy, make no presumption against the doctrines against which they vent only a senseless noise . . . There is no branch of human knowledge more entitled to respect; and the men who affect to hold it in contempt afford indication only against themselves. [James Mill, 1966, p. 382]

Harold Wincott I am sure would have relished these words, believing as he did that politicians tended to avoid the main issues of economic policy not only through ignorance but also through funk. He used the dialogue as a technique of exposition very much in the manner of James Mill and, as Lord Robbins said of him, 'there is little that is alien to his lively eye and penetrating comment' (Foreword to Wincott, 1968).

While it is tempting to pursue this parallel in the British pamphleteering tradition, it is the contrast in the positions of James Mill and Harold Wincott which makes the theme of this lecture. One senses in Harold Wincott's later writings that he saw himself trying to stem a flood-tide of plausible but specious arguments attacking the market economy, whereas James Mill, like many of his sympathetic contemporaries, wrote as if on the crest of a wave.

In James Mill's time, the intellectual sons of Adam Smith were a close-knit fraternity, facing no professional rivals of their quality and influence in Britain. They had an effective propaganda machine in the form of the famous Reviews, such as the *Edinburgh* and the *Westminster*, and, with the possible exception of their controversial views on population, they were popular with the increasingly influential bourgeoisie and even with the radical politicians, for their attacks on what James Mill called 'regal and aristocratical servitude'. Even as late as 1872, it was to his son John Stuart Mill that Emily Davis, the first Mistress of Girton, wrote for a list of questions to be studied by her class in Political Economy (1972, Letter 1730). (The imagination boggles at the thought of the present Mistress of that institution seeking such advice from, say, Milton Friedman.)

Today's intellectual descendants of the classical political economists – the liberals with a small 'l' – face a very different situation.

Consider our present preoccupation with trying to match our productive performance with the level of popular aspirations in growing real income, and add in the liberal prescription that the matching process must be compatible with maintaining individual freedom. It is widely assumed by those influential in policy discussion that liberal objectives are mutually incompatible anyway and that growth aspirations can be achieved only by much more (and not much less) economic planning associated with selective governmental intervention in the economy and further curtailment of individual freedom. It is further believed that liberals appeal to the wrong motives in emphasising the spur offered by material rewards within a competitive system, rather than by the call of 'patriotism' and close co-operation between the industrial 'estates of the realm' and government in the 'public interest'. In consequence their policy recommendations and the associated instruments, such as the reduction in high marginal rates of tax on earned income, the maintenance of profitability in private industry, and the improvement in the allocation of capital through a properly working capital market in the private sector, are manifestations of mortal sin.

These attacks on traditional liberal political economy are misconceived, particularly those which brand both Classical economists and their heirs as rampant supporters of *laissez-faire*; but strong vested interests have been created in a mythology of liberal economic thought, especially among those who wish to remain protected from the rigours of market forces. Thus a Minister of the Crown whom I heard announce that he was 'deeply devoted to the distortion of the free market' may be emitting in James Mill's words 'a senseless noise' or be badly advised, but he is clearly far from being on the defensive.[2]

Though I must say something about a liberal view of our present troubles, I am more immediately concerned with how it has come about that what may fairly be described as an eclectic body of economic thought with a long and honourable tradition may now be fighting for survival in political and governmental, if not in academic, circles.

I am therefore in much the same position as my friend, Thomas Keir, a Minister, not of the Crown but of the Kirk, who writing 30 years ago did not question the tenets of his faith but sought 'to discover what impedes their acceptance' (1947, Introduction). Only if we examine what he called 'the intellectual and emotional occasions of hesitancy' which confront liberal solutions to our present difficulties can we discover what are the best ways of removing doubt and making the voice of reason both welcome and influential.

II. THE BACKGROUND

I can obviously assume familiarity with the major propositions of liberal political economy and the kinds of attack which have been made on them. In offering some background to the present problem of maintaining and extending the credibility of liberal views, I need only refer to the contrast between the growth of the public sector and its influence on all aspects of our daily life and on liberal support for Adam Smith's 'system of natural liberty' which, though not laissez-fairist, associates the wholesale exercise of authority over the use of resources by the state as damaging to both individual freedom and economic progress.

Consider the present controversy over the size of the public sector. A good deal of the argument is concerned with the short-term problem of stabilisation. That problem is certainly made more difficult by the pressures on governments to increase the size of the public deficit, thus affecting the money supply and interest rates. It is also concerned with the general problem of re-allocating resources, as the Public Expenditure White Papers show, between public and private consumption and investment so that something like the long-term average investment/Gross Domestic Product ratio can be restored. I am not concerned here with this problem, except to say that it is easy to sympathise with any government trying to undo past mistakes which make budget adjustments of this kind so difficult today.

Less obvious but just as important are the immense distortions produced in the economy by a large, expanding, and highly centralised public sector. Such distortions constrain individual initiative and therefore reduce the efficiency with which resources are used. Such distortions are compounded by the use of regulatory instruments on top of financial controls whose effects often appear to cancel one another out.

The first distortion might be called 'motivation' distortion. Let me give an example. A private firm, in order to survive, must be able to make a return on its capital which is at least as high as the return which could be made by the alternative use of its capital funds. However, to perform this operation now requires an important set of skills which have increasingly less to do with satisfying the needs of current and potential final consumers. An enormous amount of time and effort has to be devoted to determining how and to what degree the actions of government are likely to determine the profitability, location and even the products of business operations. The acquisition of investible funds is becoming increasingly dependent on the decisions of a handful of civil servants entrusted with the onerous and awesome task of administering grants and loans under the Industry Acts. The reputation of major firms becomes more dependent on the public activities of its directors as members of government bodies of all kinds. To be seen working for the common good has some bearing on how a firm may be regarded when it comes to the negotiation of government support and the award of government contracts.

A whole panoply of measures as old as the companies legislation of the 19th century and as new as the Employment Protection Act must be scrutinised in order for firms to keep on the right side of government. It was recently estimated that a public company has to keep track of at least 100 major Acts of Parliament to do so. The results of the augmentation of selective government intervention and further attempts to influence firms through 'planning agreements' add a new dimension to what must be regarded as a major deterrent to the efficient operation of business, namely the high opportunity cost of 'interface with government' alongside the forgone alternative of concentrating on the job of producing what customers want and meeting delivery dates.

The second distortion relates to the production 'mix'. It seems in the nature of things that large, centralised government not directly subject to the discipline of the market generates both allocational inefficiency and production inefficiency – the wrong things produced at more than minimum average cost. The most dramatic example of misallocation is provided by the enormous expenditure on 'launching aid' for aerospace projects. Over a period of nearly 30 years from 1945 governments underwrote losses of at least £1.3 billion at 1974 prices. It would require a great feat of imagination to believe that the uncovenanted benefits, in the form of technological spin-off and national morale, given the alternative uses of resources, could make up the loss difference.[3] Latterly the policy of constraining the pricing and investment decisions of the nationalised fuel industries by government income redistribution objectives makes nonsense of any attempt to simulate competitive conditions – an attempt which experience suggests is bound to fail – in the public corporation sector.

The mistakes of saddling a public corporation with vaguely defined social objectives, on top of even vaguer financial criteria, are repeated in the guidelines for the National Enterprise Board. If one wanted to be sure that the Board's role should conform to the main object of the current industrial strategy, it would seem sensible to judge its success in terms of the speed with which it could return convalescent industries to the private sector – subject to the strict condition that it should raise new capital not from government (i.e. taxpayers) but from re-invested profits and/or the capital market. This would at least give it a veneer of economic respectability.

It follows that the first two distortions imply a third one – the misallocation of factor inputs. This misallocation is worsened by government legislation which perpetuates imperfections in the labour market and hinders labour mobility by a housing subsidy policy which does not even achieve its supposed objective of helping the poor. I want only to emphasise the special skills and ingenuity required in operating a system of economic controls, ranging from price and wage policies to micro-intervention in industry, not to speak of important social services, when the market is set aside as a method of allocation. It is no wonder therefore that the inevitable accompaniment of a large and growing public sector is the draining of skilled manpower into the bureaucratic machine – and one can't altogether blame those who have taken on the task of beating the market at its own game.[4] It is significant that the certainly unintended effect of the educational expansion of the late 'sixties has been to man-up traditionally labour-intensive services in the non-market sector, where productivity gains must be relatively low.

One must be careful here for, in principle at least, there is no reason to believe that the technology of government services is invariably labour-intensive, but as they are not marketed, the usual spurs to technical innovation are lacking and permanent employment contracts instituted for other reasons make any process of change operate slowly.

It would be easy to produce a compendium of statements by a wide cross-section of the community, public servants included, which would offer general support to this analysis. So the question remains why there is so little public pressure on politicians in Britain to make radical changes. One possible reason is lack of opportunity for individuals, as voters, to participate in the political process to anything like the extent available to voters in more decentralised democracies.

A more powerful reason is that the influence of the public sector is so widespread, and so important financially to individual households and firms, that the benefits of a reduction in its size to any given household seem uncertain. It might be generally agreed that the public sector should be reduced in size, but few have a direct interest in offering to forgo the advantages they derive from government services, subsidies, grants, etc. if others cannot be enjoined to do the same. Moreover, a double bargain has to be struck covering not only the amount and the form of cuts in public expenditure, but also the distribution of the resultant gains in the form of cuts in taxes. Even if there were no bargaining costs incurred in seeking agreement, and if there were much greater participation in the political process, there could be no guarantee that the desired result could be achieved.

This kind of problem is supposed to confront liberals with a difficult dilemma; for if large-scale, centralised, public action were the outcome of freely expressed choices, simulating as near as possible freedom of choice in competitive markets, why should liberals oppose them? The answer is simple but somehow mystifying to the mathematicians of fiscal politics. Liberal political economists will support those democratic systems and market systems which give full expression to individual choice but they do not necessarily have to like the results. The dilemma of liberals lies not in their dislike of some of the outcomes of a democratic system of choice which they themselves fought to introduce, but in how to persuade and certainly not to force the community to make choices which preserve their own freedom. But before considering a strategy of persuasion, I must examine why the credibility of liberal economics is called in question.

III. THE SUPPLY OF LIBERAL POLITICAL ECONOMY

The vigorous and critical examination of the political economy of government, and of suggestions for its reform, is therefore as important today as it was to Adam Smith in his famous attack on the Mercantile System.[5] It calls for a wide knowledge of the structure of society and of economic history, analytical skill and practical insight. If, as a result of such examination, the political economist finds himself nailing his colours to the liberal mast and becoming imbued with a crusading spirit, he faces the exhausting though exciting prospect of public disputation, and, in the present climate of opinion, the risk of being pilloried for his pains. The first impediment to the acceptance of liberal political economy therefore lies in the high opportunity cost attached to acquiring the necessary knowledge, skill and stamina to maintain the supply of ideas and policy recommendations.

The task I have outlined for an economist anxious to put forward his views on the state of society contrasts markedly with the role which academic economists assume in their daily lives. In the course of my academic life-time, the economics journals have become incomprehensible to anyone except the cognoscenti. (I date the fateful moment when economists became members of an exclusive professional coterie from the day about 25 years ago when Tom Marshall, one of our most eminent sociologists, announced in the LSE common room that he had regretfully cancelled his subscription to the *Economic Journal*. He was prepared to accept that he might not understand most of the articles but the moment of truth came when he could not even decipher the meaning of the title 'Does the Matrix Multiplier Oscillate?'.)

I do not wish to provide knocking copy for those who would jeer at these developments since marvellous and good things may come from the workshops of economics researchers which may be of ultimate benefit to mankind. However, the illusion that mathematical skill is a protection against the penetration of ethical bias and a complete substitute for imaginative insight into the workings of the economic system is widespread. Those of you who would seek inspiration and instruction from the normal staff and graduate seminars need to be warned that they are often arid, joyless affairs. A fashionable hypothesis is considered, reasons are given why it may be incomplete, an extra term may be added to the basic equation purporting to represent some behavioural characteristics of economic agents, a standard econometric testing procedure is deployed to show how the modified hypothesis stands up. There is then some discussion about the speaker's knowledge of the literature, about the quality of the data and the suitability of the tests, and above all the elegance of the model. Then everyone adjourns to the bar satisfied that the subject is still open and that fortunately the speaker has observed the proprieties of discourse by concluding that 'further research is needed' – hopefully to be financed by the research councils.

This widely practised ritual is indicative of the motivation of the younger creative members of the economics profession. Though interested in the efficiency of the market they are largely immune from its immediate pressures; in such circumstances it is only natural that they should seek to maximise their reputation within their peer group rather than concern themselves with the training requirements of the employers of their students or with public enlightenment. Moreover, it is in their economic interests to do so provided they wish to remain in academic life, for their promotion prospects will be geared to what their universities and faculties consider important, notably the strength of publication in the top academic journals. In this situation why incur the time and energy costs of seeking to reform the world with the further prospect, for a liberal political economist, of retailing 'reactionary' ideas which embarrass one's academic colleagues?

Of course, I have exaggerated and must add two important qualifications to my argument. The first is that there are outstanding liberal members of the profession who combine a reputation as influential writers on policy matters with important contributions to the scientific development of economics but, following the predictions of their own analysis, they have an understandable tendency to emigrate! The comparative advantage they may have, together with other distinguished overseas economists, in supplying *us* with liberal ideas is more apparent than real. They are no longer in the line of fire.

The second qualification is represented by the strong hold still exercised over a large section of the profession by the branch of the subject known as welfare economics. The tenets of its most fashionable version, going back to Pareto and Pigou, are considered as the foundation of 'sound' views on policy matters and are based on a number of propositions which might appear attractive to liberal economists. Ignoring finer points of interpretation,[6] it is initially assumed that individual welfare is what counts and that individuals are the best judges of their own welfare. From familiar assumptions of economic behaviour, prescriptions about the optimal production and the allocation of resources and sometimes the optimal distribution of resources are put forward which at first sight seem to imply strong support for a free market system with the government confining its activities to certain basic services, such as defence and law and order, for some transfer measures to remove major disparities in the distribution of income and wealth (though this usually requires further initial value and behavioural assumptions), and for measures which promote competition in factor and product markets.

It is interesting to observe that as welfare economics has developed it has tended to support more and more government intervention. Latter-day Pigovians continue to discover new examples of 'market failure'. Goods such as education are under-provided by the market because producers cannot capture those benefits of supply which accrue to the community at large. Producers may impose costs on others, e.g. through pollution, which are not reflected in their costs of production. Cases where social benefits and costs diverge from private benefits and costs certainly abound, though the divergences may be very difficult to quantify; but the existence of market failure leads welfare economists all too readily to assume that there is an efficient and costless form of government action always at hand to rectify the market's deficiencies. The range of suggested action varies with each example of deficiency from elaborate tax and subsidy schemes to direct controls and public take-over of production as in the so-called 'natural monopoly' case. Seldom are the costs of the control methods themselves evaluated and the kinds of distortion inevitably associated with bureaucratic control, which I have already discussed, are conveniently forgotten.

The curious idea that welfare economics is innocent of political judgements, or at least is based on a set of value statements that only morons would oppose, is difficult to explain but, as Lord Robbins has recently reminded us (1976, p. 3), the notion displays a lack of sophistication in marked contrast to the Classical economists. The fact remains that its adherents appear to believe that they have made notable advances in the field of public policy whereas what is normally found in their speculations is a curious blend of often penetrating observation of the workings of the market system with an astonishingly naïve view of the political and bureaucratic process. Moreover, insofar as the forms of government intervention are specified, one fortunate side-effect is support for the generation of employment opportunities for economists!

IV. THE EMOTIONAL RESISTANCE TO LIBERAL POLITICAL ECONOMY[7]

I now turn to the demand for liberal ideas in order to examine the nature and if possible the extent of sales resistance, beginning first of all with 'the emotional occasions of hesitancy'. This is a large and treacherous field of inquiry and what I have to say can at most be suggestive.

It is ironic that the most striking contemporary example of Keynes's dictum that 'practical men . . . are usually the slaves of some defunct economist' is to be found in the influence of Keynes himself. We all know that a rounded view of his work would lead one to be wary of concluding that he believed capitalist economies would suffer from long-run under-employment of resources, and would need large and continuous government deficits to raise output and employment. The fact remains that these are the central ideas with which he is widely associated. Unfortunately these ideas gave strong encouragement to one of the most influential fantasies among otherwise intelligent beings, namely that the problem of scarce resources and the conflicts of choice to which it gives rise are pure inventions.

The popular, highly vulgarised, version of Keynesianism – that the problem of production has been solved by maintaining aggregate demand, and that the only economic problem is distribution – is a marvellous tonic for those who have utopian visions of society. To give only one example, Lewis Mumford in his famous book *The Culture of Cities,* on which generations of town planners have been reared, stated that

> Fortunately, our civilisation as a whole is now at a point technically where it is feasible to give the population as a whole that basis in good breeding and good nurture which has hitherto been the exclusive possession of aristocracies. [1944, p. 464]

Only appropriate distributional and allocational policies were needed to turn megalopolis into paradise because splendid housing and perceptive planning would produce moral regeneration alongside economic sufficiency.

There are copious examples which replicate Mumford's dream of gracious living coupled with transformation in the human character, the latest being associated with the bucolic paradises of radical economists in which market relations disappear and in the process peaceful co-operation will replace competition to produce a life of 'luxe, calme et volupté'.

The obscene heresy of liberal economists has been to continue to support two propositions derived from the teaching of our intellectual antecedents. The first, derived from Hume and Smith, is that human nature changes little. In Hume's words,

> men are not able radically to cure, either in themselves or others, that narrowness of soul which makes them prefer the present to the remote. They cannot change their natures. All they can do is to change their situation . . . [1951, pp. 84–5]

The second proposition points to the limits to change in man's situation imposed by the problem of scarce resources which have competing uses, that is to say, the rejection of the vulgarised, popular view of the Keynesian message of abundance. If we couple these two constraints, derived from introspection and empirical observation, with the liberal's preference for personal liberty – only restricted to the extent that is necessary to ensure adequate realisation of and access to its benefits for all – then pronouncement of the anathema by those who believe they know what is good for us is a sure thing, because the inevitable consequence of the liberal position is that there is no possibility of an orderly heaven on earth. At most, we approach a tolerable, perhaps almost comfortable, though certainly unstable existence, constantly having to adapt to changing economic circumstances, e.g. the energy crisis, threat from illiberal dictatorships, etc.

One might have interesting arguments with those who claim that economists exaggerate the constraints on resources and take a rather narrow view of the behavioural characteristics of human beings; and that they possibly under-estimate the extent to which state action, through social services, can alter not only the economic and social situation of individuals but improve their behaviour. In a reasonable world, these matters can be decided by appeal to empirical observation and examination of the inferences drawn from such observations. At the very least, one can separate out questions of fact and logic from questions of value. Unfortunately, in areas where such debate is of vital public interest – for example, in social policy – there is all too often little opportunity for rational discourse with supporters of collective provision only of social services, such as health and education.

I could offer countless examples of the sense of moral outrage which permeates the work of sociologists and social administrators when, with obvious distaste, they feel obliged to mention the hard facts of economic life. With some reluctance, for some of us knew him well and liked him, I single out as typical one quotation from a work of Richard Titmuss. In his book *Social Policy: An Introduction,* used throughout the length and breadth of this country as a textbook, he describes various models of social policy of which the one associated with liberalism is what he called 'Model A – The Residual Welfare Model':

> There are . . . some social phenomena that may be studied with a certain degree of cold rational disinterestedness while never achieving the lack of involvement displayed by the mathematician analysing a quadratic equation. But this is not possible with the study of social policy or, to take another example, social deviation . . . One of the value assumptions, for instance, concealed in Model A – *The Residual Welfare Model of Social Policy* – is that the residual non-market sector (the public social policy sector) should concern itself with social deviants; the 'bad actuarial risks', those who are unwilling or unable to provide for their own needs – and the needs of their families – through the normal mechanism of the market.
>
> The definition of deviation means an aberration, turning from the right course, obliquity of conduct. Language is not a mere symbolic tool of communication. By describing someone as a deviant we express an attitude; we normally brand him and stigmatise him with our value-judgement . . . [1974, p. 133]

There is a temptation to match this ugly allegation against liberal thinkers with angry polemic, rather in the manner of Ludwig von Mises's brilliant diagnosis of what he labelled the 'Fourier Complex'.[8] But the idea that liberal economists want to promote social conformity *in order* to isolate the morally delinquent and deviant poor is manifestly absurd. To restore communication, and hopefully mutual understanding, with those who have been influenced by this kind of view may already be easier because of the rude shock provided by the energy crisis. It should at least dispel any illusion that 'social need' is an absolute and the scarcity concept a contrivance of mean-minded market economists.

V. 'The Intellectual Occasions of Hesitancy'

I now turn to the intellectual sales resistance. By this I do not mean the opposition to liberal political economy found among the socialist writers from Marx onwards, who share neither the liberal view about how the economy functions nor its definition of the tasks of the state. This is essentially an unending academic debate which, however fascinating, is only of vestigial interest in the present context. I am more directly concerned with how it has come about that intelligent, fair-minded and perceptive civil servants, members of senior management and some trade unionists have come to regard continuous state intervention on a large scale as at least a regrettable necessity given general recognition of the gap between British economic aspirations and our industrial performance. There may be no positive urge to solve our economic problems, if that were possible, solely by government action, but there seems to be something akin to a general belief that 'liberal political economy must know when to abdicate' in the teeth of the stern realities of an illiberal world. There is a coherent defensible position of some intellectual respectability, which requires serious consideration once one accepts the constraints on the operation of the market system its supporters regard as binding. Nor is this position a simple over-reaction to the immediate problems associated with the economic crisis of the 1970s.

The diagnosis of our economic condition (by the opposing groups, liberals and interventionists) is much the same, with the emphasis shifting very much more towards the inefficient use of factor inputs and away from the more simplistic views of the 1960s in which large-scale investment in physical and human capital was popularly considered both a necessary and sufficient condition for growth. In particular, the diagnosis points towards improving competitiveness in internationally-traded goods and particularly in manufacturing.

Then we reach the dividing line between liberals and interventionists. The sceptical pragmatist will argue that there is little that the free market can do to improve performance. Internally we have to accept the monopoly power of the trade unions as a datum; and therefore we must also accept a whole range of restrictive practices in the labour market, and political support for collectivist social policies which pre-empt a large share of the annual output flow and generate pressure for further nationalisation.

Externally the development of export markets on the scale necessary to pay off our foreign debts (even allowing for North Sea oil) will bring manufacturers and exporters of services increasingly face to face not with private buyers but rather with public officials acting on behalf of governments in oil-producing countries and industrialised socialist countries. 'Common property resources' in the sea and in the air are liable, so it is held, to be 'over-exploited' by private enterprise since they cannot be priced. Efficiency in their use will call for inter-governmental agreement, and at a minimum individual governmental regulation.

Reluctantly, so the pragmatic argument continues, the only solution will be to extend selective intervention by government. Indeed, in an international economy riddled with externalities, this will be the only prudent way to ensure that private enterprise will be able to function efficiently at all. Paradoxically, therefore, selectivity will be the principal means of preserving rather than destroying the market economy.

From this familiar line of argument to the understanding of the logic of specific proposals is a big jump. The *rationale* of those parts of the new industrial strategy which are *not* governed by political shibboleths is principally grounded in the belief that consensus can be reached in respect of both diagnosis and cure of our economic ills, and action to promote the cure lies in labour–management co-operation at the industry level. The government is not there simply to organise a 'jaw-boning' exercise but to assess the value of specific proposals for improving efficiency, and to use its fiscal and financial controls, if they can so be used, to alter the structure of industry in line with efficiency criteria.[9] At this stage of such an ambitious, elaborate and fascinating exercise, one can predict with some confidence that all parties will continue to agree that they are against sin and can discern the common path of virtue, provided it is not too clearly delineated. The crunch will come when there is (as there clearly must eventually be) a plain statement, a brutal indication of who is to bear the costs of change. At that stage the full implications of the rigidities produced by trade union and industrial restrictive practices will have to be faced.

Easier to appreciate is the gist of the argument supporting government action on the international front. The organisation of effective bargaining with foreign governments to sell our goods and to negotiate over the distribution of property rights in the sea and in the air clearly makes something of a case for a stronger diplomatic capability; the support of large industrial consortia, if only on a temporary basis, to face the risks of dealing with rich overseas governments; and the use of selective methods of export promotion, if only as bargaining counters in the game of minimising international discrimination in traded goods and services.

The crux of the argument of the intelligent sceptics is that rigidities in both the national and international economy produced by the power of strong vested interest-groups cannot be removed. At best they can only be neutralised and by methods which will often go counter to the workings of the free market. As an erstwhile civil servant I have come to respect their views and their integrity; but I believe they offer us a counsel of despair, notably in relation to our domestic economy. Moreover, I contend that selective state intervention could proliferate across the whole of government, producing precisely the result that many of them are anxious to avoid – an administered centralised so-called planned economy, and an inefficient one at that.

VI. Retaining and Expanding Credibility

I have advanced two main propositions. First, the skill and courage required to perceive and proclaim how liberal ideas apply to the operation of the economy have a high opportunity cost to professional economists. Secondly, the emotional sales resistance to liberal ideas is particularly virulent among those who play a crucial role in promoting government services which directly impinge on the everyday lives of citizens (the social services), while intellectual scepticism towards liberal policies is both marked and influential among those who run our industrial affairs inside and outside the public sector.

However, in trying to retain and expand the credibility of liberal political economy, it may not be the right course of action to concentrate only on persuading the patricians in our society. The main thrust of any campaign to remove the threat of individual freedom which is bound to result from the growth of collectivist policies must concentrate on improving the individual's chances of influencing governments, and on persuading voters in all sorts of elections that their interests are best served by voting in representatives who are not beholden to powerful minority interest-groups intent on fragmenting and ultimately destroying the market economy.

There is one particularly important dilemma encountered in trying to move towards a more liberal society. Individuals may accept the need for the restoration of incentives and the promotion of individual freedom as ultimate goals, but may not be prepared to suffer the costs of change in moving towards them. Thus it is quite possible that support could be enlisted for legislative changes which would eradicate coercion by simple majorities, for example through the safeguards proposed by Professor Hayek in the Fourth Lecture in this series (1973). However, the process by which such changes would have to be instituted, and the uncertainty attached to the distribution of the burdens and benefits of change, make it reasonable for many individuals to refuse to face the risks. Moreover, as the vacillations over the form and extent of devolution have made patently clear, it is only when there is determined, persistent and extensive pressure that governments will consider constitutional changes which may in the long run circumscribe their own powers.

Despite what I have said earlier, there is perhaps a glimmer of hope for liberals in the growing discontent with the conduct of government, as reflected in the unpopularity of the long-term income prospects (including index-linked pensions) with security of tenure of civil servants, and of the disincentive effects of the present social security and income-tax systems. Is this perhaps a hint that voters believe that those who work for, or benefit from, government services should be paid something akin to their marginal productivity? It may not be evidence that voters wish to see major changes in the tasks of government, but it may show that as taxpayers they have a growing interest in seeing that these tasks are carried out more efficiently. A potentially dangerous situation arises when alienation among voters takes the form of avoiding or evading tax obligations on a large scale (including recourse to emigration) or making them feel impelled to organise in Poujadiste-type movements which defy the rule of law, instead of channelling their efforts through the normal political procedures.

We may have reached the stage in Britain at which voter pressure to change the whole electoral system can be mustered much more easily than at any time I can remember. My colleague, Charles Rowley, has come to much the same conclusion.[10] I agree with him that even the relatively simple (but not minor) constitutional change to the Single Transferable Vote offers the prospect of removing the power of the extremists in our two main parties to coerce their colleagues into immoderate action; for then there would be a strong probability that coalitions would become the conventional make-up of any government rather than government by a party with an absolute majority of seats.

Many of us would want to go much further than that in order to avoid the continuance of a system by which governments buy voters' support through lavish spending programmes. I have argued elsewhere the case for a form of political devolution which reduces voter alienation by greater participation in the political process and thereby offers an incentive to understand both the workings of government and, one hopes, recognition of its limitations (see chapter 5 of this volume). However, this and other constitutional reforms, such as a review of the representation and functions of the House of Lords, rest on the creation of a political atmosphere in which the big issues raised can be properly discussed and, therefore, are not introduced under the pressure of immediate political events. The reflection of moderate, rational opinion in Parliament through electoral reform offers the best chance that this will occur.

In order to tie in the interests of the working community with the need for removal of distortions caused by large-scale public intervention (which inhibit our economic advance and impair individual freedom), advocates of liberal political economy need to look closely at the genuine fears of work-people that removal of imperfections in the labour market may work to their disadvantage. The traditional liberal view on this has been to point to the advantages to the consumer of more efficient allocation of resources produced by wider competition and new deployment of labour. If the price of winning acceptance for dismantling restrictive practices by labour unions, while retaining collective bargaining arrangements, is more worker participation in running industry, encouragement of labour-managed firms (as Peter Jay argued in the Sixth Wincott Lecture, 1976) and the promotion of what Sam Brittan (1976) has called 'property rights in jobs', then I am all for experimentation in such directions. There is no categorical imperative for liberals which requires us to accept that the organisation of productive activities along traditional hierarchical lines must be sanctified in our company legislation.

The real problem is how to devise systems of worker participation and control which are compatible with the survival and growth of the firm under competitive conditions, as John Stuart Mill realised over a century ago. He wrote, as I do, more in the hope than in the confident expectation that this problem could be solved; but surely his broad conclusion is correct:

> . . . what is now required is not to bolster up old customs whereby limited classes of labouring people obtain partial gains which interest them in keeping up the present organisation of society, but to introduce new practices beneficial to all. [1871, IV.vii.7]

'New practices' of genuine appeal and capable of implementation again require time for discussion and debate – and in a saner political atmosphere than we have been experiencing.

Clearly the tentative agenda I have put forward needs filling out. It certainly calls for considerable adjustment in the attitudes and range of expertise of professional economists who have a genuine interest in the great issues of our day. There are obvious dangers in directing one's intellectual energies towards support of one's philosophical position, but there surely cannot be anything reprehensible in directing our skills towards the study of issues which those most affected by them consider important, and in trying to persuade them that a liberal solution should claim their support. The commitment offers at least as much excitement as withdrawal into more purely intellectual and professionally fashionable pursuits . . . but remember the warning of the master about those who try to avoid the general contagion of faction:

> All such people are held in contempt and derision, frequently in detestation, by the furious zealots of both parties . . . The . . . impartial spectator, therefore, is upon no occasion at a greater distance than amidst the violence and rage of contending parties . . . Of all the corrupters of moral sentiments, therefore, faction and fanaticism have always been by far the greatest. [Smith, 1976b, pp. 156–7]

Trying to expand the credibility of liberalism is certainly not an occupation for the faint-hearted or the pessimistic.

NOTES

1. Seventh Harold Wincott Memorial Lecture, 1976. A number of colleagues read and commented on an earlier draft of this lecture, notably James Buchanan, Douglas Dosser, Ralph Harris, Keith Hartley, Graham Hutton, Michael Jones-Lee, Alan Maynard, Charles Rowley and Arthur Seldon. I am most grateful to them. Reproduced with minor amendments from Institute of Economic Affairs, London, 1977.
2. Curiously enough the same Minister was heard by me to remark that 'so far as small firms are concerned, I believe implicitly in the wisdom of Adam Smith'.
3. It says a good deal for the Department of Industry that it allowed the publication of the excellent study by Mr Nick Gardner, 'Economics of Launching Aid' (1976), from which these figures are derived. It was the former Secretary of State for Trade, Mr Edmund Dell, who remarked (before he became a minister) that 'Doubtful as governments might be of their ability to promote economic development in general, in aerospace and nuclear energy they seemed to have no doubt. Though the costs far exceeded the costs of empire, they have gone on. They have spent magnificently . . . the pressures of national prestige and of the thousands of persons employed in these industries are likely to determine the nation's future course rather than any more scientific calculations regarding investment and return' (1973, pp. 30–1).
4. Here I simply echo Adam Smith's remarks about the officials of the East India Company: 'It is the system of government, the situation in which they are placed, that I mean to censure; not the character of those who have acted in it. They acted as their situation naturally directed, and they who have clamoured the loudest against them would, probably, have not acted better themselves' (*The Wealth of Nations*, 1976a, Vol. II, p. 641).
5. The contemporary relevance of Adam Smith's attack on mercantilism to the economic analysis of government is perceptively analysed in Ricketts (1978).
6. For further analysis of modern welfare economics and its deficiencies, see Rowley and Peacock (1975).
7. In this section I have concentrated on the emotional resistance to liberal political economy by social reformers in the narrow sense, i.e. those concerned with the development of social services on a collective basis. I have avoided the temptation of reviewing another and very potent source of resistance, namely the 20th-century counterparts to William Blake and John Ruskin who so despised the liberal political economy of their own day. A splendid essay on this theme by a well-known English scholar is George Watson's 'The Myth of Catastrophe' (1976); he reviews the attitudes of Orwell, Connolly, Eliot, Auden and others to capitalism.
8. After the French utopian socialist. The 'complex', to von Mises, amounts to a neurotic hatred of those who question utopian schemes on the grounds that they ignore the principle of scarcity (1962, Introduction).
9. For a skilful exposition of the 'new' industrial strategy, see Lord (Second Secretary, HM Treasury) (1977).
10. In a provocative and stimulating paper (forthcoming). See also the conclusion of Jo Grimond (1976).

REFERENCES

Brittan, S. (1976) 'The political economy of labour monopoly' *Three Banks Review* No. 105, September.
Dell, E. (1973) *Political Responsibility and Industry* Allen & Unwin, London.
Gardner, N. (1976) 'Economics of launching aid' in A. Whiting (ed.) *The Economics of Industrial Subsidies* HMSO, London.
Grimond, J. (1976) *The Bureaucratic Blight* Unservile State Papers No. 22, Liberal Party Publications, London.
Hayek, F. A. (1973) *Economic Freedom and Representative Government* Occasional Paper No. 39, Institute of Economic Affairs, London (2nd impression 1976).
Hume, D. (1951) 'Of the origin of government' in *Essays Moral, Political and Literary* (edited by F. Watson) Nelson, London.

Jay, P. (1976) *A General Theory of Employment, Inflation and Politics* Occasional Paper No. 46, Institute of Economic Affairs, London.

Keir, T. H. (1947) *Faith and Response* Hodder & Stoughton, London.

Lord, A. (1977) 'A Strategy for Industry' Sir Ellis Hunter Memorial Lecture No. 8, University of York.

Mill, James (1966) *Selected Economic Writings* (introduced and edited by D. Winch) published for the Scottish Economic Society by Oliver & Boyd, Edinburgh and London.

Mill, J. S. (1871) *Principles of Political Economy* Book iv, Chapter vii (University of Toronto Press edition 1965).

Mill, J. S. (1972) *The Later Letters of John Stuart Mill 1849–1873* (edited by F. Mineka and D. Lindley) University of Toronto Press, Toronto.

von Mises, L. (1962) *The Free and Prosperous Commonwealth* Van Nostrand, Princeton, N.J.

Mumford, L. (1944) *The Culture of Cities* Secker & Warburg, London.

Ricketts, M. (1978) 'Adam Smith and the economics of bureaucracy' in *Economics of Politics* Readings 18, Institute of Economic Affairs, London.

Robbins, Lord L. (1968) Foreword to H. Wincott *The Business of Capitalism* Institute of Economic Affairs, London.

Robbins, Lord L. (1976) *Political Economy Past and Present* Macmillan, London.

Rowley, C. K. (forthcoming) 'The British disease: A public choice and property rights perspective'.

Rowley, C. K. and Peacock, A. T. (1975) *Welfare Economics, A Liberal Restatement* Martin Robertson, London.

Smith, A. (1976a) *The Wealth of Nations* (edited by R. H. Campbell and A. J. Skinner) Clarendon Press, Oxford.

Smith, A. (1976b) *The Theory of Moral Sentiments* (edited by D. D. Raphael and A. L. Macfie) Oxford University Press, London.

Titmuss, R. (1974) *Social Policy: An Introduction* Allen & Unwin, London.

Watson, G. (1976) 'The myth of catastrophe' *Yale Review* Spring.

PART III

The Economic Analysis of Government Policies

INTRODUCTION

The articles in this Part are of a more conventional character, being largely applications of economic analysis to policy problems. It may nevertheless be useful to the reader to offer a few words of introduction to their widely diverse contents.

The first three articles develop the argument concerning the causes and consequences of public sector growth already examined in chapter 1. Chapter 7 suggests reasons why public goods theory and the economic theory of politics generally can offer only a point of departure for the examination of this growth. This is because they emphasise the allocational objectives of individual taxpayers and voters as the spur to growth. As de Tocqueville realised, the extension of the property right in voting coupled with inequality in income distribution draws the attention of 'disadvantaged' voters to the use of the budget as a redistributional device. Further, public goods theory rarely has anything to say about the influence on expenditure growth of the costs of providing public services. The relative increase in the costs of important government services, particularly welfare services, is regarded by economists such as Baumol and Oates as the inevitable consequence of the labour-intensive nature of these services. Both chapters 7 and 8 offer reasons why this labour-intensive nature may be a function of the discretionary behaviour open to bureaucrats not subject to the full rigour of market forces rather than a function of technological constraints. Chapter 9 complements these arguments by revealing the slender basis of public goods theory as a guide to which services will actually be provided by the public sector and how these services should be priced. It is hoped that the reader will find some of the earnest tone of analytical discussion relieved a little by the historical digression on the Isle of May lighthouse!

Chapter 10 is more closely linked to the previous discussion than might appear from the subject matter. The arts have become a fashionable area of examination by economists and justification for growing public support has been based partly on market failure arguments and partly on the impossibility of reaping productivity gains in theatrical and music performance, which are regarded as highly labour intensive. I have offered a critical examination of this argument elsewhere (see Mark Blaug, 1976, pp. 70–83). I have sought in this companion piece on an 'upstream' industry to examine the case for public intervention in the market for musical composition, where the incidence of 'failure' is high but where, given particular guarantees by the government that require separate justification, an efficient market may be organised without large-scale subsidy to composers.

Chapters 11–14 enter familiar fields of study in public finance. I would only remark about chapter 11 that, whatever I may have said about the theory of economic policy in chapter 1, I find it has useful logical properties in demonstrating conflicts between different economic policies.

Chapter 15 redresses the balance by questioning the tendency among specialists in the economics of public finance and public policy generally to believe that they have no obligation to make their views known (and intelligible) to the taxpayers who support so many of them. This offers me the opportunity to poke a little mild fun at the recondite nature of recent developments in public finance theory. A little rigorous self-examination from time to time does not come amiss.

REFERENCE

Blaug, Mark (ed.) (1976) *The Economics of the Arts* Martin Robertson, London.

CHAPTER 7

The Problem of Public Expenditure Growth in Post-Industrial Society[1]

Wherever the poor direct public affairs and dispose of the national re-
sources, it appears certain that, as they profit by the expenditure of the
State, they are apt to augment that expenditure. [Alexis de Tocqueville
Democracy in America (1835), World Classics edition, p. 157.]

The deplorable truth is that a taste for jobs and a life at the public
expense is not, with us, confined to a single party, but is the great and
permanent weakness of the nation itself; it is the combined effect of the
democratic constitution of our civic society and the excessive centralization of our government. This is the hidden illness that has gnawed away
at every ancient authority, and will do the same to all others in the
future. [Alexis de Tocqueville *Recollections* (1850), Anchor Books edition,
pp. 41–2.]

I. Introduction

The purpose of this paper is two fold. It offers, first of all, a critical review
of recent discussion of the determinants of the growth of government expenditure in industrial countries. Secondly, it isolates and expands those parts of
the discussion which appear to have relevance to the problems of post-
industrial society.

The paper begins (section II) with a brief survey of the problems
encountered in examining government expenditure growth using the tools of
the economist. This can do no more than review the relevant literature, its
purpose being to explain why I wish to concentrate on the supply rather
than the demand factors governing government expenditure growth. Section
III advances the argument that the productivity of government services may
be markedly influenced not so much by the technical characteristics of supply,
as emphasised by Baumol, but by the lack of incentive to introduce 'process'
and 'product' innovations by bureaucratically organised production. Section

IV examines the recent economic theory of bureaucracy and its power to explain the interrelation between supply and demand factors in the process of government expenditure growth. A final section (section V) develops the argument that post-industrial societies, by definition committed to respond to growing demands for publicly produced output of goods and services, face a major problem in strengthening the collective will to have these services provided efficiently.

II. Determinants of Government Expenditure Growth: A Brief Survey

Major industrial countries in Western Europe together with the United States and Canada have uniformly experienced long-term growth in government expenditure (including transfers and subsidies) relative to Gross Domestic Product, often coupled with growing centralised control of public expenditure. The associated growth in government revenue as a proportion of GNP is equally striking. In Sweden, for example, government revenue as a percentage of GNP nearly doubled (25.9% to 50.1%) between 1950 and 1972 alone.[2]

General explanations of these phenomena are couched in terms of both demand and supply conditions for publicly provided government goods and services. On the demand side, attempts have been made to develop a dynamic theory of choice between privately and publicly produced services. What reasons can be advanced to suggest that, over the last fifty years or so, the income elasticity of demand for 'social' consumer and capital goods will be higher than that for private goods in these categories? Musgrave and Musgrave (1976), to quote well-known authorities, emphasise the growing complementarity between both public and private consumer and capital goods, as average income rises. Thus expenditure on education at secondary and higher levels is a complementary input to the changing technology associated with economic growth in industrial countries, as are both railway tracks and highways, though in the latter case complementarity may be associated with leisure activities. It is assumed that many of these complementary inputs generate benefits which are largely external so that public finance (though not necessarily public provision) will be required to generate their supply. Clearly both the relative size and composition of publicly provided consumer and capital goods will be affected by population change.

A major problem in attempting to apply dynamic consumer theory to explain the phenomenon of government expenditure growth lies in the fact that it is financed not by voluntary payments by consumers but by taxes. The political mechanism by which expenditure decisions come to be made modifies the process of choice, as compared to the market, in two important ways. First of all the distribution of 'purchasing power', as found, for example, in the voting system, may differ markedly from the distribution of purchasing power as reflected in the prevailing (pre-tax) income distribution, either at the constituency or at the Parliamentary level, and may vary markedly through time in a particular country. Secondly, the mode of decision-taking through voting must inevitably imply some degree of coercion, because the cost of obtaining unanimous decisions on all issues of public finance is clearly prohibitive save in the case of very small political units. The political facts of life are one of the major barriers to the deployment of econometric time series analysis in exploring the determinants of government expenditure growth using GDP or GDP per capita, or some such variable, as the main explanatory factor. The empirical testing of this sort of hypothesis which postulates that per capita income is of strategic importance in explaining this growth rests on the assumption that all other variables, notably the political system, which may change markedly through time, are so unimportant that they can simply be thrown into the error term.

Undismayed by these difficulties, attempts have been made to relate government expenditure growth to the structure and evolution of the political decision-making process, as explored in the now well-established economic theory of democracy. Some writers, notably Buchanan (1967), prefer to employ a paradigm in which the essential characteristic of democratic decision-making is the translation of voters' preferences into action by legislators. I take this opportunity of paying tribute to the writer who appears to be the first to hypothesise a connexion between the growth in government expenditure and the evolution of democracy and whose contribution seems to have gone unrecognised. In Chapter XII of Part I of his famous *Democracy in America* published in 1835, Alexis de Tocqueville associates the size of the government expenditure and therefore the 'burden' of taxes with two important variables: the spread of the franchise and the distribution of property. The growth of government expenditure is positively related to the extension of the franchise and the degree of inequality in the distribution of property. Thus

> in countries in which the poor should be exclusively invested with the power of making laws no great economy is to be expected: that expenditure will be considerable, either because the taxes do not weigh upon those who levy them, or because they are levied in such a way as not to weigh on those classes. In other words, the government of the democracy is the only one under which the power which lays on taxes escapes the payment of them. [p. 150]

This view does not offer sufficient reason for a change in the amount and composition of expenditure compared with a situation where a despotic or aristocratic regime obtains, but merely a reason for the distribution of tax payments. The distribution of property, the second determinant, plays a crucial role, for in a country of pronounced inequalities in the distribution of property the extension of the franchise to the poor offers the opportunity for instituting positive measures designed to improve the lot of the majority:

> the perpetual sense of their own miseries impels the rulers of society to seek for perpetual ameliorations. A thousand different objects are subjected to improvement; the most trivial details are sought out as susceptible to amendment; and those changes which are accompanied with considerable expense are more especially advocated since the object is to render the condition of the poor more tolerable, who cannot pay for themselves. [pp. 151–52]

De Tocqueville does not 'close the loop' by speculating whether the levelling effect produced by a redistributory tax system coupled with growing public expenditure will ultimately call for a lowering of the tax exemption limit. However, he speculates that 'the extravagance of democracy is, however, less to be dreaded in proportion as the people acquire a share of property, because on the one hand the contributions are less needed, and, on the other, it is more difficult to lay on taxes which do not affect the interests of the lower classes' (pp. 151–2). (It was for this reason that he believed that the universal suffrage in the United States would be 'less dangerous' than in the U.K. or France where property was concentrated in few hands.) He also adds the interesting speculation that a check on the cost of government exists in the strong interest of the electorate in a democracy in parsimonious treatment of officers of state. The salaries of secondary officials will be in line with those paid in comparable employment in the private sector, but principal officers will be poorly paid relative to their subordinates: 'in general democracy gives largely to the community and very sparingly to those who govern it. The reverse is the case in aristocratic countries, where the money of the State is expended to the profit of the persons who are at the head of affairs' (p. 156). We shall have cause to consider this speculation later in this paper.

The de Tocqueville–Buchanan approach emphasises the operational significance of consent of the governed in explaining the workings of the public sector. Others, including myself and Jack Wiseman (Peacock and Wiseman, 1967), have placed more emphasis on the power of representative governments to coerce the electorate, though this is not to deny that any attempt by a government to maximise its length of time in office must be subject to a vote-getting constraint so that voters' preferences cannot be ignored. This view of the political process seemed to fit better with the observed phenomenon (though its significance has been subject to controversy), namely that the growth of government expenditure is characterised by 'jumps' associated with major upheavals in society such as wars. Thus what Peacock and Wiseman have named the 'displacement effect' has been neatly explained by Albert Breton (1974) by his theory of the individual cost of political participation.[3] The greater the degree of coercion to which individuals are subjected, as in wartime, the lower the relative cost to voters of attempts to exact promises from government to improve social and economic conditions when circumstances allow. However, relieved of the sacrifices associated with war or similar emergency, the individual voter will 'tolerate' a retention of higher tax rates than before the emergency, provided that these rates finance services from which he will now directly benefit. Both Buchanan (1967) and Johansen (1965) have argued that the explanation of the displacement effect can be couched in much the same terms without sacrificing the framework of the 'voluntary exchange theory' of public finance, the latter employing a dynamic version of Lindahl's famous model (see Johansen, pp. 160–2).

While it seems important for later discussion to convey at least the flavour of the 'dynamic demand theory' of government expenditure growth, the conclusion that the development and timing of public expenditure growth must reflect a real transfer of resources to the public sector could be partly an illusion. Attention has shifted recently to another cause of expenditure growth hinted at by Peacock and Wiseman, later discussed by Andic and Veverka (1964) and now associated with the Baumol (1967) thesis of 'unbalanced growth'. This thesis, which is examined in more detail below, claims that the productivity gains associated with economic growth in industrial countries are not manifested in public sector activities to the extent that they are in private (manufacturing) activities. This is because public sector activities, it is alleged, are characterised by labour-intensive methods of production and offer few opportunities for the introduction of technological change.

There is clearly a major problem in measuring the productivity of government services that are not produced by sale. The empirical evidence of the 'Baumol effect' has to rely on the subterfuge of measuring the relative costs of government inputs. It may be agreed that the convention of expressing public expenditure growth in terms of undeflated ratios of government spending to GDP is illegitimate, as Peacock and Wiseman pointed out in advance of the Baumol discussion. They claimed that any corrections they were able to make by separate deflation of public and private components of GDP would probably have made little difference to their results.

While I am critical of the Baumol thesis (cf. section III below), I hope to show that the 'productivity lag' may be an important element in promoting understanding of the problems presented by the growth of the public sector in post-industrial societies. The reason soon becomes obvious. The very definition of the term 'post-industrial' incorporates large-scale provision of publicly produced goods and services of a welfare character which command popular support. At the same time such services have to be financed and their scale and character are unlikely to result in a situation where, recalling de Tocqueville, 'the power which lays on taxes escapes the payment of them'. Post-industrial societies cannot therefore ignore movements in the 'terms of trade' between voters as taxpayers and the suppliers of non-marketed government services.

III. 'Baumol's Disease' and the Public Sector

The Baumol thesis (Baumol and Oates, 1975) can be expressed for our purposes in the following way. Let the 'output' of the government (G_{ot}) be produced at a constant level of labour productivity (L_{gt}), where t is a time subscript, whereas productivity in the private sector (L_{pt}) rises exponentially (where $r =$ growth rate), producing also exponential growth in output in the private sector (P_{ot}). Then

$$G_{ot} = aL_{gt}$$
$$P_{ot} = bL_{pt} \cdot (1 + r)^t. \tag{1}$$

It follows that the ratio of government output to total output (N_{ot}) is represented by the formula derived from (1):

$$\frac{G_{ot}}{N_{ot}} = \frac{aL_{gt}}{aL_{gt} + bL_{pt} \cdot (1 + r)^t} \tag{2}$$

where $N_{ot} = P_{ot} + G_{ot}$.

Now assume that government expenditure on goods and services (G_{et}) is equal to the labour costs of producing government output and that the wage rate $(\bar{w})$ is the same in both the public and private sectors. Correspondingly, private expenditure on goods and services (P_{et}) is equal to the labour costs of producing output. Then

$$G_{et} = \bar{w} \cdot L_{gt}$$
$$P_{et} = \bar{w} \cdot L_{pt}. \tag{3}$$

It then follows that the ratio of government expenditure to total expenditure (N_{et}) can be expressed as follows:

$$\frac{G_{et}}{N_{et}} = \frac{\bar{w}}{\bar{w}} \frac{L_{gt}}{(L_{gt} + L_{pt})} = \frac{L_{gt}}{L_{gt} + L_{pt}}. \tag{4}$$

Assume further for simplicity that the labour supply is constant so that $L = L_{gt} + L_{pt}$.

From (2) it follows that as $t \to \infty$, then, with a constant labour supply, the only way in which the ratio of government output to total output can be maintained constant is by transferring labour from the private to the public sector. However, in the process of doing so, given the assumptions of the model, as labour is being transferred to relatively less productive uses, then with a constant wage rate $(\bar{w})$, the ratio of government expenditure to total expenditure must rise. This proportion is clear from (4) for, as $t \to \infty$, then $L_{gt}\uparrow$ while $L_{gt} + L_{pt}$ is constant. In other words, if government goods and services in real terms are to remain as even a fixed proportion of total goods and services in real terms, government *expenditure* as a proportion of total *expenditure* must rise through time. Intellectual history repeats itself; Baumol's theory of unbalanced growth is the modern counterpart of Wagner's famous Law of Increasing State Activity.

To complete the thesis in a way relevant to our theme, all that has to be assumed is that major public services will be financed largely by taxes. In a later addition to the thesis (Baumol and Oates, 1975) this assumption is specifically made. Education services, urban transport systems, environmental services, are becoming increasingly the responsibility of lower-level governments in the u.s. and would, in the view of the authors, require ever-increasing federal subsidies in order to be maintained at 'acceptable' levels. Under the strict assumptions of the analysis, any proportionate expansion of the progressive (private) and unprogressive (public) sectors requires that the average tax rate on wage income must rise over time. (See Baumol and Oates, 1975; Skolka, 1977.)

Is it true that public welfare and environmental services are inherently labour intensive? It is easy to imagine the possibility that this is not the case. Consider medical diagnostic services. It is now possible to make health checks on individual patients by having them answer a series of questions which can be fed into a computer and an assessment of their health characteristics can be made in minutes. The rebuttal of this kind of example, which can be replicated in many different fields, e.g. programmed learning, is that it ignores consumer evaluation of the utility of personal attention. The physical presence of the labour input is a constituent of output. This argument strikes one as sound, but, as argued below, it also offers a convenient rationalisation.

Could not the negative substitution effects associated with the growing costs of public services be offset by positive income effects as real personal incomes grow? Baumol and Oates rightly see this as a problem of ensuring that suitable tax regimes are introduced which make it 'easier' to generate the requisite funds. Their argument is worth quoting in full:

> If the demand for public expenditure does in fact increase more than proportionately with income, we then have the choice of adopting income-elastic revenue systems that will automatically provide (at least the bulk of) the necessary increments in revenues, or, alternatively, of periodic discretionary increases in tax rates. At a pragmatic level, the latter option does have one attraction: it forces the populace to reevaluate from time to time its desired level of public outputs in relation to their costs. On the other hand, this alternative brings with it the possibility of revenue shortages and less-than-optimal supplies of services associated with the frequent delays and political obstacles to increases in tax rates (or the institution of new taxes). Some sort of fiscal illusion may well be present, and it may impede seriously the adoption of socially desirable increases in tax rates. [1975, pp. 267–8]

Whether or not the growing cost of public services will generate tax resistance is an empirical one. It is conceivable that this resistance may be mild when progressive increases in revenue necessary to finance unprogressive sectors can be achieved without increased tax rates, but much will depend on whether real disposable incomes are still likely to grow simultaneously with such tax increases. Resistance is therefore likely to be a positive function of the progressivity of revenue increases (not to be confused with the progressivity of the tax structure) and a negative function of the rate of growth of the economy. However, to describe this resistance, as Baumol and Oates appear to do, as somehow irrational or socially undesirable means adopting a very arbitrary stance on whose preference systems are relevant.[4]

These two questions raised by the Baumol thesis are considered further in later discussion, but a more interesting feature of the thesis and the controversy following it is displayed in the concentration on technology as the main determinant of costs in the public sector. It presupposes that there are no barriers erected to prevent or to control the speed with which technology is introduced. Such barriers are apt to crumble rather quickly in those parts of the private sector where firms have only limited control over price, for both process and product innovation then become necessary in order for firms to survive. In the case of government undertakings that have a monopoly or near monopoly of the output of a particular service and that do not sell the product, there is a strong presumption, which is justified further in the next section, that the pressures to remove the barriers to technical progress are much lower. Bureaucrats are therefore able to maximise objectives other than profit and to allocate their budgets in ways other than to maximise the output of services. The expression (1) above may be just as compatible with a desire to eschew the use of technical progress, provided that the output can be 'sold' to legislators and taxpayers, as with the limitation on the possibility of improving technology.

IV. Bureaucracy and Public Expenditure Growth

Writers on public sector economics have recently turned their minds towards the application of economic analysis to bureaucracy (Niskanen, 1971; Breton, 1974). A model is constructed consisting of an objective function (e.g. maximise the output of the 'bureau') subject to a budget constraint. An essential element in the model is that the sole source of information on the bureau's production function available to purchasers of their services is the bureau itself. It is then shown that bureau managers within the available constraints maximise output beyond the optimal point determined by the usual condition that $MC = MR$. The precise point of intersection of the marginal valuation curve of 'purchasers' and the supply curve of bureaucrats will depend on the extent to which the latter wish to exploit 'X-inefficiency'.

This is a short-term theory concerned principally with static equilibrium conditions and therefore is not wholly appropriate for our immediate purpose. It does not directly explain the *penchant* of bureaucrats to promote labour intensity.

What has to be explained is why 'purchasers' (legislators) will have no incentive through time to induce bureaux to reduce the degree of labour intensity. A suggestive paper by Noll and Fiorina (1978) maintains that this process is established through the voter–legislator–bureaucratic nexus. In general terms, they argue, voters do not pay directly for these services and their individual tax payments bear no direct relation to the services available. They seek to minimise the cost of access to these services by choosing the legislators who can facilitate access. Incumbent legislators have a strong incentive to beat off competition from challengers by improving 'facilitation services'. Legislators are therefore strong supporters of bureaucratic organisations that promote the services voters want. Bureaucrats with a monopoly of services are in a strong position. They have also a clear incentive to maximise personnel inputs, for direct voter–bureaucrat contact will 'humanise' government and provide useful information on how to expand services according to voters' wishes. The process may eventually be self-defeating for whereas the voters as a whole may object to growing tax burdens, individually or collectively within a constituency they have no incentive to reduce their own opportunities for gain from government services.

The Noll/Fiorina analysis clearly bears the stamp of u.s. experience, but I find it suggestive. In countries with more centralised governments and less opportunities for voters to participate in the political process, access to bureaucrats has to be exercised in other ways, for example by pressure groups such as trade associations representing common interests that have little to do with voters' location. It is also not certain that bureaucratic action to satisfy pressure groups necessarily presupposes the kind of labour-intensive organisation that Noll and Fiorina associate with social programmes. Discretionary control over subsidies and tax concessions, as found in the growing phenomenon of selective intervention in the economy common to post-industrial societies, may be of equal importance. Nothing in what I have said to supplement their thesis denies their basic contention of the power placed in bureaucratic hands by the individual interests of voters and legislators. Indeed, there are other factors at work which may strengthen their argument. The first is the influence of public service unions rather than bureau chiefs on bureau activities including the factor-mix. Centralisation of such activities, which makes the government a powerful buyer of particular labour services, has encouraged the growth of countervailing power, particularly through the formation and militancy of professional public service unions. The second is the growing importance of bureaucrats as *voters* as the public sector grows. In the u.k. it used to be accepted without question that all but the most junior ranks of the civil service were not to engage in political activities, but there is now considerable pressure from civil servants to have this rule relaxed. In at least one German *Land*, it is possible for *Staatsbeamter* to sit as members of the legislature.

V. Controlling Public Expenditure Growth in Post-Industrial Society

The argument so far has endeavoured to explain why post-industrial societies committed to devoting a considerable proportion of their domestic output to the provision of collective services of a welfare and environmental character may find that, at present levels of efficiency in their provision, taxpayers/ voters will have to be prepared to countenance the transfer of an ever-growing proportion of their personal income for public sector use. As the problem has been put by a sociologist, '. . . at high levels of economic development the revolution of expectations must be channelled and contained because mass demands for benefits and services are outrunning the capacity of governments to meet them; people are happy to consume government services but increasingly restive about paying for them. How to contend with this "tax-welfare backlash" is a crucial problem for all democratic governments' (Wilensky, 1976, p. 8). It would take me too far away from my main theme to discuss the dimensions of this 'backlash' problem, but clearly it is characterised by individual and collective action either to avoid or evade payment, weighing the costs and benefits of both legal and illegal action, which leads to a heightening of interest in the distributional effects of financing government services.

One possible way of reducing backlash is suggested by the famous thesis of 'fiscal illusion' put forward by the Italian fiscal economist, Puviani, eighty years ago (see Buchanan, 1967, Chapter 10). Governments can disguise the 'burdens' on taxpayers by a series of devices and can use 'scare tactics' to secure tax compliance. Examples of disguise are to be found in specific excise taxes which are incorporated in the price of goods and thus require no written specification sent to the purchaser, and at least since Adam Smith's day it has always been recognised that the nearest thing to painless extraction of taxes is obtained by combining payment with some felicitous event such as receiving an inheritance or getting married. Examples of 'scare tactics' are more difficult to specify, though a common modern ploy of bureaucrats is to engineer a campaign that stresses the disastrous results of spending cuts. Puviani was writing at a time when in Italy a small minority held power and the large majority of taxpayers had little education. One reason for mentioning it is because Wilensky (1976) has claimed that 'backlash' is positively correlated with the 'visibility' of the tax structure in advanced industrial countries, i.e. countries relying on a high proportion of tax revenue in which the individual strikes treaties with the tax authorities (such as personal income taxes and property taxes) appear to breed more tax resistance than those with a low proportion. There are some subtle twists to his argument and some statistical problems which I must ignore and Wilensky is very careful not to overplay his hand. Still, he concludes that 'corporatist' democracies, such as Italy, France, Belgium and the Netherlands, which rely heavily on 'invisible' taxes, have a better chance of dampening backlash effects.

While Wilensky introduces an idea which is well worth further discussion and development, I remain sceptical of reliance on altering the 'tax-mix' as a long-run solution to the problem of matching demands for collective services with means for paying for them, coupled with all the other policy objectives which industrial countries will continue to seek to attain by the use of fiscal instruments. My principal objection is that the thesis ignores the learning process undergone by taxpayers in the course of governments' attempts to manipulate the expenditure- and tax-mix. This process is surely facilitated by the increased understanding of the distributional impact of the tax system following the improvement in educational standards that post-industrial societies are so anxious to promote. In some countries there is strong pressure to develop and improve statistical information on the distribution of income and wealth that fully displays the impact of budgetary transactions, difficult though this impact may be to measure in a satisfactory way. Therefore, relying on the techniques of the illusionist is neither something that supporters of the aims of post-industrial society could easily justify nor are they likely to retain taxpayer/voter support for governments promoting those aims.

The crux of the problem of keeping government expenditure under control lies in the fact that, whereas there may be general support for preventing a rise in the size of the public sector relative to GDP, few, if any, voters will have a direct interest in forgoing the advantages they derive from improved government services, subsidies, grants. The problem is made all the more difficult because a 'double bargain' has to be struck not only regarding the amount and form of cuts in public expenditure growth but also regarding the distribution of any resultant gains in the form of cuts in the growth in tax burdens. This being so, the logical method of procedure would be to institute some *general* rule of expenditure control requiring that government expenditure should not exceed a fixed percentage of GDP.[5] I am well aware of the technical difficulties that such a rule encounters, quite apart from the opposition that it might engender, particularly from bureaucrats. This could only come about if the constraint on government spending increases was sufficient to induce a major reduction in 'X-inefficiency' (as the pundits now describe it) in government services and there were no technological bias which supported the Baumol thesis.

Nevertheless the rule, if adopted, could perform an extremely useful function. It produces an analogue to the budget constraint facing taxpayers in their private spending plans, whereas in its absence voters can support political 'packages' of government expenditure while attempting to exploit the strategy of having others pay for them as de Tocqueville predicted. It would more readily put pressure on political parties to reveal their preferences in considerably more detail. Again attempts to monitor the growth in expenditure on *individual* programmes, e.g. by programme budgeting and cost–benefit analysis, frequently run up against the 'information barrier'; for those who have the most direct interest in the promotion of the programmes, the bureaucrats, are often the monopoly suppliers of information on which monitoring exercises are based. Faced with a situation where they are forced to compete more vigorously against one another for Pounds or Kroners rather than against private suppliers of services to taxpayers, bureaucrats in their own interests may have a greater incentive to improve their efficiency, particularly if their jobs are at stake.

I am well aware of certain technical difficulties which cannot be explored here. Government programmes have to be planned well ahead and public debate within the confines of the 'rule' would require the government to prepare and publish macroeconomic forecasts in *current price* terms. The announcement effects of such forecasts, particularly in times when inflation may be difficult to control, are likely to alter the data on which the forecasts are based. Further, an inflexible rule places a constraint on the use of the government budget as a stabilising instrument.

VI. Concluding Remarks

In this paper I have concentrated on the influence of the growing cost of supplying government services on government expenditure growth, rather than on the demand for public services generated by dynamic economic forces, tastes and preferences and income, and by the changing modes of their expression in political choice systems. I hope I have made it clear that I am aware that both the supply of and demand for government services interact in subtle ways. I have tried to show how a modified version of the Baumol theory of unbalanced growth points toward an important problem facing post-industrial societies – how to develop a collective incentive that improves the efficiency of the suppliers of government services. The paper is stronger on diagnostics than on remedies and is tainted with speculation rather than impregnated with hard evidence. If all it does is to stimulate discussion it will have achieved its purpose.

NOTES

1. Reproduced with several amendments from Gustafsson (1978).
2. Apart from studies of long-term growth in the public sector mentioned elsewhere in the text, attention should be drawn to the work sponsored by the Uppsala economic historians in the preparation of data and its interpretation. See, in particular, Gustafsson (1977) and notably the contributions in Gustafsson (1978) by Forsman, Werin and Rodriguez. See also references in this chapter.
3. The concept has been critically examined by many writers. For a useful summary of the discussion, coupled with a spirited defence of the concept, see Diamond (1977b).
4. It is worth noting that Baumol and Oates use 'fiscal illusion' of the taxpayer in almost the opposite sense in which it is normally found in the literature of public finance. They clearly mean taxpayer myopia concerning the benefits derived from public services, whereas in the standard literature 'fiscal illusion' is a device used by the tax authorities to 'con' taxpayers into believing that they are paying less taxes than they actually are!
5. Readers may be aware that successive Netherlands governments employed the so-called Structural Budget Margin in the 1960s which bears a superficial resemblance to this (simpler) rule. Study of its chequered history would not lead one to be too optimistic about the likelihood of success of the present proposal. For details, see Oort and de Man (1968) and Diamond (1977a).

REFERENCES

Andic, S. and Ververka, J. (1964) 'The growth of government expenditure in Germany since Unification' *Finanzarchiv* Vol. 22, No. 2, January.
Baumol, W. J. (1967) 'The macroeconomics of unbalanced growth' *American Economic Review* Vol. 57, June.
Baumol, W. J. and Oates, W. E. (1975) *The Theory of Environmental Policy* Prentice Hall, Englewood Cliffs, N.J., Chapter 17.
Breton, A. (1974) *The Economic Theory of Representative Government* Macmillan, London.
Buchanan, J. M. (1967) *Public Finance in Democratic Process* University of North Carolina Press, Chapel Hill, North Carolina.
Diamond, J. (1977a) 'The new orthodoxy in budgetary planning: A critical review of Dutch experience' *Public Finance* Vol. 32, No. 1.
Diamond, J. (1977b) 'Econometric testing of the "displacement effect": A reconsideration' *Finanzarchiv* Vol. 35, No. 3.
Gustafsson, B. (ed.) (1977) *Den offentliga sektorns expansion* Uppsala Studies in Economic History 16, Uppsala.
Gustafsson, B. (ed.) (1978) *Post-Industrial Society* Croom Helm, London.
Johansen, L. (1965) *Public Economics* North Holland, Amsterdam, Chapter 6.
Musgrave, R. A. and Musgrave, P. (1976) *Public Finance in Theory and Practice* 2nd edition, McGraw-Hill, New York.
Niskanen, W. A. (1971) *Bureaucracy and Representative Government* Aldine, Chicago.
Noll, R. and Fiorina, M. (1978) 'Voters, bureaucrats and legislators' *Journal of Public Economics* Vol. 7, No. 2, pp. 239–54.
Oort, C. J. and de Man, G. (1968) 'The Zijlstra standard in theory and practice' *Economic Quarterly Review of Amsterdam-Rotterdam Bank* June.
Peacock, A. T. and Wiseman, J. (1967) *The Growth of Public Expenditure in the United Kingdom 1890–1955* revised edition, Allen & Unwin, London.
Skolka, J. V. (1977) 'Unbalanced productivity growth and the growth of public services' *Journal of Public Economics* Vol. 6, No. 1, May.
de Tocqueville, A. (1835) *De la démocratie en Amérique* Part I (translated as *Democracy in America* by H. Reeve, Oxford World Classics, 1965 reprint).
Wilensky, H. L. (1976) *The 'New Corporatism', Centralization and the Welfare State* Sage, New York.

CHAPTER 8

Appraising Government Expenditure: A Simple Economic Analysis[1]

Who ponders national events shall find
an awful balancing of loss and gain.
[William Wordsworth,
Sonnets dedicated to Liberty and Order No. 6, 1842]

I. Introduction

There are three levels of budgetary choice. The first level concerns the division of the annual output of goods and services between public and private use and the methods – taxing, borrowing – by which these goods and services are transferred to government, central and local, for public use. At the second level, the transferred resources are divided between alternative uses. At the third level, within individual categories of government expenditure, programmes have to be devised which fit with the instructions of government. All three levels are inter-related, as any analysis of government action will reveal. The estimates of government expenditure for a particular period of time which are presented to the 'sovereign' body for approval are clearly influenced by the calculations made of the cost of particular programmes, as well as vice versa. The expenditure programmes, once executed, generate reactions from those affected by them – the 'electorate' – which influence their voting behaviour and hence the direction of pressures on the government to revise their budgets.

A dynamic theory of the determination of public expenditures is a fascinating area of exploration, as several recent contributions have shown (see, for example, Buchanan, 1967), but is too broad and too familiar a topic to require elaboration here, although it is a necessary background to the discussion in this paper. I view my task as a more modest one, which is to concentrate on discussion on the third level where cost–benefit analysis

118

and PPBS have been commonly employed as techniques of budgetary decision-making, derived from economic analysis. I shall not forget the other levels of decision-making for these are bound to influence the way in which cost–benefit analysis and PPBS may be used.

I shall begin by presenting a highly simplified model of a government 'production unit' which assumes familiarity with the essentials of PPBS and cost–benefit analysis, which have already been explained in several recent works. (See, for instance, Hinrichs and Taylor, 1969; Lyden and Miller, 1968; and in particular because of its international flavour, Recktenwald, 1970.) This model is used as a point of departure for a discussion of efficiency in making budgetary choices.

II. The Government 'Department' as a 'Firm'

A government department may be regarded as a special kind of firm. It may produce several 'products', but these are not sold to individuals through markets, but are normally provided free, being financed by compulsory levies designed by bureaucrats, approved by governments in power, and legalised by some constitutional procedure such as a vote in Parliament. On the other hand, ignoring circumstances in which resource inputs are commandeered, the inputs of labour services, raw materials, etc. for their production are bought in the market. The management problem of the government department is to devise methods by which resource inputs are effectively employed in producing the required products or services. PPBS has made a major analytical contribution in the application of modern statistical, economic and managerial techniques to this problem.

Let us assume that the government in power has issued instructions that these techniques are to be consistently applied. I shall now attempt to show, as supporters of PPBS must come to recognise, that the problems of economy in resource-use are not suddenly solved by altering the framework of decision-making along the lines suggested by systems analysis and related tools of the trade.

Imagine a government department which is responsible for state education at all stages. The first problem is to define its 'output', and we shall follow recent suggestions that output can be thought of in terms of economic, social and cultural 'outputs', to which each stage of education contributes (cf. Blaug, 1970, ch. 9). For simplicity we assume there are only two outputs: an economic output, which is measured by the contribution of the whole system to economic growth, and a cultural 'index', which is measured in terms of the output of pupils/students at all levels, weighted in some fashion according to the subjects and the length of time they are studied. There are also only two stages of education. Each 'output' is, in some sense, 'desirable' and each stage of education contributes towards these outputs in fixed proportions, but, for any given budget allocation to each stage of education, a different 'mix' of outputs is produced. The problem for the department is how to allocate a given budget (call it K) in an optimal fashion, given the objectives.

We can now present our highly simplified model as follows:

(1) Maximise $U = U(x, y)$
(2) Subject to $x = a_{1x}K_s + b_{2x}K_u$

$$y = a_{1y}K_s + b_{2y}K_u$$

$$(K_s + K_u = K)$$

where x, y are units of output and the a's and b's are fixed, non-negative, coefficients. K_s and K_u are the budget allocations for 'school' and 'university' stages of education respectively. Clearly, we have here a very simple example of a non-linear programming model.

A particular solution can be shown by a diagram (Fig. 8.1). We assume that the utility function is subject to familiar restrictions so that

$$\frac{\partial u}{\partial x}, \ \frac{\partial u}{\partial y} > 0, \ \ \frac{\partial^2 u}{\partial x^2}, \ \frac{\partial^2 u}{\partial y^2} < 0,$$

and $U(x, y)$ along a contour such as I_1 in Fig. 8.1, has a constant value so that

$$\frac{\partial u}{\partial x} \cdot dx + \frac{\partial u}{\partial y} \cdot dy = 0.$$

On the abscissa and ordinate we register units of output. $0P$ is a ray which represents all combinations of x and y which can be produced at 'school' level of education, $0A$ of x and $0B$ of y representing the maximum combination of outputs consistent with allocation of the whole budget K to this level. $0Q$ is drawn in a similar fashion for the 'university level'. A line drawn between P and Q represents the 'opportunity slope' given the fixed budget. *Provided* that the highest indifference curve is tangential to a position, say L, on the line but between P and Q, the total budget must be split between the two levels of education.

This kind of model suggests all kinds of 'Denksport'. The objective function can be made more elaborate by the introduction of further arguments, output coefficients can be made variable instead of being fixed, more stages of education can be introduced, budget allocations can be decomposed into demand for various types of factor inputs.[2] These complications make the intellectual game more interesting, but for our purposes there is no need to explore these possibilities, which would require the building of an elaborate programming model, although academic convention demands that we show that we are aware of them.

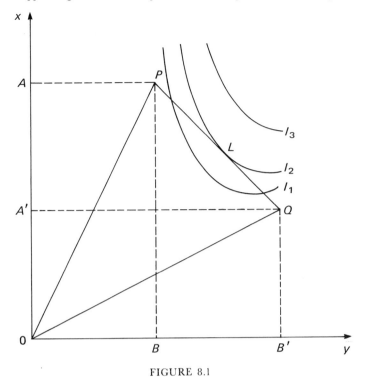

FIGURE 8.1

Even in this simplified form, the model can be used to introduce discussion of two aspects of efficiency in budget-making. In Section III, we endeavour to show that efficiency in the sense of maximising the objective function is a question not solely of economic analysis, but also of political evaluation. In Section IV, we explore the difficulties of achieving efficiency in budget-making in the sense of economising in the use of resource inputs.

III. POLITICAL EVALUATION AND EFFICIENCY

Whether the department is operating efficiently, *given*, for the moment, the technical relations between inputs and outputs, can only be determined in the light of *political choices*. Individual multi-product firms operating in a competitive environment may maximise profits, but then they sell divisible products for money to individual buyers. The 'trade-off' between production of one good as against another can be measured in terms of the marginal changes in the units of money profit which result from different 'mixes' of projected outputs. The 'maximisers' are the controllers of the firm. While there are superficial similarities, at a technological level, between a multi-product firm and a government department, the differences are all-important. The maximiser is the 'political master' of the bureaucracy who must judge the outputs in terms of utility derived from them. In order to specify the objective function (1), we need to have information of a different kind from the objective function of the private firm. We need to know the functional relationship between the utility of the 'maximiser' and variations in individual outputs, and also the 'trade-off' in utility terms between one output and another, in our example how many units of 'economic contribution' of education will be given up at the margin for units of 'culture'.

It is not denied that in any empirical investigation it may be difficult to identify the maximiser. Even if one can pin him down, it may be difficult to get 'him' or 'them' to articulate objectives fully. Governments may lack information on the link between specific programme objectives and their political aims. It may be impossible for them to gauge, for example, what is the connexion between their political survival and the relative mix of outputs produced by any part of the resources employed by government. Even if they can discern such a connexion, there is no reason to suppose that the utility function will be stable. Political preferences for particular programmes will be sensitive to changing pressures from the electorate. There may even be political advantage to be gained by not being closely identified with a precise commitment to particular programmes which may be popular one moment and unpopular the next. But, in the end, whether or not politicians choose to specify the objective function or, within broad limits, leave it to be specified by the Ministry of Finance or the individual department responsible for maximising it, the utility function is an expression of political choice.

These are obvious points, but perhaps their full implications are not understood, even by economists. There is a tendency in the profession to judge government programmes principally in terms of the very narrow criterion of measurable so-called 'economic' benefits and to regard other elements in the objective function as less important because they are less susceptible to quantitative expression. This gives rise to two important misunderstandings about the role of economics in budgetary choices. Firstly, it gives the impression that economics is only applicable to government choices which are concerned with maximising GNP. The first lesson in economics is surely that one must avoid confusion between 'material ends' and 'economising'. As our simple model shows, economic analysis indicates how to set out a departmental task for maximising *any* chosen objectives, 'material' or 'non-material' (the labels are convenient if misleading). Secondly, rightly or wrongly, economists become accused of using their skills for justifying a particular political end and of setting themselves up as judges of other people's welfare.[3]

IV. EFFICIENCY IN RESOURCE INPUTS

Operating efficiently certainly requires us to specify objectives, for otherwise resource inputs could be wasted on irrelevant and superfluous activities. However, if objectives are carefully specified and ways of achieving them are known, this does not guarantee that resource inputs are minimised. We have to look further into the question of the incentives, if they exist, to economise in public provision of goods.

This is an area of investigation on which recent discussion of the relation between market forms and efficiency may throw some light, but only the briefest of summaries of this discussion can be offered here.[4] Neo-classical theory demonstrates, using particular assumptions about firms' behaviour, that consumer welfare is maximised when, in the absence of externalities, there is no divergence between price and marginal cost. Under monopoly, therefore, losses of consumer welfare will arise from profit maximising behaviour which results in prices being charged which are above marginal cost. The standard defence used against this proposition is that, whereas market power may result in losses of consumer welfare as a result of price effects, such losses have to be 'traded off' against the scale economies which may result from mergers and other devices which consolidate production in a smaller number of units. The counter-attack against this position has been led by Professor Leibenstein in a series of articles which introduce the concept of 'X-inefficiency' into economic analysis of the firm. His analysis adopts the standard assumption of profit maximisation for the firm, but makes the telling point that labour as a factor input cannot be treated as a passive factor in the production process alongside physical inputs. Labour, including both operatives and management, seeks goals such as leisure, security, which are in conflict with the enterprise objective of maximising profits. The firm is under the strongest pressure to induce labour to conform with the profit maximisation objective and labour is also under pressure to co-operate when the firm produces in a competitive environment, i. e., is a 'price-taker'. Where a firm has control over price, it will be under less pressure to incur the 'policing costs' associated with achieving consistency between the objective function of the firm and that of its labour force. Consequently, scale economies displayed in movements along the 'industry' marginal cost curve where monopoly conditions obtain may be offset by 'X-inefficiency' resulting from the relaxing of pressure to incur policing costs, and this will be reflected in an upward shift in the marginal cost curve, as compared to a situation where competition obtains.

It is difficult, of course, to specify what precisely is the market form which governs the operation of any particular government service. The monopoly parallel seems close enough in the case of a service such as defence where the state normally refuses to countenance the possibility of private production on a competitive basis for the usual reasons, and where the services it offers can only be provided to a limited extent by alternative forms of government production, e.g., diplomatic negotiation. It follows that if the 'X-inefficiency' argument has substance, economy in the use of resources can hardly be guaranteed. There are two additional features of government production which reinforce this proposition. Firstly, there is the difficulty of specifying exactly what the objectives are and of quantifying them. Secondly, uncertainty may surround the precise contribution which any particular input, e. g., some form of Inter-Continental Ballistic Missile, may make towards the movement in whatever output indicator is considered relevant. Therefore, the functional relationship between output(s) and input(s) may be very difficult to define and waste of resources difficult to detect. The more cautious defenders of PPBS have taken this point and have implicitly exemplified X-inefficiency by drawing attention to the conservative tendencies which PPBS sometimes introduces into appraisal of new projects. The effectiveness of a new project, e.g., a new defence missile, is apt to be judged in terms of the functions of the old projects, while the new projects may themselves have other functions which accord with the ultimate objectives of the defence system (cf. Enthoven, 1968). This bias will be reinforced by those whose functions come under review and who have to bear the 'costs' of changes, say, in learning new skills or in facing uncertainty in their promotion prospects. They would be less than human if they did not act in a fashion similar to their counterparts in a private firm whose individual objectives are not in tune with the firm's overall objectives.

The possibility of scale economies resulting from the organisational changes implicit in PPBS may offer a gain in efficiency to offset the losses which may result from X-inefficiency. There is a natural bias in PPBS to promote centralisation of decision-making, particularly when objectives of policy are national ones (cf. McKean, 1968, Part 3). Economies may result from the more intensive employment of central management services, and centralised control may make it easier to economise on resource inputs through standardisation of equipment and bulk purchase. In the U.S.A., however, the emphasis on centralised decision-making as the apparent logical consequence of PPBS produced a political 'feed-back', for it presupposes acceptance of the transfer of power from State to Federal government. (There is a parallel here with the standard objection to monopoly in private industry, viz., that it has the undesirable side-effect of creating concentration of political alongside economic power.) It is clearly fallacious to conclude that any such political side-effects point to a defect in the technique of PPBS *per se*. What they indicate is the necessity to embody judgements about the desirable distribution of political power between central and provincial government in the 'objective function' or in the constraints of the PPBS model. In short, the ability or otherwise to take advantage of scale effects, if these exist, depends on an initial political judgement, although it is conceivable that this judgement might be revised in the light of the information about the relationship between the costs of alternative programmes and the structure of government which a PPBS analysis could reveal.

V. Concluding Remarks

Two conclusions may be drawn from the above analysis:

(1) Techniques such as PPBS and CB analysis are useful in displaying the consequences of governmental choices, but offer no reason for removing these choices from the political arena. In fact, the best strategy for PPBS devotees is to see to it that politicians fully understand its uses and also its limitations, for example by appropriate changes in procedures for exercising political control of public expenditure.[5]

(2) The improvement in information provided to government administrations by these techniques may reveal behaviour patterns by government employees which are inappropriate for the achievement of efficiency, but the techniques by themselves can do nothing directly to change such behaviour. Those who believe in the market as a disciplining force will want to see new techniques supplemented with methods of simulating the market in government services. (For example see Hitch and McKean, 1961, pp. 221–4.) Those who do not share this belief would presumably prefer to find methods to ensure that bureaucrats are disciplined by a strong moral or ideological commitment to the aims of government. On the choice between methods for changing behaviour patterns, an economist had better remain silent!

NOTES

1. Reproduced with minor amendments from *Public Finance* Vol. 27, No. 2, 1972.
2. Those familiar with linear programming will realise that I have 'rigged' the example in order to avoid 'corner' solutions, and other awkwardnesses. I am grateful to Alan Williams for spotting an error in an earlier draft which led me to be circumspect in this presentation.
3. Even if measurable economic benefits are the sole objectives of a government programme, it can be shown that, in cost–benefit calculations, important elements in the objective function such as the choice of a social discount rate and the amortisation period are not technical desiderata but involve political choices (see Peacock, 1973).
4. See Comanor and Leibenstein (1969), and the excellent survey by Crew and Rowley (1970) upon which the following account is based.
5. For some practical suggestions in a British context, see Peacock and Wiseman (1969) and Williams (1969).

126   *The Economic Analysis of Government Policies*

REFERENCES

Blaug, M. (1970) *An Introduction to the Economics of Education* Allen Lane, Penguin Press, London.
Buchanan, J. M. (1967) *Public Finance in Democratic Process* University of North Carolina Press, Chapel Hill, North Carolina.
Comanor, W. S. and Leibenstein, H. (1969) 'Allocative efficiency, X-efficiency and the measurement of welfare losses' *Economica* Vol. 36, August.
Crew, M. A. and Rowley, C. K. (1970) 'Anti-trust policy: Economics versus management science' *Moorgate and Wall Street* Autumn.
Enthoven, A. (1968) 'Systems analysis and the navy' in Lyden and Miller.
Hinrichs, H. and Taylor, G. (eds) (1969) *Program Budgeting and Benefit-Cost Analysis* Goodyear Publishing, Pacific Palisades.
Hitch, C. J. and McKean, R. (1961) *The Economics of Defense in the Nuclear Age*
Lyden, F. J. and Miller, E. G. (eds) (1968) *Planning, Programming, Budgeting: A Systems Approach to Management* Markham Publishing, Chicago.
McKean, R. (1968) *Public Spending* McGraw-Hill, New York.
Peacock, A. T. (1973) 'Cost-benefit analysis and the politics of public investment' in J. N. Wolfe (ed.) *Cost-Benefit and Cost-Effectiveness Analysis* Allen & Unwin, London.
Peacock, A. T. and Wiseman, J. (1969) 'The economics of public expenditure and its consequences for parliamentary control' *First Report from the Select Committee on Procedure* House of Commons Papers, 410, July.
Recktenwald, H. C. (ed.) (1970) *Nutzen-Kosten-Analyse und Programm-Budget* JCB Mohr, Tübingen.
Williams, A. (1969) 'The economics of public expenditure' *First Report from the Select Committee on Procedure* House of Commons Papers, 410, July.

CHAPTER 9

The Limitations
of Public Goods Theory:
The Lighthouse Revisited[1]

I

In his comprehensive work *Die Steuern* (1964) Heinz Haller provides a detailed
critique of the benefit principle of taxation. As he shows, the operation of the
principle rests on the assumed existence of market failure, which is associated
with the quality of 'publicness' displayed in important goods and services.
While he has been concerned with the difficulties of producing a political
analogue to the market by which benefits and taxes can be brought into
equilibrium, this contribution in his honour is concerned with two prior
questions that need to be considered before the benefit principle can be in-
voked. The first is identifying goods and services that embody *and retain* the
characteristic of publicness. The second is that of justifying taxation rather
than pricing as a method of financing a public good. My concern with
these matters arises from two apparently unrelated activities. The first is
growing scepticism at the use of static Paretian-type welfare economics as a
guide to public policy (cf. Rowley and Peacock, 1975), and the second is an
accidental journey down a historical by-way stimulated by the famous article
by Coase (1974), which is the point of departure of this contribution. My
contention is that the 'parable of the lighthouse' inaugurated by Coase has
much to tell us about the limitations of public goods theory.

II

The beam of light shed by a lighthouse to guide ships at sea safely past
navigational hazards has been frequently used in economics as the prime
example of a 'pure' public or social good, that is a good that it is impossible

to prevent anyone from enjoying (the characteristic of non-excludability) and that can be equally enjoyed by all (the characteristic of non-rivalness in production). The strong policy conclusion often drawn from these characteristics is that only the public sector can supply such a good and that it ought to supply it at zero cost.

The most ardent supporter of this proposition has been Samuelson, who developed the theory of public goods in a series of famous articles (e.g. Samuelson, 1969). Indeed, in his equally famous textbook (Samuelson, 1970) he used the lighthouse as the most telling example of this conclusion:

> The fact that the lighthouse cannot appropriate in the form of a purchase price a fee from those it benefits certainly helps to make it a suitable social or public good. But even if the operators are able – say by radio reconnaissance – to claim a toll from every nearby user, that fact would not necessarily make it socially optimal for this service to be provided like a private good at a market-determined individual price. Why not? Because it costs society *zero extra cost* to let one extra ship use the service, hence any ships discouraged from those waters by the requirement to pay a positive price will represent a social economic loss – even if the price charged to all is no more than enough to pay the long-run expenses of the lighthouse. If the lighthouse is socially worth building and operating – and it need not be – a more advanced treatise can show how this social good is worth being made optimally available to all.

Coase (1974) was the first to question the use of the lighthouse as the prime example of a public good and in so doing has opened the way for an interesting attack on the value of the whole concept. Coase was principally concerned not with the conceptual problems associated with the definition of public goods but with the simple fact that it is not historically true that lighthouses have been exclusively publicly provided and have not been able to charge. Nor was he specifically interested, except parenthetically, in the issue whether or not, in the light of welfare criteria, lighthouses should charge for their services. I now supplement Coase's historical evidence with a rather interesting example from Scots history, but conclusions different from Coase's may be drawn from the evidence.

III

It is perhaps useful for later argument to examine first of all how the difficulties of operating the exclusion principle in the case of public goods happen to arise. It has become widely recognised in the public goods literature that exclusion is always likely to be technically possible. However, the costs of exclusion is the crucial factor in determining this element of 'publicness' and must be such as to make it uneconomical for the producer to provide the service, given the alternative opportunities available to the suppliers of his capital.

If one detects 'publicness' in a particular good resulting from the prohibitive costs of exclusion and employs the familiar static analysis associated with Paretian-type model-building, the policy conclusions about the provision of the good will be based on the assumption that, save in small number cases, market failure is staring us in the face. However, policies take time to be agreed and, in the course of time, techniques of production can change and also consumer tastes and preferences. If these changes are ruled out of consideration, then the possibility of technical innovation that affects the costs of exclusion will be neglected. This may take the form of 'process innovation' by which means are found to deny customers service unless they are willing to pay. Alternatively, it may take the form of 'product innovation' by which an entirely new product is fashioned that satisfies the existing preference of consumers by different and more efficient means.

Paradoxically, perhaps, the point may be illustrated by a counter example. The development of modern offensive weapons of war has produced a situation where the defence capability of one country may provide benefits (in the form of preventing attack by a common enemy) to the inhabitants not only of that country but of others. The problem of provision then becomes more complicated, for now individual nations, having solved the problem of the 'publicness' of defence by taxing their own citizens, may attempt to 'free-ride' on the citizens of other countries whose defence provision provides them with uncovenanted benefits. 'Solutions' to this problem have been extensively investigated. In trying to minimise the risk of war subject to the 'threat constraint' of a large defence programme of a potential enemy, account must also be taken of alternative instruments. Diplomatic negotiation is an example, though one may be sceptical, in the light of recent history, of the possibility that diplomatic means are likely to undergo dramatic innovations that would make them anything more than supplements to defence deterrents.

But to return to the lighthouse. It is clearly prohibitive to try to operate the principle of exclusion in directing beams of light to particular ships whose owners are willing to pay, at least by a system of direct charging. If anything, innovations in lighthouse building have exacerbated the problem of excludability as they have moved in the direction of more powerful beams and a greater range of light. However, the product desired by the final consumer is a *navigational aid* and not simply illumination. Modern radio and electronic devices of position-fixing have been developed that not only provide a useful alternative to light and fog signals but can also be operated in such a way that only those who are willing to pay can benefit. An important element of 'publicness' thus being removed, the way is clear in principle for a market solution, though whether this would be a preferred solution would depend on such factors as the availability or otherwise of alternative sources of supply of navigational aids and therefore the terms on which they would be offered alongside the traditional source of supply, the lighthouse.

The general point is clear. There may be goods that are pure or almost pure social or public goods, but they may be subject to technological and economic obsolescence so that the service they provide need no longer be subject to market failure.

IV

Imagine now an entrepreneur who invents a product for which he knows there is a demand but which is subject to the problem of non-excludability. If we were to confine our analysis of his difficulty within the usual theory of social goods and its static equilibrium framework, then the goods would simply not be provided by a private supplier. However, this is to underestimate the incentive that an entrepreneur may have to remove the *ceteris paribus* conditions, by his estimate of the costs and benefits of finding means to enforce charging. His first step may have to be the establishing of property rights in the service offered so that he is legally entitled to capture the benefits. Existing law may permit him to do this, at least in principle, or it may not. Assuming that it does, his next step is to devise some means by which 'free-riders' can be penalised by raising the price of other goods and services that they wish to purchase. This clearly entails either some form of collusion with other suppliers or the provision of some complementary service by the supplier of the non-excludable good over which he has some control over price. (It should be noted that at this stage we are not concerned with the welfare implications of such actions.)

The common defence problem provides an example. Free-riding countries who adjust their defence programmes downwards on the assumption that the elasticity of demand of inhabitants of a 'rich' country (e.g. the USA) for defence is totally inelastic may be 'charged' for the privilege by some form of economic pressure requiring, say, the purchase of defence equipment from the 'rich' country.

In his excellent account of the development of the British lighthouse system, Coase provides fascinating historical evidence of the techniques used by private entrepreneurs from the seventeenth century onwards to make lighthouses pay. The essential features of their endeavours were as follows: a petition to erect a lighthouse was made to the Crown usually backed by the support of shipowners and fishermen; an agreement was entered into with the customs or harbour authorities of nearby ports to collect lighthouse dues, the dues often being regulated by legislation; the toll varied with the lighthouse, the number of lighthouses passed by the ship and the tonnage of the vessel. Obviously the system depended on complementarity of navigational aid services with those of customs and harbour services but, even allowing for the possibility of escape by ocean-going traffic and by smugglers, it was clearly profitable. The best evidence of profitability is provided by the sums paid for the purchase of lighthouses by Trinity House, the government agency for lighthouse provision in the UK, when it took over responsibility for such aids during the nineteenth century (see Coase, 1974, pp. 360–8).

Let me supplement Coase's historical account by an example chosen from Scotland, which had a somewhat different system from England and which to this day has a separate administration under the Commissioners of Northern Lighthouses. The narrative is based on Dickson (1899). At the entrance of the Firth of Forth, on which Edinburgh is situated (and not far from Kirkaldy where Adam Smith was born), there lies an island, the Isle of May, in a commanding position. In the early seventeenth century it was acquired by Alexander Cunningham, who obtained legislative sanction in 1641 to erect a lighthouse 'to obviat the many shipwraks that frequentlie befalls vessels entering the firth in the night tyme', as the text of a later Act of 1661 relates.

A picture of the original lighthouse is shown on p. 132. Dickson records that the

> light was produced by the burning of coal in a large grate or chauffer on the summit of the tower. A ton of coal was consumed every night and the blaze was set up by placing live coals upon the heap at the top of the chauffer. There were three attendants in the lighthouse, two of whom were constantly on the watch. The fire required mending every half-hour, and, in strong gales, every twenty minutes. During the long winter nights, when high winds blew, as much as three tons of coal were sometimes consumed. On such occasions the windward side of the beacon was never lit, the keeper with impunity laying hold of the iron bars to steady himself. This Tower survived the vengeful fury of the elements for more than a century and a half. [p. 285] . . . The architect of the Tower was unfortunate. While crossing over, in a small boat, from the island to Pittenweem, he was overtaken by a storm and drowned. Some more unfortunate old women of that town got the credit for causing the catastrophe, and, in accordance with the superstition of the times, they were burned as witches. [p. 287]

One is not surprised to learn that there were frequent complaints about the reliability of the light and that manning it was a hazardous occupation. In 1791, the superintendent and his family of seven were burned to death in their sleep by fumes from a mass of falling cinders.

The owners of the lighthouse were allowed to levy a regulated tonnage charge on vessels plying between the North and the South East coast of Scotland with a discrimination in favour of native vessels. The charge was collected by customs officers on the Fife coast who were compensated for

View of original lighthouse

their services by the agents of the lighthouse owners.[2] The shipowners and fishermen constantly complained about the unreliability of the service and hoped to pressurise the government to take over responsibility for its operation, in the hope that dues would be abolished. An Act of Parliament of 1784 empowered a new Northern Lighthouse Board, a government agency, to erect four lighthouses in Scotland, but light dues were kept in being. So far as the Isle of May was concerned it took the wreck of two naval frigates towing a prize ship whose pilots were misled by the failure of the light before finally the May light was taken over by the Commissioners of Northern Lighthouses in 1815. But it cost the Commissioners £60,000 to buy the Isle, which had no alternative use, from the Duchess of Portland whose family had acquired the Isle in 1795.

The example just given offers clear illustration of Coase's thesis that private provision of lighthouses was forthcoming and was profitable. One is bound to agree with him that a lighthouse service can be provided by private enterprise *alone* within the existing framework of property rights. It is not denied that perhaps such a service could be so operated and there were instances of this happening during the period surveyed, which consisted of local cooperative action to establish small beacons at the entrance of fishing ports to benefit mainly local traffic. However, the examples chosen by Coase, which are similar to my own, indicate all too clearly that private owners of lighthouses were only willing to operate them if they were granted monopoly privileges by the government and could rely on government officials in customs and excise to deny customs clearance of their goods unless they paid lighthouse charges. The government was willing to grant these privileges partly because locational monopoly of lights was important for efficient operation – competitive lighting would confuse the mariner. It also had an interest in lighthouses because their services were a complementary input to direct expenditure on defence at sea. Naval vessels were rendered services by lighthouses but these vessels did not and still do not pay lighthouse dues. The resultant market for lighthouse services was therefore a severely regulated one. Public 'production' was a necessary though not a sufficient condition for the operation of the market.

In fact, the only substantial change that has taken place in lighthouse provision in the UK is that of ownership. Dues are still paid with discrimination in favour of native vessels, are collected by the Customs and Excise, and the proceeds are remitted to the UK Department of Trade for the Lighthouse Fund; and the whole cost of running lighthouse services is met from this fund, no grant being received from the Exchequer. The change in ownership was originally justified, as suggested, by the worries over reliability of the service and by the hope on the part of shipowners that a government service would be provided free. But there is no reason in principle, given reliable modern lighting methods and the enforcement by the government of supply by, say, performance bonds, why the older system could not now be reinstituted.

V

It is clear that, even in the most famous 'polar case' of a public good, ways and means can be found, though of a rough and ready fashion, by which the problem of non-excludability can be solved. Even if an argument can be made, i.e. made on other grounds for public provision, there is no technical reason at least why charging should not be made for lighthouse services. However, some writers, Samuelson particularly, have stressed the other characteristic of 'publicness', non-rivalness of consumption. The benefit derived by one ship from a lighthouse does not reduce the benefits to others. It is therefore argued that even if exclusion is possible, it is inefficient in such cases. Applying, therefore, the well-known welfare principle of pricing at marginal cost, the price of lighthouse services should be zero. Only a rich philanthropist could provide such a service in the private sector.[3]

The obvious problem then arises about the implications of adopting the standard optimal pricing and investment rule that $Price = LMC = SMC$. Clearly, ignoring possible congestion costs associated with crowding of shipping lines, Samuelson is right in assuming that, at any level of capacity of the lighthouse,[4] price would have to be set at zero and therefore, as Long-Run Average Cost > Price, deficits would have to be incurred.

Even within the narrow Paretian context that governs the Samuelson conclusion about pricing, the lighthouse case creates more than the usual run of difficulties in applying the marginal cost rule. With no break-even constraint in operation, the familiar problem is encountered of devising any method of financing that does not result in a deviation between marginal cost and price elsewhere in the system. With both competitive pressures absent and total costs independent of the level of output, conditions fostering the emergence of 'X-inefficiency' are favoured. So, even without invoking 'second best' arguments of the usual kind arising from market imperfections elsewhere in the system, marginal conditions for efficiency in both consumption and production are not satisfied by the Samuelsonian rule. These sorts of difficulties lie behind recent attempts in optimal taxation theory to revive Ramsey-type pricing rules, by which the budget constraint is met within the firm but with the minimum distortion in the allocation of resources as represented by the deviation of marginal cost and price.

For those who do not feel impelled to operate within the confines of Paretian static analysis, any distortions resulting from deviation from the traditional welfare pricing rule in order to meet the budget constraint may be of minor significance as against the need to promote incentives to improve new techniques of production and to generate conditions that accelerate their adoption. In the case of the lighthouse, as in other activities, pricing at above marginal cost, whatever allocational distortions it may produce, retains the interest of purchasers in efficient production and in the search for cheaper long-run alternatives, e.g. electronic devices. Samuelsonian pricing once conceded, then, as in so many other cases where charges are not made for public services that benefit *specific* activities, strong vested interests may be created designed to achieve the maximum transfer of the costs of operations on to the general taxpayer. Economy in the use of resources for the operation of such services becomes no longer of interest to direct beneficiaries and, given the usual arguments about the policing of non-market activities, may not be in anyone's direct interest to achieve.

VI

The lighthouse case is therefore instructive if for reasons other than those deduced from the evidence by those who have considered it.

As the paradigm par excellence of 'publicness' it offers no support for the view that private operation cannot be achieved in cases where non-excludability is a technical phenomenon, though, historically, such operation, *pace* Coase, had to rest on public cooperation. Neither does it offer unequivocal support for applying the rule $MC = P$, even within the narrow confines of Paretian analysis. If allowance is made for long-run factors that cannot be handled successfully by Paretian static analysis, notably the influence of technical change on production methods and costs, the lighthouse illustrates how the existence of 'publicness' in a good may be *transitory* and not permanent. This raises important issues concerning the influence of methods of charging for publicly produced goods on the incentives to seek out and to institute more efficient methods of production resulting from technical change.

The so-called 'publicness' characteristics of goods therefore are a very shaky foundation on which to build either a normative or a positive theory of public expenditure and its finance, as many public analysts, including the author, have increasingly come to recognise. As Goldin (1977, pp. 69, 70) sums up the issue, the problem for normative analysis is one not of classification but of the choice between equal and selective access to services. For positive analysis, it is a question of finding reasons why equal access is chosen in some situations and not in others. In the case of the latter pursuit, there is great scope for the kind of detailed study of institutional arrangements and their change through time pioneered by Coase.

NOTES

1. This chapter will also appear in the *Festschrift für Heinz Haller* JCB Mohr, Tübingen (forthcoming).
2. It was off the Isle of May that the famous American rebel commander, John Paul Jones, was sighted in 1779 by a revenue cutter. A warning was issued by the Navy by none other than Adam Smith in his capacity as a Commissioner of Customs and Excise (see Mossner and Ross, 1977, pp. 408–9). The wily Captain Jones was probably the most famous 'free-rider' benefiting from the Isle of May light!
3. There are some early examples of the provision of shore lights by private individuals and corporations without any attempt to recoup costs from beneficiaries. This kind of behaviour could be explained along Hochman/Rodgers lines, though without assuming that the satisfaction derived by providers of the free service required a redistribution from rich to poor.
4. In the short run, capacity is given and there would be some costs associated with the maintenance and operation of a lighthouse, but these costs would not vary with output, the latter being approximated by the number of ships using the light. In the long run, capacity can be changed by varying the height and power of the light. The distance of the sea horizon in nautical miles is given by $1.25\sqrt{h}$ where h is the height of the light in feet. This means that the area served by the light is highly sensitive to its height. Output (in terms of number of ships served) will therefore be a function of h, though the quality of output may vary inversely with the distance from the light, as a warning of 'danger'. These technical desiderata do not alter the fact that $LMC = SMC = 0$. (I am indebted to Mr Richard Goss for the technical information.)

REFERENCES

Coase, R. H. (1974) 'The lighthouse in economics' *Journal of Law and Economics* Vol. 17, October.

Dickson, J. (1899) *Emeralds Chased in Gold; or, The Islands of the Forth: Their Story Ancient and Modern* Oliphant, Anderson & Ferrier, Edinburgh.

Goldin, K. D. (1977) 'Equal access v. selective access: A critique of public goods theory' *Public Choice* Vol. 15, No. 1.

Mossner, E. C. and Ross I. S. (eds) (1977) *The Correspondence of Adam Smith* Clarendon Press, Oxford.

Rowley, C. K. and Peacock, A. T. (1975) *Welfare Economics: A Liberal Restatement* Martin Robertson, London.

Samuelson, P. (1969) 'The pure theory of public expenditure and taxation' in J. Margolis and H. Guitton (eds) *Public Economics* Macmillan, London.

Samuelson, P. (1970) *Economics* 8th edition, McGraw-Hill, New York.

CHAPTER 10

Public Policy and Copyright in Music: an Economic Analysis[1]

I. INTRODUCTION

In the course of a long professional association with Professor Elisabeth Liefmann-Keil, it would be impossible not to be impressed by her knowledge of music as well as by her standing in her chosen specialism of the economics of social policy. It therefore seems appropriate to offer as a contribution to these essays in her honour a subject which forms a link between her professional and cultural interests. An economist who loves music is in a dangerous position when he comes to examine its economic organisation, for he can hardly bring himself to subject the composer or executant to the rigid tests of the market in assessing his value to the community. While acknowledging my prejudice, I have tried my best to retain a posture which bears some semblance to objectivity, and in any case believe that market analysis offers some insights into the problems which arise in developing a public policy which allows the composer to establish his rights in his intellectual property. But Elisabeth Liefmann-Keil will understand better than most how difficult it is to regard composers of music solely as a peculiar sort of entrepreneur, and will appreciate what Bernard Shaw meant when he called music 'the brandy of the damned'!

II. BACKGROUND TO THE ANALYSIS

Typically today in the UK, the 'serious' composer obtains about one-third of his total earnings from composition, and the remainder from other musical activities, notably teaching and performing. About 70 per cent of earnings from composition are derived from *performances* of his music with only 10 per cent derived from sales of copies of the compositions themselves. The

137

remaining 20 per cent is derived from commissioning of works, usually for music festivals or some special musical celebration.[2] The distribution of earnings from composition is heavily skewed with over three-quarters of composers earning less than the average, and earnings rise progressively with age but fall dramatically towards the end of working life. Moreover, perhaps as much as a quarter of all earnings from performance royalties accrue to composers' heirs, and this situation probably prompted Honegger's remark that the first requirement of a successful composer was to be dead.[3] Performance royalties and therefore the economic fortunes of composers crucially depend on public policy decisions about the determination of property rights.

In this contribution, I assume that commonly accepted normative propositions found in economic analysis are operative, and are therefore used to guide public policy. The consequences of accepting these propositions are then examined in some detail and with particular reference to the contemporary situation in which composers and publishers combine in all major countries in order to collect performance royalties.

III. Criteria

The first general criterion, which is widely accepted as a guide to the value of the services of any occupational group, is that this value should reflect the tastes and preferences of the consumer. The consumer is the ultimate judge of the product. He expresses his preferences through the market and, as these preferences change, so should the market be so arranged that the effort of producers is adjusted to reflect the change. Accordingly, the consumer interest is best served by a freely working pricing system such that there is quick and efficient adjustment in the prices of products and remuneration of those who produce them in response to consumer demand. It follows that no group of sellers or buyers at any production stage should be able to 'rig' prices; in other words markets for products and productive services must be competitive. The greater the number of alternative sources of supply, the greater the range of opportunities for the consumer and the lower the prices that he has to pay for alternative products.[4] This criterion has never been accepted without admitting important exceptions, notably the collective control over the pricing of labour by trade unions, but it forms the basis of industrial legislation designed to eradicate monopoly abuses and restrictive practices in many Western countries and is a fundamental article of faith embodied in the Treaty of Rome signed by EEC countries.

Although consumer sovereignty and competition are widely accepted as a guide to economic policy, their operation in the field of the creative arts has often been questioned. For instance, while the British Broadcasting Corporation

(BBC) claims to make 'a systematic study of the tastes and preferences of its many audiences' (BBC *Handbook*, 1972, p. 152) it is under no obligation to relate its activities solely to public demand, and its very method of finance – by a fixed licence fee – removes the necessity for the close adaptation of its music programmes, for example, to popular taste. It is only in fairly recent times, that, in the UK, competition in broadcasting services has become accepted as a method of offering greater range of choice to consumers. It has also become fashionable for serious composers to deny that they should be under any obligation to relate their activities to the satisfaction of consumer demand. As the American composer Milton Babbitt (echoing Stravinsky and Schönberg) has put it (1966):

> I dare suggest that the composer will do himself and his music an eventual service by total, resolute and voluntary withdrawal from this public world to one of private performance and electronic media, with its very real possibility of complete elimination of public and social aspects of musical composition.

It is true that this view is not without some influence on those bodies, including public institutions, which dispense patronage, but we shall not consider it further in this contribution.[5]

The argument so far suggests that the consumer interest is best achieved by private enterprise producing for profit and selling in the free market. However, it can happen that the market might lead to an understatement of preferences because there may be benefits to consumers arising from provision of a 'product' – music, as we shall see, being a good example – over and above what customers are willing to pay. For most physical products, those who wish to enjoy them must be prepared to pay, and their enjoyment precludes others from doing so. Musical performance presents some difficulties in this respect. It is possible to exclude non-payers from a concert hall, but the costs of reducing 'free listening' mount rapidly when certain forms of mechanical reproduction, e.g. radio receivers, are used, because it is difficult to enforce charging both for the use of receivers and also for the intensity of their use. Furthermore, enjoyment of a broadcast performance by one person does not preclude enjoyment by another, for all those within reasonable listening range can benefit.

In addition, some members of society may derive pleasure and prestige from supporting composers directly through commissioning new works or indirectly by subsidising musical performances, as instanced in private foundation support. It is also frequently argued that music should be supported by public subsidy because it provides a supplementary collective benefit in the form of international prestige and of the improvement in cultural education (see Peacock, 1968; 1969).

The problem of defining the market for musical composition draws attention to an important assumption upon which the operation of our general criterion depends. Society has to devise rules to determine not only how property rights are to be exchanged, but how they are to be acquired in the first place. Our second general criterion governing the value of musical composition is that we are dealing with a society in which the system of private property is accepted, so that its legal system embodies machinery for defining property rights and assigning them as between individuals. This second criterion is chosen for the same reason as the first – its wide acceptability in Western-type democracies. In such countries individual members of society are more or less free to use their physical and 'brain' capital as they wish in order to optimise their own welfare, although it is common for them to accept collectively that some redistribution of capital, e.g. through inheritance taxation and death duties, should be instituted as an equity measure.

Unlike those members of society whose capital comprises physical assets, owners of intellectual property have experienced great difficulty in establishing their rights. Defining rights in musical composition to include performance as well as publication of music, has encountered stiff resistance from music users. Furthermore, whereas owners of tangible property have had no time limit placed on the period of ownership of rights, although its transfer to heirs may be taxed, rights in intellectual property are normally constrained by a time limit, e.g. rights are exhausted fifty years after a composer's death in many countries. Defining such a limit offers occasion for much more controversy over property rights than normally accompanies ownership of physical property.

IV. Public Policy and the Establishment and Enforcement of Copyright in Music

The difficulties in establishing and negotiating property rights in musical composition lie at the heart of the problem of determining its economic value, so we consider them at some length.[6] Even if property rights are confined only to control over publication of compositions, difficulties have arisen in instituting legal action against piracy. The problem is still an important one, now that publication can take the form of recordings, and even though in major record-producing countries there are laws aimed at legal protection against unauthorised records. Detection of pirate production within these countries is difficult enough, but there are still countries which do not afford such legal protection. Taiwan, for example, allows copying of records without royalty payment, provided the records are not exported – but such records appear in markets all over the world. It has been estimated that in the late 1960s as many as one hundred million disc records were already being made and sold each year without payment to composers and authors, as well as performers, of which about 70 per cent are made in the Far East (cf. Sterling, 1970, pp. 216–17).

Of course, piracy is an age-old problem in music. When Haydn's fame first spread abroad in the 1770s, his symphonies were not only published in Paris originally without his knowledge but also without any remuneration to him from sales. Publishers also capitalised on Haydn's popularity by issuing compositions of less known Austrian and other composers under Haydn's name. The business-like Haydn soon took the opportunity of selling his symphonies direct to a Paris publisher in order to protect his financial interests.

Secondly, the extension of property rights to cover performance as well as publication of music, reasonable in itself, has been fraught with problems. It is generally accepted, for example, that the author's economic exploitation of his work should be extended at least to public performance, but the history of case law in England indicates how difficult it has been to determine the meaning of 'public' (cf. Whale, 1971, Ch. 4). Furthermore, if royalty payments for performance are to be related to the extent of performance, i.e. some measure of performance 'output', difficulties of definition are legion when enjoyment of the product by one individual does not preclude enjoyment by another. For example, should 'production' of broadcast music be defined in terms of the size of audience who listen to it, or by reference to the number and price of broadcast receiving licences?

Thirdly, even if public performance can be defined in an acceptable fashion, the problem remains of dividing the royalties received between those who establish rights in performance, e.g. publishers, performers, as well as composers. Of course, this problem is not unique to music, and applies to the whole range of commercial transactions where bargains have to be struck over terms of sale.

Fourthly, the negotiation and enforcement of property rights in composition rests on accurate information of the occurrence and frequency of performance, either 'live' or 'canned'. This could mean that if an individual composer were left to discover for himself whether in fact his works were being performed, the 'tracing' costs would almost certainly outweigh the returns he would be able to negotiate with users of his works.

Fifthly, the mass media of radio and television have become a major means of public performance, but these media, for public policy reasons, have been restricted in the number of outlets in many countries and, in the cases where they have been wholly or partly operated as public corporations, these corporations have not had to follow commercial practice in realising their policy objectives. On the receipts side of their budgets, for practical as well as political reasons, they do not negotiate charges for different kinds of programme service. On the expenditure side, they have been able to exercise market power in purchases in excess of that which could be obtained if there were free competition in broadcasting. This has meant that composers have had difficulty in obtaining agreement with broadcasting companies on the proportion of their income which can be attributed to musical performance and, in the absence of 'countervailing power', would in any case be at a disadvantage in negotiating royalty payments with powerful buyers of their product.

The above mentioned difficulties in establishing, enforcing and negotiating rights for the composer have had the consequence that public authorities in many countries have been continuously under pressure to intervene on composers' behalf. The general problem facing governments in recognising that 'intangible' rights of composers and authors should be protected has been to devise legislative provisions which at the same time do not conflict with policy objectives other than the 'fair' distribution of property rights, notably the interests of the final consumer of composers' services. Briefly put,[7] Western governments accept the following general provisions for the protection of composers' rights:

(a) Legal recognition, following the analogy with tangible property which can be owned and inherited, for the length of life of copyright. Thus there is widespread acceptance of the proposition that copyright in publication and performance should last until fifty years after the death of the composer.

(b) Legal recognition that copyright covers performance as well as publication of music, which has been particularly important in broadcasting. This recognition has not come without a struggle and countries differ considerably in the breadth of definition of performance. Thus the US legislatures and courts, for example, have only grudgingly accepted the application of extension of the term 'performance' to cases in which music represents an ancillary means of attracting custom, e.g. the juke-box.

(c) Legal provision to uphold 'moral rights' of composers by which composers may control the form which performance may take, e.g. arrangements of their works, but, as a protection to the consumer against exclusive dealing arrangements, not to prohibit performance altogether. Thus record companies may be able to record a composer's music without permission provided that a royalty is paid. An interesting example which reflects both the problem of defining performance and controlling it is provided by 'home-dubbing', by which private persons record works on tape recorders or video records. In Western Germany the copyright law extends beyond public performance, but while there is no prohibition exercised against home-dubbing, it is accepted that the composer is entitled to a royalty. The method of collection has been through a levy on the manufacturer's price of a tape or video recorder of 3 per cent. However, an attempt to extract 5 per cent on the value of imported recording apparatus fell foul of the EEC authorities because it represents discrimination against foreign competitors.

(d) The acceptance of the fact that the costs of collection of performance royalties to individual composers so far outweigh the revenue benefits that they should be allowed to combine in order to negotiate terms of payment, licences, etc. and to decide methods of royalty distribution between members. In the UK, this acceptance was made all the more necessary by the presence of the BBC as a powerful buyer with a strong influence on the terms of sale of compositions for performance, particularly as in this instance the state had deliberately conferred monopoly rights on one of its own public corporations. Again, a problem arises concerning the compatibility of protecting composers' rights and the consequential acceptance of collective action by them to exploit such rights, and the interests of final consumers in obtaining access to musical enjoyment on the cheapest terms possible. What constitutes a 'reasonable' exercise of the powers of exploiting such rights, especially under conditions where economies of scale in royalty collection lead to the emergence of only one national collecting agency, is considered later.

(e) The surveillance by government of the actions of collecting and negotiating agencies in the light of restrictive practices legislation. Thus governments may also set up arbitration bodies to which either sellers or buyers of performing rights can appeal, as the natural concomitant to the acceptance of the necessity for collective bargaining over the rights themselves. The principles which should govern the judgments of such bodies is clearly a matter for controversy. Furthermore, when countries decide to harmonise their commercial law, as in EEC, conflicts between existing national and 'community' law will have to be resolved.

V. DETERMINING THE ECONOMIC VALUE OF COMPOSITION

The above discussion points to three important policy issues which arise in appraising the arrangements by which composers are remunerated, given the general criterion of satisfying consumer needs. The first issue is that of the 'reasonableness' of the economic privileges conferred on composers by copyright law. The second concerns the potential threat to consumer interests resulting from the manner in which these privileges are exercised, viz. the development of 'collective bargaining' in the negotiation of performing rights. The third issue – a much neglected one – concerns the definition of the 'consumer' for the purpose of identifying who should be charged for the use of music, and how these charges should be levied.

The first issue concerning the period of copyrights has given rise to some discussion of the tests which might be applied in assessing the reasonableness of the 'fifty-year' rule. Thus it has been argued that the correct test to be applied is that it must somehow be proved that, were the present degree of copyright protection reduced, the supply of composition would fall, i.e. at the margin, composers and would-be composers would divert their talents and efforts to supplying other goods and services. At the time of the discussion of the reform of copyright in the UK during the early fifties, Sir Arnold Plant (1953) argued that it was reasonable to suppose that the present protection to composers' successors was too generous to both composers and publishers. His view was that there was no presumption that, even if current levels of output of musical works were considered satisfactory, a reduction of the period of copyright protection would substantially affect it. A fair proportion of music, he held, is produced without reference to copyright protection at all, particularly 'serious' music, and would continue even if copyright protection were abolished. In other words, some composers maximise objectives other than purely commercial success, such as the prestige they gain among their fellow-musicians. If the current level of output were to be affected by change in copyright protection, so he argued, it might be the case that a *reduction* in protection would increase output rather than diminish it. So far as both publishers and composers were concerned, it could be admitted that they were both jointly involved in a risky occupation comparable, say, with the fashion industry, but received far greater protection than industries where the risks were comparable. It was further admitted that, whereas the costs of production were evenly spread through time, income from composition might be sporadic and subject to a wide dispersion from the life-time average, but the correct remedy for this situation might be some alteration in the tax laws rather than the continuation of the present copyright situation.

Plant's general approach to the problem, i.e. to relate the remuneration of copyright beneficiaries to the 'elasticity of supply' so that composers, for example, should be paid no more than is necessary to achieve some 'desired' output, is at least a useful starting point for discussion.[8] Unfortunately there is practically no evidence to go on, but even if his analysis is accepted and any performance right resulted in a redistribution of economic rent between consumers and producers of music, without a fall in the quantity and quality of output, society may still accept that any allocational improvement resulting from the transfer of the resources released from production of musical compositions to other economic activities does not offer sufficient reason for instituting the change. Consider the implications of making the change. First of all, it further restricts the right in intellectual property when, as already argued, no time limit is placed on the enjoyment of a return from physical capital, given the right of bequest of physical property. Secondly, it implicitly invokes a principle by which all property rights should be assigned with reference to allocational effects only, but only seeks to make the adjustment to an optimal distribution of these rights within one narrow sphere of economic activity, viz. composition and authorship, and without compensation to those affected. In short, society may wish to stop short of what could be argued to be a double discrimination against human as distinct from physical capital, particularly if it is unwilling to reassign *all* property rights simultaneously in accordance with the allocation principle.

The second problem is more directly related to the consumer interest. If composers and publishers have to combine in order to make the benefits of copyright negotiation and enforcement within the law outweigh the costs of doing so, how are restrictions on the sale, performance and recording rights to be avoided? Before attempting to answer this question, it should be noted that the emergence of monopoly is a function of the falling marginal costs of collection, which can be achieved by collective negotiation of rights on behalf of composers and publishers and does not necessarily arise from any desire on their part to increase control over prices charged to final consumers. The problem is complicated in practice, as we have repeatedly stressed, by the incentive to composers and publishers to combine in order to protect themselves against radio and record companies with a powerful hold on the market for musical composition as monopolistic buyers.

The most radical solution to this problem would be for the government itself to undertake to marry the interests of producers and consumers of music by forming a single nationalised collecting agency. There are two advantages which might be claimed for such a system. The first is that there would be no need for consumers to negotiate with producers of music over rights of performance and recording. They could be allowed to perform and record as they pleased, subject to the law on 'moral rights', but would presumably be required by law to disclose to the government when they did so. The second advantage is that government pricing policy could 'simulate' a competitive solution where there was a case for subsidising particular sorts of consumer or where charging was difficult or impossible. In addition, payments by the government to composers could be adjusted so as to reflect the wider community interest in encouraging (or discouraging) particular sorts of music which 'best' reflect collective benefits.

The issue as to whether the best solution to a potential monopoly situation is nationalisation cannot be resolved without reference to initial value judgments. Clearly, a nationalised royalty collecting service would not appeal to a large proportion of producers, if only because, among other things, it could too easily become a tool of censorship. It is perhaps more fruitful to consider the technical objections, of which three could be listed:

(a) There is no reason to suppose that a nationalised undertaking would be any better at identifying consumer use of copyright work than a private organisation. Also, a nationalised undertaking would inevitably be under less pressure to do so than a private organisation in which composers and publishers would be directly represented.

(b) Insofar as charges to consumers were to reflect the administrative costs of collecting royalties, there is no reason to suppose that these costs would form a smaller proportion of total revenue than in the case of a private organisation, which was the main collecting agency.

(c) Nationalisation is not required in order to give effect to any community interest in influencing the production of music in any particular way, e.g. by subsidising orchestras or composition of 'serious' music. Indeed, there is no particular reason why a royalty collecting agency should have any say in the matter of defining what this community interest should be.

Although we rule out nationalisation of royalty collection, our general criterion of consumer satisfaction requires the formulation of some form of 'code of good practice' which will govern the operation of royalty collection by a single private company. As the GEMA case illustrated,[9] EEC law would suggest a code which is based on anti-monopoly legislation, the object of which is to protect the consumer interest. No attempt is made to formulate such a code, but the following elements would need to be embodied in it:

(a) Freedom of entry into royalty collection including entry of foreign companies.
(b) Composers and publishers to be able to enter or withdraw from any royalty collection agency without any unreasonable delay.
(c) No discrimination, e.g. between foreign and domestic composers, in the methods of royalty payment.
(d) No collective restriction of output by composers and publishers and, by implication, no restriction on 'imports' of musical composition, other than to enforce 'moral rights'.
(e) Some arbitration procedure to resolve disagreements over charges.

Such a code of practice would obviously have to take into account the extent to which composers and producers might be disadvantaged in negotiating performance royalties with powerful buyers – broadcasting companies have been mentioned repeatedly. In addition, composers and publishers might reasonably claim that the extent to which they should co-operate over international free trade should depend on how far other countries are willing to follow suit.

It should be noted that, insofar as consumers do not consider that their interests are sufficiently safeguarded by voluntary negotiation of licences and charges for performance, the intervention by a public body, such as the Performing Right Tribunal in the UK, requires some 'guidelines' for the determination of charges, which are recognised as 'reasonable' and 'just'. This is a problem common to all situations where a public body has to survey the operations of monopoly organisations.

The third problem of major concern arises from the rapid rate of technological change in both sound and video recording. When the area of consumer utilisation of composers' services could be regarded as more or less co-terminous with public performance, defined to include radio and television broadcasting, it was reasonable to confine royalty collection to commercial producers of performances, to broadcasting companies, and to producers of records. The improvement in both radio and record production, combined with improvements in tape, has made good reproduction of performance for personal use, including video recording, a reality. There is no firm evidence on which to make a prediction of the effect of these developments on composers' incomes. Producers of these new or improved methods of recording will argue that audio and video cassettes will increase the perishability of composition, and thereby the demand for 'new' music.[10] On the other hand, it is feared by composers, and publishers, record manufacturers and artists, that reproduction for personal use will result in no net increase in demand for their services, as it will reduce further the demand for 'live' performance and for records. Moreover, detection of 'free listening' may be almost impossible and, even if it were possible, the costs of collecting a royalty through the normal means of licensing would be prohibitive.

If, in a free market, consumers voluntarily choose to change the mode of transmission of music (bearing in mind the costs to them of doing so, which are not negligible, e.g. the cost of attending concerts compared with the capital cost of a tape recorder and the purchase of tapes), then presumably this will increase their satisfaction. But should consumers be faced with the further cost of a royalty on reproduction of performance for personal use? If one were to accept the 'incentive' test as the method for determining the distribution of property rights, it is doubtful if a case could be made, given the Plant assumptions about the 'elasticity of supply' of musical composition. On the other hand, accepting society's present judgment of the rights in intellectual and cultural property, it would be illogical not to extend the law to cover reproduction for personal use, particularly if 'home-dubbing' led to a decline in consumer demand for other methods of consumer access to music.

The practical problem is how to devise a method of charging consumers which is both efficient and equitable. Given the costs of detection of reproduction, it would seem to be impossible to devise a system which could be operated through the normal methods of royalty collection. Forbidding private reproduction would be ineffective and even if it were not, would reduce the welfare of both producer and consumer. The alternative would appear to be some form of taxation which would be related to consumer use of the musical product.

The only country to have allowed such a system to operate has been Western Germany, which permits a levy which may not exceed 5 per cent of the manufacturer's price on tape and video recorders. The objection to this method of charging is that it is not related to consumer use of the musical product. It would seem more equitable as between consumers if the tax were related to the length of *playing time* available to consumers through recording. This suggests a tax on tapes, varied according to their length, rather than on the recording apparatus.[11]

VI. MARKET FAILURE

So far it has been argued that, subject to satisfactory arrangements about property rights, our criteria suggest that the market can be used as the vehicle for determining the remuneration of composers, due attention being paid to some of the problems which arise in identifying consumer benefits and in regulating the methods by which composers' royalties are collected. Nevertheless, composers frequently complain – and they have many supporters outside their profession – that their remuneration through the channels of the market is not a reflection of their 'true worth'. Economists are justifiably sceptical of schemes of remuneration which are based on completely arbitrary 'job evaluation' systems, but are bound to recognise that there are areas in which benefits other than those emanating from the market may accrue to consumers, so that the question of 'market failure' in composer remuneration is worth further investigation.

There seem to be two sorts of extra-market benefits which those who argue the case have in mind. The first is the familiar one that even those who do not pay to listen to their work derive satisfaction from pride in their achievement, for example, from the international prestige associated with the dissemination of culture abroad. The second is more germane to this study. The serious composers are the musical innovators, both in regard to developments in musical forms and in the exploitation of new sound patterns and new instruments, such as electronic devices. These innovations 'filter through' to the other members of the profession and help the development of light and popular music. The point was put very well forty years ago by Constant Lambert in a detailed analysis of the musical features of jazz:

> The sudden post-war efflorescence of jazz was due largely to the adoption of raw material of the harmonic richness and orchestral subtlety of the Debussy–Delius period of highbrow music . . . The harmonic background drawn from the impressionistic school opened up a new world of sound to the jazz composer, and although the more grotesque orchestral timbres, the brute complaints of the saxophone, the vicious spurts from the muted brass, may seem to belie the rich sentimentality of their background, they are only thorns protecting a fleshy cactus – a *sauce piquante* poured over a nice juicy steak. [1948, pp. 149–50]

The first kind of benefit, that which accrues directly to the final consumer, suggests the need for some form of public subsidy to serious composers, including tax measures designed to induce private persons or foundations to support them. It has no direct bearing on the question of the division of royalties between different classes of composers, although it may affect their relative earnings. Serious composers have benefited increasingly in recent years from public patronage through the commissioning of new works and award of fellowships by a wide variety of state and municipal bodies in

European countries. The amount of support is generally considered by composers to be woefully insufficient and the choice of 'grantees' much criticised. Although London orchestras, for example, receive about 20 per cent of their income from public grants, the 'mix' of their programmes reveals that, currently, the works of British living composers form less than 8 per cent of the total works performed (see Annual Reports of the London Orchestral Concert Board, 1970–71). There is no practical remedy which can be suggested, which has not been tried before. In any case the argument based on 'extra-market' benefits of composition is one which has wide applicability and not only in the sphere of culture.

The 'uncovenanted benefit' which serious composers confer on other composers, as distinct from the public at large, presents a different order of problems. Major publishers of serious music have long believed that it is in their long-term interests to support contemporary serious composers by profits earned from the works of past masters whose works are out of copyright in the expectation that new additions to the catalogue will in time earn them profits which can be used in part to support future generations of composers.[12] This transfer mechanism worked by publishers is in danger of falling into disuse, both because of the fall in income experienced from sales of non-copyright works and also because of the greater risks associated with the publication of avant-garde music with a much more limited appeal than the new works of the past. There is no doubt that popular and light composers recognise their debt to serious composers, but it can no longer be expected that the publisher will act as the intermediary by which 'hits' will offer support for serious works as well as himself bearing some of the risks of their publication.

Economic analysis has recently devoted a good deal of attention to this problem of uncovenanted benefits. The problem is one of getting the beneficiaries to reveal their preferences. If potential beneficiaries will gain from a particular service whether or not they are willing to pay, then they will not be prepared to pay unless *everyone* pays. (In a market situation this does not arise, because the service can be denied to those who are not prepared to pay for it.) A method by which everyone can check on everyone else to see if they pay 'their due' would have to be devised, and this could be prohibitively expensive to make effective, particularly if beneficiaries were not known to one another. A 'voluntary' solution may be impossible to reach; and if the alternative is that the service may be in danger of not being provided, potential beneficiaries may be prepared to submit to an 'imposed' solution, as happens when a community agrees to be taxed in order for a service to be financed which it would otherwise not be possible to provide by unsubsidised private enterprise, e.g. defence.

The combination of composers of all kinds and publishers to form a royalty-collecting organisation offers a convenient method of reducing the transaction costs which are incurred in any voluntary negotiation of un-covenanted benefits. It is worth noting that performing rights organisations frequently do operate a system of royalty distribution which favours the serious composer. Common elements in such a system are (a) an initial classification of compositions which awards higher royalties to symphonic works and chamber works; and (b) payment of a royalty which discriminates in favour of works according to their playing time. It cannot be claimed that this distributional system reflects exclusively the production externalities received by 'light' and 'pop' composers from serious composers, but certainly these externalities are recognised as one element governing its operation.

VII. CONCLUSION

This contribution has shown that there are special problems encountered by the composer in obtaining his 'just rewards' in the light of criteria commonly accepted as relevant in contemporary economies where the market allocates resources. Composers, as suggested in the earlier quotation from Milton Babbitt, are commonly supposed to adopt a posture which reflects either aloofness from or contempt of material rewards, and of the judgment of a 'bourgeois' capitalist system of their 'worth'. Yet the remoteness from material existence suggested by Arnold Schönberg in his *Schöpferische Konfessionen* (epitomised in his statement 'der Mensch ist das was er erlebt; der Künstler erlebt nur was er ist' – 'Man is what he experiences; the artist experiences only what he is') is in strong contrast with the realities of their economic position for, whatever composers may think about the economic system we live in, they certainly actively participate in organisations designed to protect their economic interests. As a counterweight to much that is written by composers about their position in society, it is difficult to resist quoting the down-to-earth judgment of a serious composer on the contemporary scene, for, even if it is no more than a pithy impression, it seems to be more in accord with how they act:

> So few composers are professional writers. They have this quaint nineteenth century idea of being pens in the hands of God. But it's so presumptuous, especially these days when a lot of our jobs are being taken over by the radiophonic workshops. There's nothing wrong with what they do, so long as we remember that they're electricians and not composers. But we mustn't be arrogant. We have no special inner life. We're just the same as everyone else.[13]

Nothing in this statement need lead anyone to lose his respect for the creative artist or to enjoy his (or her) product any the less.

NOTES

1. I am grateful to my York colleagues Tony Culyer, Alan Maynard, Keith Hartley, Alan Williams and Jack Wiseman who offered criticisms of this paper which spanned the whole dynamic range from *piano* to *fortissimo*. Much though I would like to, I cannot hold them responsible for any remaining discords which I may have failed to resolve. The article is reproduced, with minor amendments, from Bernard Kulp and Wolfgang Stützel (eds) *Beiträge zu einer Theorie der Sozialpolitik: Festschrift für Elisabeth Liefmann-Keil zum 65. Geburtstag* Duncker and Humblot, Berlin, 1973.
2. These data are extracted from an unpublished survey of composers' earnings by the author made in 1972.
3. 1984 has a special significance for composer remuneration in the UK, for in that year the copyrights in the works of Delius, Elgar and Holst simultaneously lapse!
4. Ignoring externalities and income distribution (both considered later).
5. For further discussion, see Peacock (1968).
6. It is not our purpose to discuss the philosophical basis of a composer's right. For a useful analysis of this matter, see Whale (1971) Chapter 2.
7. No attempt can be made here to summarise even the main legal provision made in such countries, nor is this necessary for the purpose in hand. We are only interested in those general characteristics of copyright protection which have a bearing on the problem of defining the economic value of musical composition. For the evolution of performance rights in music in the UK, see Peacock and Weir (1975).
8. See also Thomas (1964) and Economic Council of Canada (1971). The latter document summarises the economist's approach as follows: 'We have found it more helpful and illuminating not to *start* with the grant by governments of legal protection to certain rights, but to commence at an earlier stage and focus more on the incentive *purpose* of the grant' (p. 142).
9. In 1971, GEMA (Gesellschaft für Musikalische Aufführungs- und Mechanische Vervielfältigungsrechte), the German collecting agency for composer royalties, formed one of the important test cases under the EEC cartel law. GEMA was given six months to alter its commercial practices, notably its policies of confining ordinary membership to German composers and of levying discriminatory charges on imported recording apparatus.
10. 'The audio-visual recording may consume product – as television audiences voraciously consumed all available visual programming – at a rate never dreamed possible in the music business' (Young, 1970).
11. It will be noted that we do not deal here with the problem of the licensing and negotiation of royalties for the commercial use of video-cassettes, e.g. in places of public entertainment. We are assuming in the case of commercial use, existing negotiating machinery with performing right and mechanical right agencies could be used.'
12. On this point see Roth (1969) Chapters 6 and 7. His personal experience as a publisher of new music is typified by the following passage: 'I, like many other serious publishers, have not only printed immature works in order to encourage a young man, but also paid fixed salaries or guaranteed incomes to real or presumed talents: like many other publishers, too, I have often been disappointed. . . . One of whom I was not alone in expecting great things and for whom I procured a ballet commission, absconded on that occasion with a girl from the corps de ballet and was never heard of again. But the few who fulfil or exceed expectations compensate for all the failures and mistakes, for the wasted labour and money. One feels oneself confirmed in one's task and, rightly or wrongly, believes one has rendered a service to the art perhaps even to mankind' (p. 129).
13. Elizabeth Lutyens in an interview, *Sunday Times*, 27 February 1972. For a similar view, see Hindemith (1953) Chapter 11, which offers excellent advice to young composers on business matters.

REFERENCES

Babbitt, M. (1966) 'Who cares to listen' quoted in G. Chase (ed.) *The American Composer Speaks* Louisiana State University Press, Baton Rouge.
British Broadcasting Corporation (1972) *Handbook* BBC, London.

Economic Council of Canada (1971) *Report on Intellectual and Industrial Property* Ottawa.

Lambert, C. (1948) *Music Ho!* Pelican edition (1st edition 1934).

Hindemith, P. (1953) *A Composer's World* Harvard University Press, Cambridge, Mass.

Peacock, A. T. (1968) 'Public patronage and music: An economist's view' *Three Banks Review* No. 77, March.

Peacock, A. T. (1969) 'Welfare economics and public subsidies to the arts' *Manchester School* December.

Peacock, A. T. and Weir, R. (1975) *The Composer in the Marketplace* Faber (Music), London.

Plant, Sir A. (1953) *The New Commerce in Intellectual Ideas and Property* Stamp Memorial Lecture, Athlone Press, London.

Roth, E. (1969) *The Business of Music* Cassell, London.

Sterling, J. A. C. (1970) 'Piracy of recordings' in *The Music Industry: Markets and Methods for the '70s* New York.

Thomas, D. (1964) *Copyright and the Creative Artist* Institute of Economic Affairs, London.

Whale, R. F. (1971) *Copyright: Evolution, Theory and Practice* Longman, London.

Young, R. L. (1970) 'Audio-visual technology and the law' in *The Music Industry: Markets and methods for the '70s* New York.

CHAPTER 11

Stabilization and Distribution Policy[1]

I. INTRODUCTION

When asked to explore the problem of the possible conflict between stabilization and distribution I cast my mind back to the early days of the application of Keynesian economics as found, for example, in the famous discussion by Beveridge in *Full Employment in a Free Society* (1944). He saw no conflict because, if mature economies suffered from a permanent lack of aggregate demand sufficient to ensure full employment, redistribution policy would be complementary to and not in conflict with stabilization policy. The pursuit of the kind of social policies which he advocated, notably the extension of state-supported social security schemes, and a national health service, involved redistributing income to those whose propensity to consume was higher than those who bore the costs of this policy. The aggregate average propensity to consume would shift upwards, and this would be a useful way of stimulating aggregate demand. Of course, it followed that if a permanent lack of aggregate demand were not to obtain and there might at least be periods when ex-ante aggregate demand exceeded aggregate supply at the full employment level, then the opposite policy – taxing those with a relatively low marginal propensity to consume and therefore the poor rather than the rich – would be the logical corollary of Beveridge's argument. One could go on to show that if stabilization policy required the cutting of aggregate demand, subject to the constraint of leaving the disposable personal income distribution unchanged, then a greater tax revenue would be required than would be necessary if taxation were used to make private disposable income more unequal, and this might be an additional consideration to bear in mind in deciding which policy instrument to use.

Since those optimistic days major changes have taken place in the scope of welfare policies which, if not exclusively designed to promote redistribution of income and wealth, do have this result. The simple Keynesian model has been transmogrified in order to take account of the larger number of 'target variables' of policy relevance, the improved specification of monetary forces and the balance of payments, the identification of lags in the economic system and of the sophisticated econometric testing which has found wanting some of the basic relationships such as that between income and consumption. Practical experience in the use of fiscal and monetary instruments as well as regulatory measures has made applied economists wary of being too sanguine about our ability to forecast their precise effects. It is hardly surprising that policy makers, though often convinced that they can 'square the circle' and reach some 'bliss point' of their own choosing by dramatic and popular measures, are often profoundly sceptical of the economic scenarios which are derived from Keynesian-type forecasting models.

With these analytical and policy developments in mind the short answer to the question: do redistribution policies conform to or conflict with stabilization goals must be that 'it all depends'. All that I can hope to do is to indicate how an answer might be sought. I shall employ for this purpose a simple version of the theory of economic policy using a static Keynesian-type model of an open economy with a government sector.

II. A Policy Model with Stabilization/Distribution Trade-Off

Imagine a government which chooses as its main short-term objective that of minimising the rate of unemployment and the rate of domestic inflation relative to the 'overseas' rate of inflation. Initially the economy is in short-term equilibrium with the conditions for maximising this objective function satisfied. It then decides – perhaps as a result of political pressure – to pursue a more vigorous social policy by increasing the coverage and the rate of state pensions payable to retired persons in lower income groups. Using a simple macroeconomic policy model, let us observe what happens:

Thus
$$Y = Y(X, M) \quad [f'_y(X) > 0; f''_y(X) = 0;$$
$$f'_y(M) < 0; f''_y(M) = 0] \tag{1}$$

$$U = U(Y) \quad [f'_u(Y) < 0; f''_u(Y) > 0] \tag{2}$$

$$\frac{\dot{p}_d}{\dot{p}_x} \equiv \dot{P} = \dot{P}(U) \quad [f'_p(U) < 0; f''_p(U) > 0] \tag{3}$$

$$(X - M) \equiv B = B(\dot{P}) \quad [f'_B(\dot{P}) < 0; f''_B(\dot{P}) > 0] \tag{4}$$

where Y = GDP in volume terms
U = the rate of unemployment
$\dot{p}_d$ = domestic rate of inflation
$\dot{p}_x$ = 'overseas' rate of inflation
X = volume of exports
M = volume of imports

Equation (1) simply states that GDP depends on the volume of exports and volume of imports, the multiplier being given. This assumption can easily be varied in accordance with the needs of our exercise.

Equation (2) is a simple inverse production function.

Equation (3) assumes a Phillips-type relationship except that we have allowed for the existence of external influences in the form of the rate of inflation abroad. Thus a higher rate of inflation abroad, given the domestic rate of inflation, is consistent with a lower rate of unemployment.

Equation (4) states that the higher the rate of domestic to overseas inflation, the lower the volume of exports and higher the volume of imports. Of course this is a highly simplified assumption and embodies the further, important, assumption that the exchange rate is fixed. Clearly, exports and imports with a fixed exchange rate could be expressed as a function of the difference between the absolute domestic and overseas price level for tradeable goods but, as will be clear later, the concentration on differential rates of inflation is determined by the kind of objective function which we wish to consider. While it is recognised that equation (4) is 'fudged', a more extended formulation would not make any difference to the main argument.

On inspection of this system of equations it is soon clear that there is an equilibrium solution, given p_x as exogenously determined. It may be useful to offer a diagrammatic version of the system in the usual four-quadrant presentation with all axes positive (see Figure 11.1). Of course this equilibrium is a short-term one, for the persistence of balance of payments deficits or surpluses would in practice put pressure on the government to adjust the exchange rate, which in turn would alter the relation between domestic and overseas prices.

The quadrants are numbered according to the equations and the functions drawn in accordance with the information in the equation. Perhaps equation (1), which will be manipulated, needs a word of explanation. It can be written out explicitly as $Y = K \cdot (X - M)$ where K is a multiplier reflecting the marginal propensity to consume and to tax, the consumption and tax coefficients being constant and < 1. The initial equilibrium position is shown by the rectangle *ABCD*.

We now introduce the objective function of the government:

$$W = W(U, \dot{P}). \tag{5}$$

In our diagram we maximize this function at the point of tangency, *A*, of the Phillips-type curve and a 'government' indifference curve which is concave to the origin, though this is not to suggest that the origin is necessarily some 'bliss point'.

The trade-off depicted in (5) could represent the conflict between stability

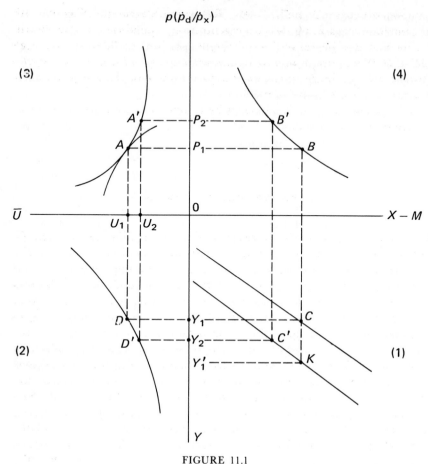

FIGURE 11.1

(as measured by the inflation rate) and *factor* distribution of income on the assumption that the factor shares altered in favour of wage incomes as unemployment fell. However, rather than seeking to confirm or deny this relationship between unemployment and factor shares, let us assume that the government decides to employ an 'active' social policy, as previously suggested, by introducing a pensions scheme for retired workers who are assumed to spend all the receipts. For the moment, the government makes no alterations in tax rates. Equation (1) may now be written explicitly as $Y = K[(X - M) + S]$ where S is the exogenously determined transfer expenditure on pensions. The straight line in quadrant (1) has now to be shifted downwards to the left to reflect both the initial expenditure S and its multiplier effects. Aggregate demand increases, unemployment falls, but the rate of domestic inflation rises and the balance of payments worsens. Again an equilibrium position will be established with the equilibrium level of Y

somewhere between Y_1 and Y_1' at Y_2. Rather than obscure the diagrammatic presentation by showing the convergence to an equilibrium, we arbitrarily fix the final 'position of rest' in this simple economy as shown by rectangle $A'B'C'D'$. We notice in passing that, *ignoring the implied change in the objective function resulting from the new policy*, A represents a lower level of government welfare once equilibrium is established.

We can now use this highly simplified analysis in order to develop an answer to our basic question.

III. THE IMPORTANCE OF 'TRADE-OFF'

Semantic argument is always rather boring, so I hesitate to say that the first problem encountered in answering our basic question is how to define stabilization and distributional policies. To give an example of what Peacock and Shaw (1976) have termed the 'target variable ambiguity', seeking to establish a low and stable level of unemployment may be regarded as 'stabilization' in one sense and 'distributional' in another, depending on whether the object is to improve the bargaining position of labour as a means of 'correcting' the factor distribution or to remove the disutility which it is believed to be experienced by those who prefer more income and more work to less income and less work in the short run and who wish to reduce the degree of uncertainty attached to future employment prospects through state action. The approach in this paper is essentially pragmatic and I shall associate stability primarily with the rate of inflation and distributional objectives with transfers of income from higher to lower income groups through the budget. We need not necessarily attach either label to the unemployment target but merely recognize that it is an important argument in the government welfare function.

A further point to be made is that the idea of a 'conflict' between stabilization and distribution policies is usually associated with the constraints imposed on joint pursuit of these policies by the underlying economic conditions. We shall examine constraints shortly, but our simple model shows that it is far from being the sole and dominant factor subsumed under the term 'conflict'. The extent of the 'conflict' clearly depends on the 'taste' for these policies.

It is beyond the scope of this paper to investigate how the tastes of individuals are reflected in their utility functions and how far these become embodied in government choices. However, it is a reasonable presumption that we cannot generalize about the extent of conflict if tastes and therefore 'trade-offs' between the policies differ from country to country and over time within one country. Consider the social welfare function expressed in

(5) expanded in order to include the utility attached to subsidizing pensions:

$$W = W(U, \dot{P}, S_r) \tag{5a}$$

where S_r = the per capita payment made to retired persons below some specified income level.

This function may be written explicitly as:

$$dW = \frac{\partial W}{\partial U} dU + \frac{\partial W}{\partial \dot{p}} d\dot{P} + \frac{\partial W}{\partial S_r} dS_r. \tag{6}$$

As already shown in quadrant (3) the indifference curve fulfils the condition that $dP/dU = f'_p(U)$ with $f'_p(U) < 0$.

On the other hand we have not determined the trade-off between U, P and S_r and to keep the analysis simple and in line with our previous system of equations, let it be assumed that $S_r = \overline{S}_r$, i.e. the per capita pension represents a boundary condition with no trade-off between the other arguments in the welfare function. We can now write equation (6) in the form

$$dW = dU \left[\frac{\partial W}{\partial U} + \frac{\partial W}{\partial f'_p(U)} \cdot f'_p(U) \right] + \frac{\partial W}{\partial S_r} \cdot d\overline{S}_r. \tag{6a}$$

Let us go through the steps of the previous analysis again and assume that equation (6) is maximized as depicted in point A in Figure 11.1, i.e. the boundary condition is not met. Now introduce the boundary condition so that S_r increases from 0 to some positive amount. The righthand expression in equation (6a) is positive but though unemployment is reduced, prices increase, so that the lefthand expression must be negative given that previously the trade-off between prices and unemployment was optimal. We cannot say whether the whole expression will be negative or positive without evaluating $\partial W/\partial S_r$, but we can see that the final result crucially depends on the value of $f'_p(U)$.

The cost of introducing a distribution objective of the form represented by our boundary condition will depend on the curvature of the indifference system representing the trade-off between U and $\dot{P}$. Given tangency at A between the Phillips-type curve in quadrant (3) and alternative indifference systems, then if U and P are perfect substitutes $f'_p(U) = -1$, $f''_p(U) = 0$. The 'cost' of adding the boundary condition is clearly less in this case than in the 'normal' trade-off case where $f'_p(U) < 0$ and $f''_p(U) < 0$. In short, 'conflict is in the eye of the beholder', and the extent of the conflict will therefore depend on the delineation of the trade-offs, given for the present that there is no dispute about the economic model which is used for policy purposes.

To underline this point in a slightly different way, imagine that we have a 'blow-up' of quadrant (3) as in Figure 11.2. We have a government with trade-off represented by indifference system I_1 with a point of tangency to the Phillips-type curve at A. In contemplating the introduction of the pensions

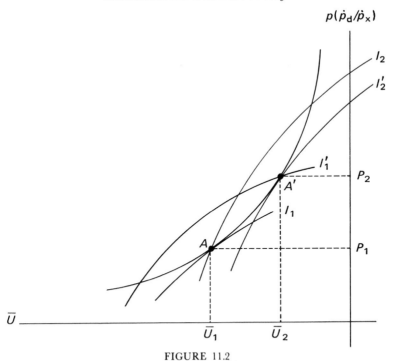

FIGURE 11.2

boundary condition, a move from A to A' must take place. There is a conflict of objectives in the sense that the evaluation of the rise in per capita pension has to be balanced against the loss of welfare resulting from the government having to accept a higher domestic rate of inflation though lower unemployment. Imagine that this government suddenly loses power to one with trade-offs represented by indifference system I_2 which is also committed to meeting the same boundary condition. Moving to meet this condition involves no conflict for A' is preferred to A by the new government.

IV. Policy Conflict and the Choice of Models

I suppose that the problem of conflict between stabilization and distributional objectives is not normally thought of in terms of the difficulties of resolution through the exploration of trade-offs, but in terms of an addition to the number of *targets*. Taking our previous example, the policy problem is how to meet the boundary condition while simultaneously maintaining the original levels of prices and unemployment (P_1 and U_1), as depicted in Figure 11.1, which are taken as target levels. This calls for some form of adjustment in one of the available policy instruments.

Our model suggests that this is an easy matter. The government can make some offsetting adjustment in expenditure or taxes which restores the system to its original equilibrium position. However, let us impose another and realistic constraint on government action, namely that it believes that the community derives utility from other expenditure programmes and that these are not to be cut. Fiscal policy action, ignoring debt policy, must then be confined to adjustment of taxation. The reason for this arbitrary addition to the arguments in the welfare function is justified by the need to demonstrate that our view of the degree of conflict between stabilization and distribution policy and, the possibility of its resolution, and the determination of the methods of resolution depends on which model we consider is appropriate for the economy under scrutiny.

The 'old style' Keynesian expenditure model which still dominates our textbooks, tells us that there is a simple answer, as I have already indicated in the Introduction, and that is to cut private consumption by taxing income so that, in terms of Figure 11.1, income is restored to the level Y_1. Thus if

$$Y_1 = K_1(X - M + A), \qquad k_1 = \frac{1}{1 - a[1 - t_1(1 - r)]}$$

$$Y_2 = K_2(X - M + A + S), \qquad k_2 = \frac{1}{1 - a[1 - t_2(1 - r)]}$$

$0 < t_1, t_2 < 1$ where t_1, t_2 are proportional tax rates on income

$\quad 0 < r < 1$ where r is an exemption limit which is a fixed proportion of income

$A =$ exogenous terms in the multiplicand $(I + G)$
$a =$ consumption coefficient
$S =$ total transfer payment to pensioners spent entirely on consumption.

For Y_1 to equal Y_2 then

$$\frac{K_2}{K_1} \cdot \left\{ 1 + \frac{S}{(X - M + A)} \right\} = 1. \tag{7}$$

With a and r given, this can only come about if $t_2 > t_1$, which is obvious enough.

Of course, while a technical solution can be offered, if this model remotely describes the real world, further policy problems may be created. The larger the value of S, the higher the tax rate. If tax resistance builds up, the government may be tempted to lower the value of r so that the distribution policy turns into one of redistribution of income between the retired population and working population rather than redistribution from upper to lower income groups.

But suppose that one is a Friedmanite in the sense that one believes that the permanent income hypothesis is accepted (*cf.* Laidler, 1973; Sumner,

1974; Peacock and Shaw, 1976). This would alter our view about the efficacy of tax adjustment. This can be most simply explained by considering the consumption function, for the tax adjustment is designed to reduce consumption. We write

$$C_n = a_0 Y_{pn}$$

where

$$Y_{pn} = e \cdot Y_n + e(l-e)Y_{n-l} \ldots \ldots e(l-e)aY_{n-a} \qquad (0 < e < l) \qquad (8)$$

Y_{pn} is permanent income at time period n and a is the number of past income periods considered relevant in its determination, while e is the coefficient relating permanent to current measured income. As usually stipulated, $e < 1$. It follows from (8) that

$$C_n = a_0(l-e)Y_{pn-l} + a_0 e Y_n. \qquad (9)$$

Tax changes limited to their impact on current income must now exert less effect on the level of aggregate demand compared with the Keynesian case where consumption depends solely on current measured income. If we express the consumption function implicit in (8) in difference equation form:

$$C = a_0 Y_n[1 - t(l-r)]$$

so that

$$\frac{\partial C}{\partial t_1} = -a_0 Y_n(1-r) \qquad (10)$$

but employing the permanent income hypothesis, and remembering that tax is levied on current measured income only, the change in consumption with respect to the tax rate is

$$\frac{\partial C}{\partial t_1} = -a_0 e Y_n(1-r) \qquad (11)$$

and clearly with $e < 1$, the impact of the tax change is less in (11) than in (10).

The resolution of the conflict through fiscal policy becomes demonstrably more difficult. It will be noted that this simple model ignores the influence of the permanent income hypothesis on the demand for money which would have to be taken into account in a Keynesian-type model embodying a monetary as well as a public sector. On this point see Peacock and Shaw (1976, pp. 56–8).

So far, working within the confines of the model, the extent of conflict in policies is presented in terms of the difficulties associated with trying to reduce the level of private consumption by fiscal policy measures to enable resources to be transferred to lower income groups. The attempts to restore unemployment and prices to their original target levels are made through the reduction in aggregate demand. Neo-Keynesian models, however, refuse to treat consumers (wage-earners) as passive adjusters to tax changes and attempt to embody assumptions about their reactions as manifested in trade union response to changes in direct taxation (Auld, 1974). In other words, there is an implicit assumption in the simple model that wage rates are fixed, whereas trade union response to a cut in disposable incomes by taxation could be to attempt to protect real take-home pay by attempting to raise the wage rate. In the short run, with a cut in aggregate demand and a rise in supply prices in response to a rise in wage rates, unemployment will be higher and the rate of inflation higher than would be the case if wage rates remained fixed. In terms of Figure 11.1, the process of adjustment entails a shift in the curve in quadrant 2 downwards to the left and the curve in quadrant 3 upwards and to the left. There is a presumption that the original targets would then be out of reach, unless some other policy instruments were brought into play, but it would be necessary to reconstruct our simple model, with more variables and lagged functions, in order to indicate what the final result would be; and once we extend the model to include the political influence of wage-earners as voters on the use of policy instruments, we would need to construct an elaborate politico-economic model of the macroeconomic process and this is beyond the scope of the paper.

The policy conflicts demonstrated with simple fiscal policy models above, can be illustrated by reference to the problems of the UK where the concept of the 'welfare state' has been all but sacrosanct.

Faced with the problem of adjusting to the adverse terms of trade produced by the rise in oil prices and other raw materials in the early 1970s, an attempt has been made to avoid the consequential fall in real disposable national income and the painful decisions of resource allocation resulting from this fall by 'borrowing our way out of the depression'. The longer-term consequences of this policy mean that when such borrowing becomes regarded as imposing too onerous a burden on the economy, a constraint has to be placed on the balance of payments deficit $(X - M)$. Our model is clearly over-simple but it throws some light on the policy dilemma. Such a constraint, given p_x as beyond the influence of UK policy-makers, places a constraint on the domestic rate of inflation (p_d) which in turn places a constraint on the achievable reduction in the rate of unemployment U, which in turn places a constraint on the use of Keynesian aggregate demand as a method of raising output and employment. Therefore a boundary condition which requires that social services, including pensions, should retain their real value, either means cutting other government expenditure or transferring resources, e.g. through taxation or non-inflationary borrowing, to the public sector, given the aggregate demand constraint. With public expenditure (central and local) at present running at 60% of GDP and a public sector deficit of 8% of GDP, it requires little imagination to see the nature of the policy conflict.

V. Concluding Remarks

The above analysis suggests some obvious conclusions, though I hope it has been worth delineating the path which leads to them. A government's degree of success in reconciling distributional and stabilization aims will be positively correlated with:

(i) a clear and realistic statement of its objectives and trade-offs between them;

(ii) a stable objective function or one which lends itself to easy prediction over the relevant policy-making period. (Clearly a problem arises in this context, if there is little consensus between successive governments about objectives and trade-offs);

(iii) recognition of the constraints which determine the maximization of the objective function though, as pointed out, the estimation of the magnitudes of the constraints depends on the skill which its advisers display in economic forecasting and estimation or in devising methods which obviate the need for prediction.

In concentrating on the short-term position perhaps it has not been made sufficiently clear that distributional aims are usually reflected in measures, such as social security schemes, public investment in human capital, etc., which take time to develop, often make firm claims on resource-use in the long term and which are difficult to adjust (particularly in a downward direction) in the short run for technical as well as political reasons. Stabilization policies are generally designed to make quick short-term adjustments to the control over resources by the private sector in order to make total resource-use compatible with control over prices, incomes and employment. It is clearly much easier for a government to make these adjustments palatable if these can be carried out while maintaining a positive rate of growth in real private disposable incomes and without increasing income inequality. This is clearly much easier for a country which is able to maintain a high growth rate without balance of payments constraints of a short- or long-term nature. Our economic analysis can indicate why this is so, but has not very much to say about how to bring this desirable state of affairs about.

NOTE

1. A slightly shortened version of a contribution to Martin Pfaff (ed.) *Grenzen der Umverteilung* Duncker and Humblot, Berlin, 1978.

I wish to express my appreciation of useful comments made by Abba Lerner and also Colette Bowe, Economic Adviser, Department of Industry, and Michael Jones-Lee, now Professor of Economics, University of Newcastle-upon-Tyne and formerly of York.

REFERENCES

Auld, D. A. L. (1974) 'The impact of taxes on wages and prices' *National Tax Journal* Vol. 27, March.
Beveridge, W. (1944) *Full Employment in a Free Society* Allen & Unwin, London.
Laidler, D. E. W. (1973) 'Expectations, adjustment and the dynamic response of income to policy changes' *Journal of Money, Credit and Banking* Vol. 5, February.
Peacock, A. T. and Shaw, G. K. (1976) *The Economic Theory of Fiscal Policy* revised edition, Allen & Unwin, London.
Sumner, M. T. (1974) 'Fiscal policy and the permanent income hypothesis' *Manchester School* December.

CHAPTER 12

The Treatment of
Government Expenditure in
Studies of Income Redistribution[1]

I. INTRODUCTION

Those intrepid souls who attempt to measure the redistributory effects of public budgets usually have their task defined for them in the following way. First, identify the pre-budget national or personal income distributed by income groups, using the individual or, more usually now, the household as the income-receiving unit. Second, find means by which the various tax and expenditure components can be allocated by income group. Finally compare the pre- and post-budget income distribution. If any income group receives more in allocated benefits than taxes paid, then that group is termed a 'net beneficiary'. In theory, given a balanced budget, the total pre- and post-budget national or personal income will be equal, but the distribution in each case will obviously depend on the allocation process. Tabular or other methods of comparison, e.g., Lorenz curve or Gini coefficient measures, may be used to show the redistributory effects.

It will be useful for future analysis to employ the following notation. Thus,

$$\sum_{i=1}^{i=m} y_i^0 + \sum_{i=1}^{i=m} (g_i^l + g_i^c) - \sum_{i=1}^{i=m} ((t_i^d + t_i^e) \equiv \sum_{i=1}^{i=m} y_i^p,$$

where m is the number of identified income groups, y^0 is the 'original' (pre-budget) income, y^p the post-budget income, g^l government transfer payments, g^c government expenditure on goods and services (later divided into g^s = 'specific' services and g^p = 'indivisible' services), t^d direct taxes, and t^e taxes on expenditure (less subsidies). As it is assumed that a given national or personal income is being redistributed, and there is also a balanced budget, clearly

$$\sum_{i=1}^{i=m} (g_i^l + g_i^c) - \sum_{i=1}^{i=m} (t_i^d + t_i^e) = 0.$$

165

Defining the task is one thing, but to carry it out is another. Even as formulated, we have oversimplified it, ignoring such complications as the scope of the budget – whether it covers all layers of government and the social security system – the extent to which certain fiscal charges should be regarded as taxes, and so on. So far as the measurement game is concerned, one can say without fear of contradiction that the major effort of fiscal economists in such studies has been devoted to the role of the theory of tax incidence in allocating t^d and t^e.[2] Richard Musgrave has been a major influence in these studies, but he has also reminded us that '. . . any meaningful theory or policy of public finance must ultimately combine the issues posed by the two sides of the budget. This, indeed, is the cardinal principle of the economist's view of public finance. The distributional implications of expenditure policy, therefore, pose an important further problem' (Musgrave, 1964).

This contribution in his honour offers a critical examination of some of the methods employed in order to put this principle into practice.

II. Some Preliminary Matters

Before examining in detail the actual methods employed in allocating government expenditure by income group, two preliminary matters need to be investigated. The first is that we must be clear exactly what is the nature of the comparison being made between pre- and post-budget income. The second concerns the argument that it may be reasonable to contract out of the allocation of government expenditure in whole or in part.

There are various approaches to the problem of comparison, but we may concentrate on examination of the most extensive discussion in recent years by Gillespie (1965a,b). He employs the good old classical technique of 'conjectural history'. One imagines a community in which at time, t, individuals exist in a state of nature (in the political philosophers' sense of the term!) with no method available for satisfying social wants by goods available for consumption in equal amounts by all, and presumably, although this is not mentioned by the author, no wish to redistribute income other than by voluntary action. At time, $t + 1$, like John Locke's percipient members of the community, a social contract is made, the 'device of government' is introduced, and, in Gillespie's words, a 'complete adjustment' is made to the public sector. A comparison is being made, therefore, between income distribution in a state of nature and income distribution after the relative position of individuals (households) has been altered through fiscal action, following the introduction of government. The technical term for this comparison is *fiscal incidence*.

There is no objection to comparing actual situations with hypothetical ones in economics – we do it all the time. One has doubts, however, about the usefulness of this particular fiction as a way of exploring fiscal incidence. For one thing, in modern societies, presumably *some* public action is a prerequisite for the existence of most income-producing activities. This point was early recognized in the literature of fiscal incidence for, as Rottier and Albert (1954) put it, 'it is not possible to conceive of an initial income distribution which does not reflect a number of important interventions by the state power' (p. 92). Secondly, the introduction of public goods presumably alters the factor and personal income distribution before any allowance is made for the measurement of the burdens and benefits of the budget. It is not plausible to assume that public production is simply substituted for private production, for the very nature of the postulated change in the economy is an alteration in the production pattern; nor does it seem reasonable to assume in a general equilibrium setting that the alteration in production structure does not alter the distribution of national income in the social accounting sense.

These points, while they must be dealt with or conveniently ignored, and, while they will crop up again in this analysis, are less fundamental than the implications for the measurement of the redistributory effects of the budget of an assumed change in taste in the community which suddenly requires the exercise of choice through the political instead of the price mechanism. The very term 'redistribution' suggests compulsion, but if the community agrees that the political mechanism is the only means by which desirable indivisible public services can be provided, in what sense does compulsion exist? As we shall argue later, the measurement of the benefits of indivisible services crucially depends on an answer to this question.

Having defined the nature of fiscal incidence, one could pass straightaway to discussion of the allocation of government expenditure on goods and services by income group. Many studies, however, for one reason or another, contract out, wholly or in part, from allocating these expenditures. Knowing in advance that allocation is difficult, it seems worth considering the rationale for avoiding what might be unnecessary trouble.

The first example is provided by those many studies which concentrate on measuring the effect of taxes and transfers on the size distribution of incomes.[3] There are two characteristics of this approach. The first is that the comparison is being made between an initial *personal* distribution of income,

$$\sum_{i=1}^{i=m} y_i^0$$

(assuming no undistributed income), and the distribution of final disposable income,

$$\sum_{i=1}^{i=m} y_i^0 - \sum_{i=1}^{i=m} (t_i^d - g_i^t).$$

It follows that there is no particular reason other than chance why the pre- and post-tax transfer income totals should be the same, i.e., why

$$\sum_{i=1}^{i=m} t^{\mathrm{d}} = \sum_{i=1}^{i=m} g^{\mathrm{l}}.$$

According to Nicholson (1964) 'income after direct taxes and benefits . . . has a more tangible and general significance than post-redistribution income', the argument appearing to be that this is the income over which the individual exercises control as well as being much more readily amenable to calculation than some final income which includes both the allocation of taxes on expenditure and government expenditure on goods and services.

It may readily be agreed that a comparison at a point in time and over time between the distribution of personal and disposable income by income groups has its policy uses. A policy for stabilization may very well require some indication of the effect of the tax structure, not only on the size but also on the distribution of disposable income, because of the possibility of differing marginal propensities to consume of different income groups. A policy for growth which places some emphasis on the need to view the effects of the tax system on personal incentives might find it useful as background information to examine the distributional effects of personal taxes and transfers, although in countries with extensive state welfare services offered in kind there is an immediate query about confining attention to money transfers only.

But the traditional and presumably the main purpose of such studies is to offer information useful for the pursuit of distributional objectives, and in this connection they are likely to be seriously misleading. A simple example makes this point. Imagine that the government increases transfer payments to lower incomes and finances them by a cut in defence expenditure *or* education expenditure *or* by an increase in the sales tax. The registered distributional effect on disposable income would in all three cases be the same, if the method under discussion were used, but clearly the real incomes of different income groups would be appreciably and variously affected by each postulated change.[4]

One possible further way of contracting out of the allocation of indivisible goods and services is to argue that those government services most likely to be directed toward the alteration of the income distribution are often of a contractual nature, such as social security schemes and welfare schemes partly financed by earmarked taxes. Even if these items cover only part of the overall government budget, the taxes and expenditures are likely to be those most relevant to the economic conditions of those for whom the community is likely to feel most concern – the lower income ranges.[5] There are difficulties encountered in carrying out even this more modest task of allocation, apart from such obvious ones as agreeing on the allocation of payroll taxes paid by employers. The first is that the very fact there is some contractual element suggests that one should compare the taxes or contributions paid and the benefits received over the length of the contract. In the case of retirement pensions, for example, the relevant redistributory effect to the individual depends on the relation between the present value of contractual benefits on retirement and the present value of the contributions to be paid over working life. In any case, this example suggests that, at a moment in time, the interest in redistribution centres not in the position of the individual income receivers, but in other groupings, such as the position of the working population *vis-à-vis* the retired population, the healthy *vis-à-vis* the sick, and so on.

A further difficulty is presented by the awkward fact that in some countries the government may subsidize social security and other welfare schemes by a contribution from general taxation. In considering the redistributory effects of the British Welfare State some years ago, the present author tried to avoid this problem by postulating that the proportions in which general taxes are raised by the government were independent of the financing requirements of welfare expenditure. Any subsidy received from general taxation was therefore assumed to be financed by direct and indirect taxes according to the proportions of these taxes in the general budget (see Peacock and Browning, 1954). In retrospect this can only be regarded as no more than a plausible subterfuge.

The analysis so far simply confirms Musgrave's conclusion that partial results are no substitute for a study of the overall effects of the budget, and are also misleading; to quote: 'Those special benefits which can be allocated tend to be distributed such that the ratio of benefits to income falls when moving up the income scale; and the corresponding benefit taxes tend to be regressive. The resulting impression is little redistribution' (1964, p. 211). Striking confirmation of this result is to be found in the calculations published by the British Central Statistical Office from time to time in the official publication *Economic Trends*. These calculations show that the welfare benefits received by households in lower income groups are, broadly speaking, much less than the taxes paid, but this result is obtained by the allocation of benefits whose total money value in the public budget is only *half* the allocated taxes! The result may have some interest, but no conclusion can be drawn about the redistributory effects of public finance.[6]

III. ALLOCATION OF GOVERNMENT RESOURCE-USING EXPENDITURES: THE ISSUES

Having agreed to invoke the Musgravian principle of allocating both sides of the budget, we have to identify the government expenditure relevant to our calculation and seek some principles for allocating it. (Government transfers to persons and subsidies to firms are already disposed of as negative direct and indirect taxes respectively.)

First of all, let us deal with two problems in social accounting. Government expenditure on goods and services is conventionally regarded in national income accounting as part of final output, and following this convention we should assume it is part of the flow of national output enjoyed currently by the community. It may not be very helpful to stir the embers of an old controversy, but there is clearly a sense in which Kuznets (1953) is right in arguing that some government expenditure on goods and services could be regarded as intermediate goods, i.e., goods used up in producing national income and which otherwise would have to be supplied, if they could be, by industry itself in order to achieve the same annual output. However, we may be content to abide by current social accounting conventions and disregard a proposition which would involve us in the gigantic task of having to redefine the national income.

The second problem is whether or not to include government capital expenditure as a benefit to individuals in the year in which it occurs. Aaron and McGuire (1970) have criticized this procedure, which has been used in several studies, on the grounds that the only benefits relevant to individuals are the current benefits and these may accrue to additional government investment not only in the current but in future years. Highway expenditures are an obvious example, but the same argument could conceivably be applied to human capital formation and therefore to at least some part of government expenditures on education. They describe the problem as 'serious'. It seems to me that two issues need to be distinguished. Remembering that what we are trying to do is to reallocate a *given* national income, what is recorded in the national income accounts is that taxes are being levied on persons in order to add to capital formation by the government, assuming that there is an overall budget balance. This represents a reallocation of national expenditure by political forces, presumably on the grounds that this would achieve a better allocation of resources than would otherwise take place if the market were the only mechanism of choice. There is no reason, therefore, why the money value of government investment expenditures should be treated any differently from the money value of current expenditures on goods and services and not be allocated to the period in which investment occurs, for the value of the investment at the margin is the present con- sumption forgone. Investment takes place now presumably because the community derives a present satisfaction from conferring benefits on future users of government services which is greater at the margin than the satisfaction derived from a transfer of resources to either private use or to public use as current expenditure on goods and services. For the purpose of defining the scope of government expenditure to be allocated in any redistribution study, the allocation of the stream of benefits generated by investment incurred now is irrelevant, although such investment, as in the case of investment in human capital, may have a pronounced effect on the amount and distribution of future national income. The issue as to how to *allocate* such investment expenditure among income groups is a separate one, and one may very well question the procedure by which, for example, the annual increase in the capital stock of highways is allocated by the simple expedient of estimating individual use of highways (cf. Gillespie, 1965b, pp. 140–5).

Having defined the scope of the expenditure on goods and services to be allocated, the next set of problems concerns their distribution according to income group. We would have an exact analogue with tax allocation if the government provided specific services for certain defined groups in the community. Just as money transfers to individuals may be treated as negative direct taxes, the value of government services provided at zero prices could be regarded as an indirect transfer. This would be the extreme case of a negative indirect tax of the same genre as subsidies offered to private firms for the purpose of lowering prices to consumers. Although there are certainly problems encountered in determining the incidence of benefits, in principle all that we have to do is to seek some means of identifying by income groups those who directly utilize the service in question.

The division of cost of inputs according to utilization as representative of the division of benefits from the service is clearly questionable. If we take the case of primary and secondary education, consumption is compulsory. Children and even parents (where children might currently be earning) may not measure the benefits as 'worth' the value of inputs, but, given the level of service provided, presumably the 'undervaluation' by parents and children is compensated by the valuation placed by the community as a whole on the external economies of education. This suggests that some fraction of the cost of government services, which in all other respects are like privately produced services, should not be allocated to those households which utilize the service. There are two possible counter-arguments. The first is the pragmatic one that the division between 'external' and 'specific' benefit must be purely arbitrary. The rejoinder may be offered that this suggests that one makes a range of alternative estimates of the division of cost. The second counter-argument is that the externalities of consumption arise through individual utilization of the service. In the private sector we do not revalue or reallocate national expenditure to reflect consumption externalities, so why should we do so in the case of public production of specific goods? The answer surely lies in the fact that the *level* of public production is a function not of individual valuation of the services reflected in prices paid directly for them, but of a community valuation reflected in political decision-making.

So far we have argued as if the state only produced goods which could otherwise be privately produced, and which, in principle, could be priced. State services such as defence and law and order, which form a considerable proportion of expenditure on goods and services in most public budgets, do not fall into this category for the usual well-known reasons. They are presumed to be 'enjoyed' equally by all, i.e., are indivisible, and to be capable of efficient and acceptable provision only through compulsory levies by the state. This familiar public goods problem clearly poses a difficulty so far as the allocation of money value of these services is concerned which is on all fours with the identification and allocation of the money values which reflect the external benefits of specific services.

The commonly accepted way of dealing with this difficulty is to adopt one or all of a number of assumptions about the distribution of these expenditures which in some way reflects a distribution of benefits. For example, Gillespie (1965b, p. 132) distributes expenditures from defence, law and order, space research, and technology as follows: (i) per family; (ii) by income; (iii) by capital income; and (iv) by disposable income. The first method adopts an 'equal' benefit assumption, the remainder assume differential benefits according to some concept of the individual family's 'stake' in protection of its earning power or capital assets. The main criticism of this approach is that there is only implicit acknowledgment of the need to construct some sort of utility function. For example, as pointed out by Aaron and McGuire (1970), whose alternative approach is examined in detail below, the allocation of public goods expenditure equally among families implicitly assumes, if public goods are enjoyed equally by all, that the marginal utility of income is constant as income rises.

Before examining alternative approaches to the allocation of government expenditures on goods and services it may give some indication of what is at issue if one examines whether or not the allocation of expenditures by whatever method does appreciably affect the results of calculations of the effects of the budget on the distribution of income. In the extensive study of Gillespie already referred to, this is certainly the case. If one confines the study of the budget impact to the federal level of government where the major expenditure item is defence, the allocation of taxes alone would not distort the distributional picture, but only provided it is reasonable to allocate indivisible expenditures proportionately to income level. However, at the state and local level, the direct benefits are substantial and, according to the author, have a 'pro-poor' bias, with the result that the overall fiscal structure is more favourable to lower income groups than the tax structure alone would suggest. It is to be noted that Gillespie allocates specific services entirely to users and makes no allowance for any externalities.

IV. The Application of the Theory of Public Goods to Benefit Allocation

The above analysis has shown that public financiers have been unwilling to do more than to state the dilemma presented by the fact that those government expenditures on goods and services identified as indivisible cannot be allocated according to 'use'. There has been no explicit attempt, at least in the full-scale empirical studies so far available, to derive principles for allocation of these expenditures from the general theory of consumer equilibrium which embraces the case of public goods. However, in an article to which passing reference has already been made, Aaron and McGuire (1970) have stepped in where others have feared to tread, and their original contribution to the debate merits close attention.

To preserve methodological symmetry, it is useful to begin by stating how they propose public goods should be allocated. Recalling our previous notation, and slightly adapting it, we first of all calculate 'private-type' or 'product-received' income, i.e., income after all taxes, transfers, and specific benefits (g_i^s) are allocated for each income class, i.e., for income class, i:

$$y_i^r \equiv y_i^0 + (g_i^l + g_i^s) - (t_i^d + t_i^e).$$

The procedure leaves an unallocated total expenditure for public goods (which can include the imputed money value of the general benefits accruing to the community from production of specific goods). We then hypothesize a schedule of the marginal utility of private-type income which we use to distribute the residual expenditure on public goods so that $\partial U_i / \partial y^r$ times the family's share of public goods expenditure is the same for all representative families, noting that the sum of the allocations weighted by the number of families in each income class must add to the total residual expenditure. The relevant pre- and post-allocation comparison is between y_i^0 and $(y_i^r + g_i^p)$. The derivation of this allocation rule cannot be given in detail, but a brief idea must be conveyed of the difficult hurdles which have to be leapt over (or circumvented!). First of all a utility schedule is postulated for the individual, which assumes that the utilities of public goods and private goods are independent, enabling us to write

$$U_i = U_i^y(y_i^r) + U_i^p(\mathbf{P}),$$

where $\mathbf{P}$ is a vector of the physical quantities of public goods. Secondly, it is assumed that the allocation of resources to public goods is Pareto-efficient and that the average cost of production equals marginal cost for public goods $(MC_p = AC_p)$. Following the familiar Bowen–Samuelson allocation rule, the efficiency condition becomes $\sum t_i = \sum MRS_i = MC_i$, i.e., in order to obtain an efficient level of public goods provision, we *sum* the *MRS* for all individuals. The third assumption is that all family utility functions are identical so that the partial derivative of U_i with respect to $\mathbf{P}$ is the same for all families. Employing these three assumptions, it is possible to construct a very simple formula which shows that each household should be imputed a fraction of the total value of public goods proportional to the reciprocal of its marginal utility of income.

Within this framework, one is still left with the problem of identifying individual utility schedules. The authors nail their colours firmly to the Edgworthian mast and use 'plausible' (*sic*) utility functions illustrating the famous law of diminishing marginal utility of income. If MU_{y^r} declines as y^r rises, then clearly the income value of public goods rises as we move up the income scale. The results of allocating the benefits are very sensitive not only to the utility schedule chosen but also to the amount of indivisible expenditures identified. This depends not merely on the identification of the 'commonly accepted' indivisible services, such as defence, law and order, etc., but also on the proportion of the costs of specific goods which are allocated as public goods.

The authors then compare their results with those prepared for the Tax Foundation (1970) by Bishop, which allocate indivisible expenditures on a per family basis, making no allowances for any indivisible element in specific expenditures. Some specimen results showing the final net income redistribution per family for selected income groups are given in Table 12.1.

TABLE 12.1   *Net income redistribution, 1961*

	Net gain or loss ($-$) per family		
Money income class	Under $2000	$5000 to $5999	$15 000 and over
I. *Allocation NE:*[a]			
1. Tax foundation	$1493	$125	$$-$10 632
2. $U = A \log Y^c$	968	113	$-$8682
3. $U = E - C/Y^c$	691	$-$359	1790
II. *Allocation E:*[b]			
1. Tax foundation	$1427	$115	$$-$10 048
2. $U = A \log Y$	640	100	$-$7019
3. $U = E - C/Y$	313	$-$567	8373

[a] Allocation NE includes no allowance for external benefits of specific goods.

[b] Allocation E assumes the following proportions of the cost of specific goods are allocable as public goods – elementary and secondary education (0.7), higher education (0.5), public assistance and other welfare expenditures (0.3), labour (0.3), veteran benefits (0.3), streets and highways (0.5), agriculture (0.5), net interest (0), social insurance (0.3).

[c] In the utility functions, income (Y) is 'product received' income; and A, E, and C are arbitrary constants, whose values do not affect the results.

Source: H. Aaron and M. McGuire, 'Public Goods and Income Distribution', *Econometrica*, Vol. 38, No. 6, November 1970, table III, p. 919.

The authors offer a careful examination of their results, but it is sufficient for our purpose to note that these cast doubt on the view that taking account of government expenditure results in a considerable redistribution of income from higher to lower income groups.

It would be churlish not to recognize that the authors have offered the public financier a big and juicy bone to chew over, but its digestibility is a matter for debate. I do not wish to deal at any length with obvious queries. How acceptable is the assumption that the utilities of public and private goods are independent? Is it reasonable to use a utility function which varies with income, but not by family size *within* income groups? One would like to dwell for some time in the area of specific benefit allocation. It seems a little unfair for the authors to criticize others for using implicit utility functions in allocating benefits which are open to question and then to adopt only one set of weights, whose rationale is not explained, for the cost of specific goods allocable as public goods. This is particularly important in the case of direct transfer payments, which form over half the specific goods benefits in the lowest income group. If, as the authors claim, benefits are valued purely in terms of exchange value, so that infra-marginal utility gains are not included, how can one assume it possible to regard transfers as partly public goods, when transfers are additions to *income* and not to *expenditure*? The most one can do is to assume that the administrative costs of transfer schemes represent the indivisible element, but, although I have no access to relevant data, these are presumably less than 30% of the total expenditures on social insurance.

However, a much more crucial point harks back to our earlier discussion (section II) of the evaluation of political choices. It will be agreed that public goods confer utility, but are not consumed in the usual sense, and that non-excludability from enjoyment of them normally means that they cannot be provided by the market. The implicit assumption in the Aaron/McGuire analysis and, it would seem, most studies of redistribution, is that preference revelation through the political mechanism cannot be any guide to the allocation of benefits, even though such a mechanism is a necessary condition for the provision of indivisible goods. Individual members of the community must trade off the disutility of a compulsory solution, e.g., as would result from majority voting, against the disutility of nil provision of public goods. Working at the same level of abstraction as Aaron and McGuire, some allowance for this awkward fact of life must be made in individual utility functions. This is one reason why, following Musgrave, public financiers are prepared to risk the wrath of Samuelson (1969) in continuing to recognize the merits of the Lindahl approach to public goods allocation which sees an analogue in the political mechanism to a pricing solution. Followed to its logical conclusion, assuming that the system of public finance is only concerned with allocation of indivisible goods and services, Lindahl's solution is Pareto-efficient, for clearly if $MRS_i = t_i$ for all households, the condition $\sum MRS_i = \sum t_i$ is met. The allocation rule which follows is that public goods benefits are distributed simply according to the allocation of taxes! Even if the Lindahl solution postulates unanimity in decision-making, and is a very special case, it seems just as plausible a starting-point for discussion of the allocation of indivisible benefits as one which ignores any reference to the political bargaining process.[7]

This line of reasoning leads us toward further difficulties. The very acceptance of the externalities present in a wide range of government services which are not indivisible prompts the question why the community is willing to finance them by redistributive taxation. Unless one postulates that the tax system is totally unresponsive to voters' pressures and then only to the pressures of those who are taxed the least, the allocation procedure adopted by Aaron and McGuire can only be explained if there is interdependence among individual utility functions. More specifically, this interdependence suggests than an increase in the welfare of the poor confers a positive utility on the rich. No 'ethical observer' is needed to pronounce on the need for redistribution and no benevolent dictator to enforce it. The rich have a positive incentive to confer benefits on the poor, and this should be reflected in the tax/transfer system. If Hochman and Rodgers (1969) are to be believed, then here is evidence that the actual tax/transfer system in the u.s.a. (using, incidentally, the Gillespie data) is more than a pale reflection of this assumption. There is therefore force in the argument that the efficiency criterion which governs the process of allocation of public goods by income groups must also comprehend the distributive goal as manifested in the actual tax/transfer structure.[8]

To sum up. Once we accept that the political system is not a device simply for the imposition of government decisions which exists independently of individual choice, then individual utility functions must reflect the individual's opportunities for influencing the amount and composition of the budget. Equally, however, it would be naive to say that the political system is so perfectly adjusted to the wishes of the community that we can regard its operations as optimal in the Paretian sense, for this would mean that *by definition* the redistributory impact of the budget is always nil! It is worth passing mention that East European writers reject the use of the term 'redistribution' for it clearly implies that the planned economy would not generate an income distribution in accordance with the People's will. The distributional objectives are laid down by the Plan, so that public finance is used, not as a corrective force, but as a 'positive' planning instrument, among others, to achieve popularly accepted objectives (see Branik, 1968).

V. Concluding Remarks

Rationalizing the omission of the allocation of government goods and services in redistribution calculations is a convenient but inadmissible procedure. Attempting to derive utility functions which assume no connection between individual consumer decisions and the political process in order to attempt their allocation leads to arbitrary results.

Our previous criticisms of the way in which utility functions have been postulated point to another line of enquiry, but one which admittedly, runs into its own particular problems. Direct enquiry from households about their evaluation of government services could, in principle, be used to obtain information on preference structure but is bedevilled by technical as well as psychological obstacles. Here I can only repeat previously expressed doubts (Peacock and Shannon, 1968; see also Dorfman, 1969, pp. 271–3). Individuals asked to evaluate the contribution of public goods to their welfare may be shy of preference revelation if the answers might be used as some sort of a guide to tax policy. The kind of questions asked may relate to policy decisions, e.g., about defence policy, which seem far removed from their experience and which may seem to have little bearing on their immediate welfare. Devising questions which offer information on alternative tax/expenditure patterns is extremely difficult, and, representing purely hypothetical choice situations, such questions may not produce satisfactory answers.

At the same time, the very fact that such surveys are likely to produce such results might itself give some indication of the kinds of changes in the political system which are necessary, if it is desired to articulate more clearly the preferences of the community, including their view of the redistributory functions of the budget. This rather cryptic statement will no doubt fail to satisfy those who would prefer to be able to state, without fear of contradiction, that such-and-such fiscal measures will produce a measurable amount of change in the concentration coefficient. Those who, on the other hand, are not prepared to accept the analytical and statistical short cuts found in conventional procedures and are resigned to the resulting inconvenience of imprecision in estimation may care to recall the words of Hugh Dalton (1929, p. 15) in his attempt to extricate himself from the difficulties of explaining the principle of maximum social advantage: 'Those who are oppressed by a sense of difficulty of this calculus, should console themselves with the saying of the Ancient Greeks that "it is not the easy things, but the difficult things, that are beautiful" '!

NOTES

1. Written when the author was Visiting Research Professor in Economics at the Fondazione Luigi Einaudi, Turin, Italy. He gratefully acknowledges the support received from the Fondazione and the comments received from Onerato Castellino, Bruno Contini, Franco Reviglio, and Luigi Tomasini. Reproduced with minor amendments from W. L. Smith and J. Culbertson (eds) *Public Finance and Stabilization Policy: Essays in Honor of R. A. Musgrave*, North Holland, Amsterdam, 1974.
2. For a useful survey of modern tax incidence theory, see Mieszkowski (1969).
3. For bibliography see Musgrave (1964) and Gillespie (1965a).
4. It will again be noted how difficult 'before and after' comparisons become, for account must be taken of the multiplier effects on the size and distribution of personal income as a result of the alternative (hypothetical) budgetary changes.

5. Nicholson (1964) puts the proposition in negative terms in presenting his original estimates for the U.K.: 'The present estimates take no account of the advantages (or disadvantages) which the whole population derives from government expenditure on administration, defence, police, roads, public buildings, parks, ceremonies, and so on. Some of these things, aptly termed regrettable necessities, would not normally be regarded as bringing tangible benefits to individual households.'
6. This is only one of a number of criticisms which can be made of the British calculations. For a fuller analysis, see Peacock and Shannon (1968).
7. There is an interesting parallel here with the attempts to determine the social time preference rate in cost–benefit analysis. There is a firm division between those who would, like Eckstein (1961), derive such a rate from postulated utility functions of present and future generations and those who consider that the STP can only 'emerge' from a political decision taken by present generations.
8. It is recognized that there would be many matters left over for explanation, and particularly the important question of the *form* in which transfers are effected, e.g., as between goods in kind and cash.

REFERENCES

Aaron, H. and McGuire, M. C. (1970) 'Benefits and burdens of government expenditure' *Econometrica* Vol. 38, No. 6, November.

Branik, J. (1968) 'Le budget et la distribution du revenue national' *Public Finance* Vol. 23, Nos. 1/2.

Dalton, H. (1929) *Principles of Public Finance* 5th edition, Routledge, London.

Dorfman, R. (1969) 'General equilibrium with public goods' in J. Margolis and H. Guitton (eds) *Public Economics* Macmillan, London.

Eckstein, O. (1961) 'A survey of the theory of public expenditure criteria' in J. M. Buchanan (ed.) *Public Finances: Needs, Sources and Utilisation* National Bureau of Economic Research, Princeton.

Gillespie, W. I. (1965a) 'Effect of public expenditures on the distribution of income' in R. A. Musgrave (ed.) *Essays in Fiscal Federalism* The Brookings Institution, Washington, D.C.

Gillespie, W. I. (1965b) 'The incidence of taxes and public expenditures' in *The Canadian Economy* a study prepared for the Royal Commission on Taxation, Ottawa.

Hochman, H. M. and Rodgers, J. D. (1969) 'Pareto optimal redistribution' *American Economic Review* Vol. 59, No. 4, September, pp. 542–57.

Kuznets, S. (1953) 'Government product and national income' in G. Stuvel (ed.) *Income and Wealth: Series 1* Bowes & Bowes, Cambridge.

Mieszkowski, P. (1969) 'Tax incidence theory: The effects of taxes on the distribution of income' *Journal of Economic Literature* Vol. 7, No. 4, December.

Musgrave, R. A. (1964) 'Estimating the distribution of the tax burden' in C. Clark and G. Stuvel (eds) *Income Redistribution and the Statistical Foundations of Economic Policy, Income and Wealth: Series X* Bowes & Bowes, Cambridge.

Nicholson, J. L. (1964) 'Redistribution of income in the United Kingdom in 1959, 1957, and 1953' in Clark and Stuvel *op. cit.*

Peacock, A. T. and Browning, P. (1954) 'The social services and income redistribution in Great Britain' in A. T. Peacock (ed.) *Income Redistribution and Social Policy* Jonathan Cape, London.

Peacock, A. T. and Shannon, R. (1968) 'The welfare state and the redistribution of income' *Westminster Bank Review* August.

Rottier, G. and Albert, J. (1954) 'The social services and income redistribution in France' in A. T. Peacock *op. cit.*

Samuelson, P. A. (1969) 'The pure theory of public expenditure and taxation' in Margolis and Guitton *op. cit.*

Tax Foundation, Inc. (1970) *Tax Burdens and Benefits of Government Expenditures, 1961 and 1965, 1967* quoted in Aaron and McGuire.

CHAPTER 13

The Multiplier and the Valuation of Government Expenditures[1]

I. INTRODUCTION

In two recent contributions (Bailey, 1962, pp. 72–4; 1971, pp. 153–4; and Shoup, 1969, pp. 563–5) attention is drawn to the interesting possibility that households may value government expenditures as income and that, in consequence, private consumption, usually assumed independent of government expenditure on current goods and services, may be a decreasing function of such government expenditures. This seems reasonable, given that households' consumption may be affected, as Bailey suggests, by other forms of personal income received in kind, such as meals supplied free at the place of work.

The purpose of this note is to review and to comment on the conclusions drawn from this proposition by Bailey and Shoup, an essential feature of which is that they modify the standard results obtained from integrating public sector transactions in the conventional multiplier analysis.

II. ANALYSIS[2]

Assume that all components of national expenditure (Y) are valued at constant prices, then, following Bailey, we re-write the conventional consumption function as:

$$C + \overline{G}_c = a + b[Y + \overline{G} - \overline{T}] \tag{1}$$

where C = consumption by households

$\overline{G}_c$ = government consumption expenditure

$\overline{G}_i$ = government investment expenditure

$\overline{G}$ = total government expenditure on goods and services

$(\overline{G} = \overline{G}_c + \overline{G}_i)$

$\overline{T} =$ autonomous tax yield

$a =$ constant term in consumption functions

$b =$ consumption coefficient.

With a continuously balanced budget where $G = T$, the consumption function reduces to:

$$C = a - \overline{G}_c + bY.$$

With the further component in national expenditure represented in the usual way by $\overline{I} =$ autonomous investment, then:

$$Y = [a - \overline{G}_c + \overline{I} + \overline{G}] \cdot \frac{1}{(1 - b)} \tag{2}$$

$$= [a + \overline{G}_i + \overline{I}] \cdot \frac{1}{(1 - b)} \tag{2a}$$

It follows that, if Y is in equilibrium and government expenditure *on consumption goods* is increased and financed by an equal increase in taxes, then:

$$\frac{\partial Y}{\partial G_c} = 0, \tag{3}$$

since G_c does not enter (2a).

In other words, the 'standard' balanced-budget multiplier conclusion no longer holds when households view government consumption as part of income and value it at cost.

The same problem is treated in a slightly different way by Shoup (1969) who considers the situation in which one group of households pays taxes in order to finance goods and services which benefit non-taxed households. We reach his conclusions using an alternative formulation from Shoup which is a natural extension of (1) and (2) above.

We identify a consumption function for taxpayers and non-taxpayers. The first group receives a proportion, c, of national income and pays all (invariant) taxes but receives no benefits, whereas the second group receives $(1 - c)$ of national income and regards all government expenditure on goods and services as an increase in real income equal to the cost of the services provided. Thus:

$$C_1 = a_1 + b_1(cY - \overline{T})$$

$$C_2 + \overline{G}_c = a_2 + b_2[(1 - c)Y + \overline{G}_c] \tag{4}$$

where a_1, $a_2 =$ constant terms in consumption functions

b_1, $b_2 =$ consumption coefficients.

Substituting $C_1 + C_2 = C$ in (2) above enables us to re-write the national expenditure formula as:

$$Y = [A + \overline{G} - \overline{G}_c(1 + b_1 - b_2)] \cdot \frac{1}{1 - c(b_1 - b_2) - b_2} \tag{5}$$

where $A = \overline{I} + (a_1 + a_2)$.

Now if $\overline{G}_c = \overline{G} = \overline{T}$, as before, and $b_1, b_2 < 1$ as normally assumed, then

$$\frac{\partial Y}{\partial G} \lesseqgtr 0 \text{ as } b_2 \lesseqgtr b_1 .$$

In other words, if the consumption coefficients are the same for both taxed and untaxed sectors, the balanced-budget multiplier effect is zero, but if the untaxed sector has a higher (lower) consumption coefficient, the balanced-budget multiplier will be positive (negative).

III. COMMENT

This analysis offers a useful extension of the examination of fiscal changes on consumer behaviour, but poses a number of problems. Consider, for example, the assumption that all government expenditure is designed to benefit the untaxed group. Under what conditions is it reasonable to accept the further, strong, assumption that the untaxed households value this expenditure *at cost*? For example, if the cost is £200, then should this sum be regarded as equivalent to an increase in *total income* of £200. Households would so value these goods if they *could be traded*, i.e. could be converted into some numeraire good and, if so desired, could be exchanged for other goods. If this were so, and neglecting any costs of trading, then traded goods would have the same effect as a straight money transfer[3].

What happens, as is typically the case with several important government services, if the goods cannot be traded? In the Shoup example, where a redistribution of income is envisaged, it is very likely that the 'rich' will be willing to support redistribution to the poor (i.e. derive utility from doing so) only if such redistribution takes the form of subsidised consumption of non-traded goods, e.g. education and health services, of which they approve[4]. We can first of all conclude, given the usual assumptions about individual utility functions, that the non-taxed households will regard themselves as better off than in a situation without any government services, but not so well off as in a situation in which the goods could be traded. This follows from the proposition that, unless the publicly provided good is a perfect substitute at the margin for private consumption, the 'representative' non-taxed household will be placed on a lower indifference curve than in the case where trading is possible and where it has greater freedom to maximise. Consider, for example, hospital services provided free by the government to non-taxed households. These services can only be utilised by recipients. In such a case, there is no reason why households receiving free hospitalisation would value such a service at cost, *and* that the community as a whole (i.e. both taxed and untaxed households) would reduce total consumption expenditure by the cost of the free service, unless exactly the cost of the free service would otherwise have been spent on hospital services by the non-taxed households if they had to pay for them themselves.

A diagrammatic illustration may be helpful. Consider a 'representative' non-taxed household which has already achieved its optimal allocation of a given income $0B$ in Figure 13.1, all goods prices being constant. It is now faced with a new choice situation in which, without loss of income, it is

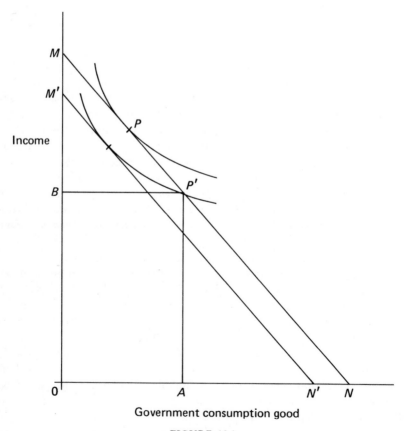

Government consumption good

FIGURE 13.1

offered a given quantum of a government consumption (g.c.) good, $0A$. If the g.c. good can be traded, then, with conventionally drawn indifference curves representing the choice between 'all other goods' (income) and the g.c. good, it will convert part of the g.c. good into some numeraire good and increase its expenditure on all other goods. In other words, its opportunity slope is given by MN, and its new optimal position will be at P. Because the household can convert, if it so wished, the whole of the g.c. good into all other goods, its valuation of the addition to its income (BM) will equal the cost of the amount of the g.c. good on offer. But if the g.c. good cannot be traded, its opportunity slope becomes $BP'A$, and the best that the household can do is to optimise at P' which is on a lower indifference curve from P. Valuation of the income equivalent is given by the point of tangency of an indifference curve passing through P' and a line parallel to MN, say $M'N'$. The new valuation of the government consumption good *as income* is now $BM' < BM$. Of course, the diagram cannot illustrate any alteration in the 'mix' of private consumption goods following from the availability of the free g.c. good.

In the Shoup analysis, if the individual values the g.c. good as income, say, £200, then total household consumption would rise by £200 $\times b_2$. If $b_2 = 0.8$, total consumption will rise by £160, but as, *by assumption*, households consume *all* the g.c. good on offer, private consumption must fall by £40. In our diagram, this is equivalent to a situation where the indifference curves are parallel with MN, i.e. there is perfect substitutability between the g.c. good and all other goods, and trading is permitted. We then have the peculiar result that the individual is indifferent between a pure transfer payment of amount BM and consumption of the whole amount of the g.c. good on offer, $0A$. On the other hand, in the 'traditional' analysis, what is being assumed is that the indifference curves of the non-taxed households, and, indeed, of all households, are horizontal, or in other words, that households value free services at zero.

We are now in a position to offer a simple general formulation based on the above comments. We postulate a 'reaction coefficient' of the untaxed households such that if the government consumption good is perfectly tradeable then the coefficient (g_2) takes a value of 1, but if it is not fully tradeable, then $g_2 < 1$, and, in the extreme case represented by the 'traditional' formulation, $g_2 = 0$. In the general formulation we assume that only untaxed households have a reaction coefficient.

Then

$$C_2 + g_2\overline{G}_c = a_2 + b_2[(1-c)Y + g_2\overline{G}_c] \tag{6}$$

and, assuming $G = T = G_c$, and substituting in (5), we have

$$Y = \{A + \overline{G}[1 - b_1 - g_2(1 - b_2)]\} \cdot \frac{1}{1 - c(b_1 - b_2) - b_2}. \tag{7}$$

In the Shoup analysis, $g_2 = 1$, so we obtain our earlier result, viz.

$$\frac{\partial Y}{\partial G} \lesseqgtr 0 \qquad \text{as } b_2 \lesseqgtr b_1 .$$

In the 'traditional' analysis, $g_2 = 0$, so we have

$$\frac{\partial Y}{\partial G} > 0, \text{ and } \frac{\partial Y}{\partial G} = 1, \text{ if } b_1 = b_2 .$$

Our analysis suggests that intermediate cases would be more usual, with $1 > g_2 > 0$, so that

$$\frac{\partial Y}{\partial G} \lesseqgtr 0, \text{ as } \frac{(1 - b_1)}{(1 - b_2)} > g_2 .$$

We cannot be sure that $\partial Y/\partial G > 0$, but there is a strong likelihood that it will be, unless b_2 far exceeds b_1. Clearly, if $b_1 = b_2 < 1$, the balanced-budget multiplier will be positive.

To sum up, Bailey and Shoup offer a useful hypothesis but, in setting it to work to modify the usual balanced-budget multiplier analysis, they use questionable assumptions about the choice situation facing consumers and about their maximising behaviour. The vital element in the choice situation is whether or not the free public consumption goods can or cannot be traded, for this affects the households' valuation of the p.c. goods as income: the distinction is ignored in their analysis. Secondly, their analysis requires that there is perfect substitutability between goods purchased in the private sector and goods provided free by the public sector – surely a rather extreme position.

NOTES

1. Reproduced from *Finanzarchiv* Vol. 30, No. 3, 1972. I am indebted to Paul Burrows and Tony Culyer for a number of useful comments.
2. This analysis is confined to the 'balanced-budget' case. For a perceptive examination of unbalanced-budget cases, see Bailey (1971) pp. 155–62.
3. If taxed households simply provide money transfers equal to the taxes they pay to untaxed households, and there is no government expenditure on goods and services, then $C_2 = a_2 + b_2[(1 - c)Y + \overline{R}]$ where $\overline{R}$ = transfer payments and $\overline{R} = \overline{T}$. In this case:

$$Y = [A + \overline{T}(b_2 - b_1)] \cdot \frac{1}{1 - c(b_1 - b_2) - b_2 .} \tag{5a}$$

The effects on the multiplier are identical to those found in (5).
4. For a useful survey of these issues, see Pauly (1970).

REFERENCES

Bailey, M. J. (1962) *National Income and the Price Level* 1st edition, McGraw-Hill, New York.
Bailey, M. J. (1971) *National Income and the Price Level* 2nd edition, McGraw-Hill, New York.
Pauly, M. (1970) 'Efficiency in the provision of consumption subsidies' *Kyklos* No. 1.
Shoup, C. (1969) *Public Finance* Weidenfeld & Nicolson, London.

CHAPTER 14

Do We Need to Reform Direct Taxes?[1]

I. INTRODUCTION

The recently published report of a committee set up by the Institute of Fiscal Studies and chaired by the Nobel Prize winner, Professor James Meade (Institute of Fiscal Studies, 1978), offers some radical proposals for the reform of our system of direct taxes. The more important of these proposals can be listed as follows:

(i) a 'new' Beveridge scheme which would raise national insurance benefits (e.g. unemployment, old-age and sickness benefits) to a minimum acceptable standard of living coupled with replacement of tax allowances with cash payments. Benefits and cash payments would be subject to tax;

(ii) a move towards some form of progressive expenditure tax taking as its base the taxpayer's total expenditure on consumption. (Various forms of expenditure tax are examined in considerable detail.);

(iii) a 'flow of funds' corporation tax designed to meet the requirement that the rate of return on a company's new capital development is not taxed unless the proceeds are distributed and not reinvested in the corporate sector. (Again, various choices of tax base are considered.);

(iv) if an expenditure tax and associated 'flow of funds' base corporation tax were not acceptable, the tax base for both personal and business income should be broadened. In the case of personal income tax, the following items, *inter alia*, would be included in the tax base: the annual value of a house over and above any rent paid; capital gains on government securities, premiums paid for life insurance (subject to some exceptions), and income from National Savings beyond income subject to the basic rate of income tax. In addition the Meade Report recommends a return to a system of depreciation allowances restricted to 'true' economic depreciation in calculating liability of businesses to payment of income tax or corporation tax;

(v) wealth taxation designed to discriminate against inherited wealth, e.g. by the replacement of the Capital Transfer Tax by an accessions tax.

186

Alternatively, if further discrimination covering wealth accumulated from own savings is considered acceptable, a progressive annual wealth tax with a high threshold coupled with a 'moderate' accessions tax is recommended.

The radical changes represented by these proposals may be judged by comparing them with those of the last official major investigation of direct taxation undertaken by the Royal Commission on the Taxation of Income and Profits which published its Final Report in 1955. Being evenly divided on the matter, the Commission had to obtain a ruling on whether or not an expenditure tax could fall within their terms of reference and in October 1952 the Chancellor of the Exchequer, Mr (now Lord) Butler, ruled it out, offering as his reason that 'it would be impossible to carry through an examination of a scheme of taxation on expenditure without also examining on fairly fundamental lines the scope and purpose of indirect taxation'.[2] The whole Commission rejected various schemes arguing in favour of linking payment of social security benefits with the income tax.[3] The majority rejected the extension of the personal tax base to include capital gains, and recommended extension of allowances for personal saving, through generous treatment of superannuation provisions. Though an annual tax on wealth might be paid out of income, the Commission clearly did not consider such a tax as within their terms of reference, though the Memorandum of Dissent by Messrs Woodcock, Bullock and Kaldor suggested closing one avenue of escape for wealth holders by recommending that transfer of property through inheritance or gifts *inter vivos* should be reckoned as realisation for the purpose of calculating capital gains taxation. This proposal reappears, incidentally, in the Meade Report.

The Meade Report is without doubt a *tour de force*. It provides alongside its recommendations an in-depth analysis of the shortcomings of our system of direct taxation that it would be difficult to surpass. While the conclusions are perhaps not original in themselves they are cogently defended and the problems of implementation are not glossed over. The difficult feat of offering an exposition that will satisfy the professional requirements of economists, lawyers and accountants yet remain intelligible to the non-specialist politician and layman is surmounted by buttressing the individual chapters with chunky appendices. It is a landmark in the development of British fiscal theory, though many of the issues it raises have been the concern for many years of us writers, notably Simons, Shoup, Vickrey, Musgrave and Goode.

The following comments and criticisms of the Report concentrate on certain methodological questions raised by it and how the Report deals with them. It also concerns itself mainly with the expenditure tax proposals, which are central to its discussion. If issue is taken with the Report's conclusions, this is in no way meant to belittle its contribution.

II. When is Tax Reform Necessary?

The word 'reform' applied to government policy suggests that changes are necessary in the policy mix because policy instruments are no longer co-ordinated with policy objectives. There are three main reasons why coordination may have ceased to exist.

In the first place, policy aims may have changed or those who have aims of their own that are different from those pursued by the government may wish to influence government towards change. So far as economic policy is concerned, this does not usually take the form of recognising new aims of policy (or 'additional arguments in the government welfare function' as the pundits would put it) but of a change in orders of priority in the pursuit of existing aims (or 'a change in the "trade-off" between "arguments" '). For example, rival parties may accept economic efficiency and reduction in inequality as aims, but their trade-offs will be different. If an incoming government changes the trade-off by favouring, say, greater equality, it may claim that this must imply an increase in the progressivity of the personal income tax. This need require a change not in the structure of the tax system, but simply in the rates of tax. More radical adherents to such a policy might demand tax reform in the sense that they might advocate the introduction of additional taxes on the rich such as a swingeing wealth tax.

In the second place, even if aims and trade-offs do not alter, the constraints on maximising the aims may have changed. The oil crisis is a striking example of such a change. Its adverse effects on our terms of trade and the consequential balance of payments problems added markedly to the difficulties of the government in trying simultaneously to promote economic growth and employment opportunities together with preventing inflation and correcting inequalities of income by budgetary means. So far as the tax system is concerned, it brought to the fore the demand for indexing tax allowances to offset the reduction in real incomes, particularly at the lower end of the income scale, caused by rising prices. Automatic indexing for inflation would certainly require major changes in the structure of the personal income tax system and other taxes, too, while simultaneously making it much more difficult to use the direct tax system as a built-in stabiliser.

Finally, even without changes in aims and trade-offs and in the constraints on maximising them, policy instruments themselves may have proved to be less effective than originally expected. This may promote a search for alternative instruments as well as for innovations to remedy the deficiencies in the existing instruments. Thus hard-pressed taxpayers attempting to minimise the reduction in their real incomes may decide to exploit unexpected loopholes in the tax laws discovered by professional accountants and others, thus forcing governments to consider how the loopholes are to be stopped or to reduce the 'tax backlash' by even modifying the policy aims themselves in extreme cases.

Clearly these three elements in the process of coordinating aims with policy instruments are closely interlinked. They also suggest a method by which one can judge how reforms in the structure of taxation might be appraised, but before extending this framework of analysis to cover this point it will be useful to examine the Meade Committee's views on the necessity for reform.

III. THE MEADE COMMITTEE'S GENERAL CASE FOR REFORM

The Meade Report does not base its case for reform on the need for any adjustment in policy aims. Indeed, it makes much of the point that 'different governments will put different emphases on the relative importance of economic incentives and of a more equal distribution of standards of living as social objectives . . . we say something on the principles underlying their choice; but we make no farreaching proposals on what in our view constitutes the best pattern. Indeed it is doubtful whether we could have reached agreement on such a question even if we had tried to do so'. Nor does it base its case for reform to any great extent on changes in economic circumstances that would inevitably circumscribe the pursuit of policy aims, though a chapter of the Report is devoted to ways of remedying the effects of rapid inflation on the tax system by various forms of indexing.

The main case, therefore, rests on the need to remedy defects in the existing tax system as a policy instrument, which ought to be so designed that it can effectively conform to different policy mixes but within the range of objectives that are commonly identified as relevant to the British scene.

The Committee therefore sees its task as the enunciation and application of tax principles that command political consensus. These principles (highly reminiscent in some respects of Adam Smith's famous 'maxims' of taxation) are: retention of incentives so as to promote economic efficiency; 'fairness' in the sense of both treating those similarly situated economically in similar fashion (horizontal equity) and removing gross inequalities between those differently situated economically (vertical equity); compatibility of the tax system with international economic relations; simplicity and ease of understanding; and absence of 'excessive' administrative costs.

I consider how these principles are applied later, but first of all it is necessary to consider the general rationale of the Meade case for reform. The aim of producing a tax reform designed to remove 'unplanned distortions' in the tax system and one that will not prejudge the political ends is laudable but it is bound to encounter serious obstacles.

The first obstacle is that objectives of policy such as maintaining incentives and equity and tax instruments cannot be so easily disentangled in the political mind. There is good reason behind this refusal to separate the two, at least in the eyes of political parties who retain their long-term support by the pursuit of party ideology and not simply by political ambition. Thus to Conservatives, it is probably questionable whether an annual wealth tax, on top of existing taxes on capital, could command political consensus even though, as the Meade Report makes clear, a Conservative government would have the option of controlling the rate of tax. There is no use creating the elaborate machinery that such a tax would require if the optimum rate of tax is considered to be zero![4]

The second obstacle is a reflection of the important fact in politics that, though political parties pursue ideological aims, they trade these off against the desire to remain in power. This requires parties to be sensitive to voters' reactions to tax changes and particularly the reactions of the 'voters in the middle' who may have a more than proportionate influence on the outcome of elections. Clearly any major tax reform of the Meade variety could produce major distributional effects, not only as between regions, occupations and industries, and illustrations of these effects might enable politicians to gauge their influence on voters' reactions. The Committee clearly did not regard it as part of its task to offer detailed illustration of distributional effects and, more importantly, of the change in the compliance costs falling on the taxpayer. It might reasonably have argued that such effects would largely depend on the rates of direct taxation rather than on the structure, the rates resting on a political decision about the revenue to be raised to transfer resources for public authorities' use. However, one is left with the impression in its Report that the taxpayer is to be treated merely as a passive adjuster to changes introduced by an independent central authority beyond his control, albeit one who arouses the protective instincts of the Committee from time to time. In this respect the Committee follows a long-standing but contestable tradition in British fiscal theory in which the doctrine of consumer sovereignty only extends to the individual's use of his post-tax income, his actions being irrelevant in the determination of the size and composition of the public budget.[5] Whatever the methodological and philo-sophical issues, no politician dares work on this assumption.

The third obstacle is that politicians might regard the Committee's approach as having limited usefulness because it tries to limit its analysis to the possible substitution of one form of direct taxation for another without considering the relative efficiency of direct as against indirect taxation. It is perfectly reasonable for the Committee to argue that there is enough to be concerned about in our direct tax system without extending its enquiries further. The point nevertheless remains that in seeking to remain in office, for good reasons as well as bad, politicians cannot work within such restricted terms of reference and their judgment of whether or not a consensus could be reached in the structure of our tax system cannot be made unless the relations between all major taxes, direct and indirect, are presented to them.

As it happens, the Committee is forced to bend its own terms of reference to consider the relation between one very important indirect tax, the local rate, and its schemes for improving the comprehensiveness of the direct tax system, particularly in respect of the taxation of the annual value of housing. Thus 'if the local rates did not exist, the case for subjecting the annual value of all categories of housing to the national tax on income and expenditure would be greatly strengthened' (Institute of Fiscal Studies, 1978, p. 218), and later, 'on the face of it a local income tax or a local expenditure tax would appear to us to be a fairer and a better measure of ability to pay than the annual value of a taxpayer's residence'. But why subject such an important tax to the judgment of one criterion when the Committee pays so much attention to others? In any case, it is doubtful if such a judgment improves the chances of promoting political consensus.

IV. The Case for an Expenditure Tax

The most original feature of the Meade Report without any doubt is the closely argued case for a universal expenditure tax as the tax most likely to fit best with the criteria of a 'good tax' already enunciated. The scope and content of these maxims might be questioned, but accepting the Committee's view that they accord with political consensus (though allowing wide differences of view about the rates of tax to be used), brief mention must be made of the shortcomings that the Committee finds in the existing direct tax system.

The first shortcoming lies in the erosion of the personal income tax base, which is a problem that has also exercised us writers.[6] The most noticeable examples are the lack of consistency in the treatment of social security benefits and the omission of imputed income from durable consumption goods that narrow the tax base. 'Unplanned' distortions result as taxpayers order their affairs to reduce their tax burdens, which militates against both economic efficiency and equity.

The second shortcoming lies in the rate structure of the income tax. The structure is not coordinated with the social security transfer system with the result that marginal tax rates at the lower end of the income scale can be extremely high. A low-income earner may add little or nothing to his disposable income by moving out of social security into work – the poverty trap – and this adversely affects his incentive to work. At the other end of the income scale, very high marginal rates of tax are in operation that reduce the incentive to save.

The separation of the system of transfer and social security payments and income tax has produced a third shortcoming associated with inflation. The lack of a comprehensive base alone is enough to produce grave inequities when price inflation alters the real value of income, but separate administration of social security benefits and personal income taxes has produced a lack of coordination in adjustments for inflation that has caused major tax anomalies, particularly at the bottom end of the income scale.

These shortcomings would seem to point towards a reform in the personal income tax base itself, for example by making it more comprehensive in coverage and by reviving the proposals for amalgamation of income tax with social security, which Professor Meade himself supported thirty years ago[7]. The Committee rejected this standard solution on the grounds that it is too difficult to produce a satisfactory measure of income for tax purposes. The famous Haig/Simon definition of income as the 'increase in economic power' within the tax year would certainly extend far beyond earnings to include net capital gains as well as windfall receipts but would lead to 'strange results'[8]. An alternative approach is no better. If we define income, not as the amount an individual could consume in one year without diminishing his wealth, but as the amount he can consume that still left him able to maintain the same level of consumption into the future, the tax base would have to be based on subjective expectations and not upon accounting data.

The alternative tax base to income is taken to be expenditure on consumption, an idea at least as old as Hobbes, and supported by a succession of economists from J. S. Mill to Kaldor.

Looking back at the 'maxims' enunciated in section III above, taxing expenditure is claimed to score much higher than the income tax when it comes to equity considerations. Taxing consumption means taxing those who are withdrawing resources from the 'common pool', exempting those who are adding to productive potential by saving and hitting the wealthy who finance consumption out of capital resources. Equally, on efficiency grounds the exemption of saving means that the yield to the saver equals the yield on his investment, so that enterprise is encouraged, whereas income tax (so older writers have claimed) results in the 'double' taxation of saving, for income is taxed as it accrues and any saving out of income as a return to investment must be taxed as income. In addition, some important 'unplanned distortions' are removed arising from the fact that individuals cannot avoid tax by adjusting the form in which they acquire purchasing power, e.g. by seeking capital gains subject to lower rates of tax rather than earnings.

These arguments are well known in the public finance literature, but the Meade Report makes a major contribution to the discussion about ways in which an expenditure tax might be levied. It is impossible to do justice to the detailed argument, but, not unexpectedly, the more maxims the tax has to meet, the greater the administrative complications. This can be illustrated by comparing Value Added Tax (VAT) with a Universal Expenditure Tax (UET), to take only two of the four variants in the Report.

In principle, the present VAT could do the job of an expenditure tax by raising the present rate and making it uniform and universal and then abolishing the income tax. There are two major difficulties. The first is that if the equity maxim requires progressive taxation, as with the present income tax, it would be difficult if not impossible to design a VAT, which would have to contain a multi-rate structure, to reflect discrimination against the rich. Secondly, though the combination of a universal VAT with the abolition of the income tax might have very complicated effects on the structure of prices, there would be a reasonable presumption that the rise in disposable income resulting from the abolition of the income tax would be offset by a once and for all rise in the cost of living. The effect on wage settlements would be important. The Meade Report argues that 'perhaps understanding of the meaning of such a shift has been made easier by the bargaining process which has gone on between the Chancellor and the trade unions in 1976 and 1977 about the relationship between earnings, levels of taxation and prices' (p. 155). One should perhaps underline the word 'perhaps'!

Granted the need for progressive rates, and this is certainly favoured by the Meade Committee, then the only alternative is to operate a universal expenditure tax (UET). This requires a record of taxpayer's total consumption calculated indirectly by obtaining information on his total receipts from all sources and subtracting from this total all payments made for purposes other than consumption. Even if the tax were in full operation, the preconditions for its ability to fulfil the tax maxims laid down by the Committee are formidable, as the Committee itself is forced to recognise. While it would have the merit of making it unnecessary to retain many distinctions between income and capital and to operate a separate Capital Transfer Tax, it would be impossible to operate it administratively without the introduction of self-assessment by taxpayers. One important maxim, preserving good international economic relations, would be particularly difficult to fulfil, given the likelihood that other countries would continue to have income taxation. With a UET, there could be immigration to take advantage of relief from saving and emigration to avoid taxation of dissavings, but, apart from this, there would be major difficulties arising from income earned abroad or by foreigners in this country calling for a complicated system of double taxation relief.

Another major problem of equity that the Committee recognises is that important household expenditures, e.g. purchase of durable consumption goods such as cars and houses, are 'lumpy' and, with a progressive rate structure, households during the years of relative low earning power in their lifetime earnings stream could be hit hard. The Committee proposes to solve this problem by removing some assets from the tax base as an averaging device, the general principle being to register only those assets on which substantial capital gains might be made. This is a difficult principle to implement and the Committee has to agonise a great deal over whether housing should be registered or unregistered assets. Even if the principle could be applied in a reasonable manner, the fact that the UET cannot be introduced overnight would mean that the distinction between registered and unregistered assets would raise immense difficulties in the transitional period. To quote a graphic example given by the Committee:

> the elderly citizen without any considerable pension rights who was just about to live in retirement on his past savings, and who had a high standard of living and therefore a high marginal rate of expenditure tax, would lose most heavily. But it would not only be the elderly unpensioned rich who suffered. Any taxpayer who had saved up for a future consumption expenditure (e.g. to furnish a home for the first time) would be liable to the new unexpected charge if savings had been invested in registered assets. [pp. 187–8]

The Committee's reaction to this problem is to consider the effect on the capital market of the shift in demand from registered to unregistered assets in anticipation of the introduction of a UET, and the consequential loss of revenue, and what could be done about it. As previously argued, this is to emphasise the passive adjustment of taxpayers to a new tax regime and ignores the alternative possibility that the path from the old to the new regime is one that taxpayers, as voters, may simply refuse to travel. In fairness to the Committee, however, it must be emphasised that it has not committed the fallacy of comparing an imperfect existing income tax with some ideal hypothetical alternative.

V. Unresolved Issues

The Meade Report has not been given the credit for the careful assessment it contains of its own expenditure tax and related proposals. It is a matter of judgment whether this assessment should lead one to reject the main proposal and to explore more fully the alternatives that the Report itself considers. In my view, there are important issues left unresolved in the Report, other than that of taxpayer reaction already emphasised in this critique, and that reinforce the case for following the Committee down the line of income tax reform rather than moving, however slowly, towards an expenditure tax system.

A 'neutral' tax structure, allowing different political preferences to be expressed in differences in tax rates, presupposes consensus on the tax base.

As we have seen, the Committee justifies an expenditure base on the grounds that we should be taxed according to what we take out of the 'common pool' of resources rather than according to what we contribute to it. There are no grounds for supposing that this view should command the consensus that the Committee must assume exists. Its presumption must be that it is beyond dispute that saving is an activity that, *in equity terms only*, has a special significance. There is no reason why this should be so. For most people, saving is an act designed to reallocate their claim on resources through time in accordance with their own preference and not some selfless act that requires special treatment. As Richard Goode has put it:

> There seems to be no principle of justice, nor even of popular prejudice, holding that taxes should be relatively heavy in periods of youth and age and years of temporary adversity and relatively light at other times. Arguments have been advanced in favour of average short term fluctuations in the tax base and even variations over the life cycle, regardless of whether income or consumption is taxed. [1976, p. 23][9]

For the large majority of people, over whose life cycle consumption and disposable income are close to equality, the substitution of an expenditure tax for an income tax is simply a difference of timing in payment.

Moving from equity to efficiency arguments, it is important to be clear on the correct methodology of tax comparisons. An improvement in efficiency produced by one tax as compared with another may be achieved at the cost of other policy objectives. A simple and commonly used method for dealing with this problem is to associate the other policy objectives with a revenue constraint. Thus, in examining the Meade Committee's claim that an expenditure tax encourages saving, and therefore enterprise and growth, we could compare the existing income tax with an expenditure tax of equal yield. Meeting this revenue constraint means that government expenditure plans would not be affected, and other policy objectives reflected in these plans could be attained.

Let us begin, as the Meade Report does (pp. 192–4 and Appendix 9.4) by assuming that the UET has no effect on saving. To meet the equal yield condition, the progressive tax structure with a UET must contain higher rates of tax so long as total consumption is less than total taxable income, for the tax base will be narrower than for an income tax. The 'announcement effects' might encourage more taxpayers' resistance even though the total tax burden would be the same. However, if, as claimed, the UET were to increase the rate of saving, the equal yield condition can only be met if the tax rate on consumption expenditure is increased *pari passu* with the increase in saving.

The problem is recognised in the Meade Report but set aside in the following way. A detailed calculation is made of the revenue effects of a change-over from an income tax to a UET with the same rate schedule, and it is initially found, on the assumption of no change in the rate of saving, that the revenue loss would have been negligible over the period 1971–75. However, this result can only be obtained by bringing housing expenditure into the expenditure base but without adjusting the income tax base to include the annual value of housing. It is also assumed that the UET is not beset by any transitional problems of the kind already described. Thus it has to be admitted that when housing expenditure is left out the total revenue loss would have been about £1.5b (at 1975 prices) out of a total income tax revenue of £11.0b (also at 1975 prices). However, as the purpose of the Meade Report is to establish that the UET would encourage saving, any increase in saving as a result of the tax change-over would have increased the revenue loss even more.

This does not stump the Committee, which produces a Kaldorian shot out of the locker (see Kaldor, 1955, Chapter 2). The revenue loss is not a matter for concern for 'paradoxically, however, the effect of this would be to permit lower rather than higher rates of tax'. This is because a 'more appropriate criterion for neutrality of tax changes is a constant level of demand in the economy rather than a constant level of tax revenue; and an increase in aggregate saving would reduce aggregate demand by more than the amount of revenue lost' (p. 193).

This seems to be quite an ingenious way out of the problem, but it only works if it is assumed that the only other policy objective we have to worry about is economic stability, though this is an objective that is barely mentioned in the Report. However, with a given tax rate structure this is a permanent and continuing loss of revenue that, if government expenditure plans (at constant prices) are to be fulfilled, requires the substitution of continuing government borrowing. It is true that the increased supply of saving, given no special reason why savers should move into cash, will increase the supply of loanable funds available to the government, but some restriction must be placed on future policy options by the need to meet future tax obligations as interest and debt repayment become due. A further point to be taken into account is that severing the nexus between taxation and government spending is not exactly the best way of ensuring that politicians in power have their minds concentrated on maintaining efficiency in public services.

The general point to be made about macroeconomic calculations of this kind is that they must be comprehensive. Whether or not one adopts the convention of comparing tax regimes with a revenue constraint, one wants to be able to know, so far as that is possible, how these regimes change not only the direction but also the magnitude of those economic variables – the growth rate, the inflation rate, etc. – that represent the constituents in the government 'utility or welfare function'. As already argued above, what these changes will mean to different governments in power will depend on the weights they assign to these economic variables, but the information system that explains how these variables are likely to move can be supplied, in principle at least, by the same macroeconomic model in which the alternative tax regimes are simulated. In examining major changes in tax policy in the USA it is now common practice, even for private as well as government investigations, to employ a computable macroeconomic model, and it is a pity that a major investigation of the Meade kind was not able to follow suit.

VI. Some Conclusions

The answer to the question posed in the title of this article is: yes. However this is not to say that the case is satisfactorily made for a move towards a direct tax system in which an expenditure tax would have pride of place. There are no grounds for supposing that the principle of equity underlying the system would command political consensus and voter support and, to me at least, has no inherent virtues superior to income as a base that would lead one to wish to persuade voters that they would be better off under an expenditure tax regime. This is sufficient reason for recommending that it would be more profitable to pursue other suggestions that the Meade Committee has put forward.

If income is kept as the tax base, then the need to maintain fairness as between those similarly situated ('horizontal equity') and those differently situated ('vertical equity') certainly makes a strong case for as comprehensive a definition of income as possible and the Meade suggestions listed at the beginning of this article, particularly the reintroduction of the annual value of housing, merit serious consideration. Furthermore, the well-argued case for combining an accessions tax with income tax, recognising the extra 'income' in the form of security that wealth provides, might command wide support. More controversial, obviously, is the case for an annual wealth tax, which would hit accumulated as well as inherited wealth.

There remains one important administrative reform upon which a move towards a comprehensive income tax, or a UET, would depend. One of the hallmarks of a properly functioning democracy is an educated taxpaying public. From time to time, the Inland Revenue have shown that the ordinary citizen does not know how much tax he pays and is incapable of performing a simple exercise in coding his own tax. However, while this may be true, it is a poor argument for perpetuating conditions where he has no incentive to take an intelligent interest in his rights as well as his duties as a taxpayer and the spur this might give him to take a critical view of how his taxes are spent. On these grounds alone the case for self-assessment for income tax, which is strongly supported by the Meade Committee, seems unassailable.[10] It is true that self-assessment would require some simplification in the income tax, particularly in the system of tax allowances, and the embodiment of a Meade-type tax credit system could only be contemplated if social security allowances were taxed, but there are equity grounds that make these changes desirable as well as necessary. True, the taxpayer would face heavier compliance costs, but these would be at least partly offset by administrative savings resulting from the abolition of PAYE and sample rather than comprehensive checking of individual tax returns. Such savings could indeed be diverted to reduce the compliance costs themselves by making personal advice and information on a major scale the principal function of the Inland Revenue. In these days in which there is much talk of encouraging greater interest and participation in the political system, one could do much worse than start by making the direct tax system less of a mystery to the ordinary citizen.

NOTES

1. A somewhat extended version of an article first published in *Lloyds Bank Review* No. 129, July 1978.
2. Quoted in para 2 of The Royal Commission on the Taxation of Profits and Income (1955). As Mr (now Lord) Kaldor pointed out at the time, the Select Committee on the Income and Property Tax 1861 (of which Gladstone was a member) had an expenditure tax included in its terms of reference though the Committee rejected it. See Kaldor (1955) Preface. Lord Kaldor's book arose out of a memorandum submitted by him to the Royal Commission (of which he was a member) in 1952.
3. Including one designed principally by Professor Frank Paish and myself for the Liberal Party!
4. For other countries' experience in the operation of annual wealth taxes, see Sandford, Willis and Ironside (1975) Part II.
5. For evidence of this, see the Meade Report (Institute of Fiscal Studies, 1978) Appendix 2.2. See also chapter 15 of this volume for an extension of this argument.
6. Pechman (1977). This work is the culmination of a whole series of Brookings studies on income as a tax base.
7. See Meade (1948). My early book on such matters (Peacock, 1952) was influenced by the Meade arguments.
8. The Haig/Simon definition can be expressed as follows:

$$Y = G - E + S - K + A$$

where G = gross earnings (including imputed value of owner occupation and income in kind), E = costs of obtaining G, S = proceeds of sale of capital assets, gifts, bequests, K = costs of assets sold, and A = change in value of assets held during the tax year. (For further discussion, see Goode, 1976, Chapter 2.) The 'strange results' could arise, for example, if capital losses caused, say, by a rise in interest rates, resulted in A taking a negative value that exceeded the value of G. *Ceteris paribus* this could produce the result that a millionaire living solely off interest income could incur capital losses that would reduce his income to zero in a particular year, making him eligible, presumably, for supplementary benefit (see Institute of Fiscal Studies, 1978, p. 31).
9. See also his *The Superiority of the Income Tax over the Expenditure Tax* (forthcoming).
10. The Meade Committee rightly commends the detailed study of self-assessment previously published by the Institute of Fiscal Studies and Institute of Chartered Accountants. See Barr, James and Prest (1977).

REFERENCES

Barr, N. A., James, S. R. and Prest, A. R. (1977) *Self Assessment for Income Tax* Heinemann, London.

Goode, R. (1976) *The Individual Income Tax* revised edition, Brookings Institution, Washington, D.C.

Goode, R. (forthcoming) *The Superiority of the Income Tax over the Expenditure Tax* Brookings Institution, Washington, D.C.

Institute of Fiscal Studies (1978) *The Structure and Reform of Direct Taxation* (report of a committee chaired by Professor J. E. Meade) Allen & Unwin, London.

Kaldor, N. (1955) *An Expenditure Tax* Allen & Unwin, London.

Meade, J. E. (1948) *Planning and the Price Mechanism* Allen & Unwin, London.

Peacock, A. T. (1952) *Economics of National Insurance* Wm Hodge, London and Edinburgh.

Pechman, J. A. (ed.) (1977) *Comprehensive Income Taxation* Brookings Institution, Washington, D.C.

Royal Commission on the Taxation of Profits and Income (1955) *Final Report on the Taxation of Profits and Income* Cmnd 9474, HMSO, London.

Sandford, C. T., Willis, J. K. M. and Ironside, D. J. (1975) *An Annual Wealth Tax* Institute of Fiscal Studies, London.

CHAPTER 15

The Promulgation of Ideas about Normative Public Finance[1]

It is a vain and false philosophy which conceives its dignity to be debased by use
[Jeremy Bentham, *The Philosophy of Economic Science* in *Jeremy Bentham's Economic Writings* (edited by W. Stark) Allen and Unwin for Royal Economic Society, 1952, p. 81.]

I

At a recent conference at which Jack Wiseman and I gave a paper, the critic and commentator was a well-known UK politician who had held ministerial office in the Treasury. He made the incidental observation that his colleagues and himself believed that there had only been one significant contribution to public policy discussion by academic economists in the UK since Keynes that had had major influence upon their thoughts and actions. What struck us about this remark was less its brutal honesty but more the fact that the work in question is regarded by practising economists whom we respect as of little analytical or practical consequence.

This incident raises the important question whether we should take an interest in the promulgation of our ideas beyond the immediate confines of the study and conference table. In the UK there is a long tradition dating back at least to Ricardo and James Mill that economics can be explained to the electorate, statesmen and bureaucrats and that professional economists themselves should do the explaining. John Stuart Mill, talking of the definition and methods of political economy, claimed that 'the principles which we have now stated are by no means alien to common apprehension: they are not absolutely hidden, perhaps, from anyone, but are commonly seen through a mist' (Mill, 1844). Granted that 'apprehension' was possible, the Classical economists set about promulgating their views with demonstrable vigour. Ricardo sums up their position in a letter to James Mill:

The grand cause, good government, is always present in my mind. . . .
in every argument with my friends I do what I can to maintain the
cause of truth, as far as I can see it, and frequently flatter myself that I
am successful. I am quite sure that the good cause is advancing, though
at a moderate step, and all we can hope to do in our time is to help it a
little forward. [Ricardo, 1823]

Those of you who are familiar with contemporary economic debate in the
UK will know that it is difficult for our economists to resist the temptation to
hurl pamphlets and articles into the arena of policy discussion, as well as to
seek experience in both the legislature and the bureaucracy. I admit that
I am no exception.

James Buchanan would take a different view and I heard him recently
warn economists against the corrupting influence of close contact with the
government and administrative machine. Politicians and bureaucrats are
better observed at a safe distance. Another facet of this view is conveyed by
Buchanan's quotation, which he approves of highly, from Wicksell's *Finanz-
theoretische Untersuchungen* at the beginning of *Public Finance in Democratic Process*
(Buchanan, 1967): 'I am ready to admit that much of my discussion may
be classified as armchair speculation . . . I never worry about the external
consequences of carrying out my theory. How much – whether any at all –
may be practically applied in the near future, practical men may decide.'
Later in the same work (p. 212) he quotes another 'heavyweight', Luigi
Einaudi, who in his Ínaugural Lecture at Torino (1949) stated that 'the
economist does not know, and should not know, and should not be concerned as to whether his theories, his models, his instruments or research,
serve or should serve, many, one, or none at all'. (I find difficulty in believing
that Einaudi faithfully followed his own advice!)

Reasonable men could disagree about the posture we should adopt towards
promulgation of our views and only a trained psychologist could, if anyone
can, tell us why we veer towards one view or another.

However, those of us who maintain the proposition that the political system
ought to be designed to reflect individual choices as far as possible can hardly
complain if taxpayers were to become curious about the utility to them of
research into public choice theory. After all, much research into problems
of public finance is financed by research councils from funds provided by
taxpayers. Can we deny that, protected as many researchers are from the
bracing air of the market economy, they are not subject to the temptation
to follow discretionary behaviour patterns? That part of public choice
theory concerned with non-market institutions, including bureaucracy, would
support my proposition. Who would therefore dispute that those giving
papers at this conference, for example, do not derive *some* utility from
maximising their reputation with their colleagues and are not solely if at all
concerned with divining taxpayers' interest in their findings? Professors who
simultaneously extol the virtues of the free market but are immune from

the market's pressures must agree that they are in a somewhat sensitive position!

I am not going to argue that freedom to follow our own bent in research pursuits cannot be defended even when such research depends on public funds. On the other hand, we should not be surprised if taxpayers or their representatives claim a legitimate interest in what we are doing and therefore it might be wise if we were able to answer any reasonable enquiry.

If my point is taken, then the difficult question remains of deciding what a body such as this would want to promulgate as the contribution of public choice theory most likely to interest the outside world. It would not necessarily be sensible to seek agreement on such a matter and, even if one did, the theory of public choice itself tells us that the costs of trying to achieve 'approximate unanimity' might be high, unless Professor Buchanan comes up with some innovation in constitutional procedures that will help to reduce them. I therefore propose to give my personal views, if only as a way of stimulating discussion.

II

Let us imagine a mythical being called 'the intelligent voter-cum-taxpayer' (vct) who makes some polite enquiries about his role in public choice theory. Such a being is only a useful expositional fiction, but no more so than the vct depicted in, say, that excellent work of Albert Breton, *The Economic Theory of Representative Government* (1974). Our vct may in general terms discern the kind of role we assign him in public choice theory as someone who recognises that there are subjective marginal benefits and marginal costs attached to provision of public services that he hopes to enjoy and that a crucial factor in the vct's assessment is the relation between what he pays *and what others pay* for these services. His practical interest in his own role will depend on what influence he may have over his fate. He may consider *a priori* that he is merely a passive adjuster to the facts of fiscal life, or he may have been led to believe by the growing evidence of a 'taxpayers' revolt' in a number of countries that he should reconsider his role.

If promulgation of our researches paraphrased the lines of approach in influential normative theories of public choice, our vct would probably be shocked and surprised at the extent to which he is regarded as a kind of circus animal subjected to certain stimuli, which make him jump through a series of hoops in order to achieve goals that are not of his choice.

This is clear enough if we look at the normative theory of public finance found in contemporary 'optimal taxation' discussion. As we all know, Edgeworth is the father of this discussion. Postulating that the objective of taxation was to maximise the welfare (total utility) of the community, by assuming that individual utility schedules were identical, marginal utility declining as income increases and income the sole source of utility, he produced irrefragable proof that taxation must be used as a means of creating equal income distribution (1897). Poor Edgeworth was very upset at his own conclusion, as much perhaps as those taxpayers would be who either already have or aspire to having relatively high incomes. So he added to his analysis: 'the *acme* of socialism is thus for a moment sighted; but it is immediately clouded by doubts and reservations'. He turns to Henry Sidgwick for further guidance as the colleague who best 'discerns the enormous interposing chasms which deter practical wisdom from moving directly towards that ideal'. We shall not follow him, but merely note that his successors, the optimal tax theorists of today, have modified the Edgeworth model in order to take account of the most obvious objection – the likely fall in the aggregate income to be distributed as a result of the disincentive effect of equalising taxation.

Stated in general terms, what latter-day utilitarians have done is to add an additional term to the individual utility function – utility is a negative function of the hours worked – and also a production function in which aggregate income depends on the skill and time input of the community. Further, skills are unequally distributed and those with greater skills have higher incomes. If total utility is then maximised, the optimal income tax schedule becomes approximately linear for 'plausible' trade-off values between income and leisure and utility schedules. The *acme* of capitalism is for a moment sighted; but it is immediately clouded by doubts and reservations! Repelled, as Edgeworth was, by their own conclusions, the optimal tax theorists do not take Sidgwick but Rawls as their guide through the misty and precipitous regions where they have landed themselves. By invoking the Rawlsian principle that the welfare function must be changed to that of 'maximising the satisfaction of the worst-off individual' (the maximin principle), peace of mind can be restored to latter-day egalitarians.

My purpose in paraphrasing optimal income tax theory is not to embark on a large-scale critique but to consider those aspects of it that would intrigue our VCT. It will strike him immediately that he plays no part in the political decision-making process. Worse still, if we took some of these writers literally, for example Mirrlees (1971) in the seminal article on optimal income taxation, 'better' results can be obtained by measures that concentrate the work load, by force if necessary, on the skilled in order to maximise income. As my colleague Martin Ricketts has satirised this approach:

One might envisage the idle classes spending their time on intellectual pursuits (always taking care to avoid acquiring any useful skills – the study of economics might prove admirable in this regard) combined with an occasional tour of the factories to cuff about the ears any workers who, now that they are working for eighteen in every twenty four hours, have the lamentable (not to say anti-social) tendency to fall asleep. [Ricketts, unpublished]

I hope that there would be sufficient of us available to convince our VCT that this form of intellectual *Denksport* has little operational significance. If one were prepared to campaign, in the manner of the Classical economists, for 'justice as fairness' along Rawlsian lines, one cannot see even the most authoritative regime countenancing redistribution of income together with relieving the relatively unskilled of the necessity of working simply because skilful mathematical economists backed by econometrics are able to 'prove' that the work–leisure trade-off demands it. If, as many of us would hope, VCTs have some power over the public purse, the more interesting question is under what circumstances, given a democratic decision rule (e.g. simple majority decision), would a Rawlsian-type policy emerge (on this point, see Buchanan and Bush, 1974). Our VCT might be relieved to know that this manner of approach is being explored, suggesting that he might at least, with others, have the function of voting restored to his bundle of property rights.

III

If we return to the modern theory of public goods, the vast intellectually absorbing literature (see, for example, Mueller, 1976) could probably be distilled into a set of ideas that our VCT could readily grasp. Let loose in a world in which the goods from which he derives satisfaction are apt to have the character of 'publicness' (they are, in standard Musgravian, 1969, terminology 'non-excludable' and 'non-rival'), he is depicted as behaving in a thoroughly anti-social manner by being tempted not to reveal his 'true' preferences. Our VCT must be subjected to 'experiments' of various kinds that induce him to reveal these preferences as 'information' for those who will then decide how much of the public goods to provide and what to charge individual taxpayers.

If our VCT has the temerity to enquire what exactly is the crime he commits by non-revelation of preferences, the public goods theorist presumably answers that the very basis of the rationale for state intervention – the existence of 'publicness' – is at stake. Moreover, if we follow Samuelson much *is* at stake, for he rejects the notion that the real world is one in which there are 'polar' cases of purely public and purely private goods with a continuum in between. 'So I now think the useful terminology in this field should be: pure private goods in which the market mechanism works optimally, and possibly close approximations to them, versus *the whole field* of consumption-externalities or public goods' (Samuelson, 1969; italics mine). On the other hand, if our VCT presses us for evidence of this wide range of goods from which no one can be excluded from benefiting and that are characterised by zero marginal costs of consumption (non-rivalness), what can we offer?

Here I am afraid that the lack of imagination, the lack of knowledge of current business practice and the lack of historical scholarship of many economists might soon have them caught on the wrong foot. As Goldin (1977) has shown, exclusion devices abound in practice and the evidence that there is a wide range of goods characterised by 'non-congestability' or 'non-rivalness' is slim indeed. I would emphasise a slightly different point in supporting Goldin's position. Even where the expected costs of exclusion to a private producer are reckoned to be so high that he would make losses, this may offer an incentive for investing in technology or for persuading governments to endow them with property rights, e.g. performance rights in music, so as to reduce exclusion costs.[2] I am not denying that such devices can be opposed on efficiency and equity grounds, but we owe it to the VCT to distinguish clearly what is feasible from what is desirable. But once this distinction is made, it is much more likely that our VCT will wonder what all the fuss is about. Why should he have to accept that economists can tell him anything about normative propositions, and therefore decide for him the agenda that should determine the nature and extent of government intervention?

IV

Let us accept, however, that the VCT is prepared to admit that economists can tell him something about the consequences of his own normative judgements and that among these consequences could be the problem of market failure in the provision of some goods from which he derives utility. The VCT's suspicions might be allayed by making it clear to him that whatever being – Leviathan, Superman, the 'ethical observer' – is going to decide on the optimum allocation of resources between public and private uses will do so by embodying individuals' own utilities in the social welfare function.

The conventional view in public choice theory has been that it is virtually impossible to produce conditions that would penalise non-revelation of preferences for public goods. This would require that (a) individuals would be faced with actual and not hypothetical choices; (b) individuals would be willing to make such choices, i.e. would not be forced to do so; and (c) individuals would know what their preferences were for public goods to some of which, such as defence and criminal justice, it is difficult for him to attach a price tag. It is a tribute to the persistence of economists, as the Tideman and Tullock contribution to this conference indicates (forthcoming), that they have tried to devise ingenious ways for circumventing these difficulties both by the design of experiments and by their actual pursuit (see Bohm, 1972). However, while we can admire their professional skill, let us try to imagine how the 'guinea pigs' might react to experiments to which they are asked to be subjected.

Firstly, there is a natural suspicion of experimentation that calls for the fullest provision of information to the 'guinea pigs'. Bohm carried out a test designed to discover whether or not a sample of individuals would be willing to cover the cost of a half-hour TV programme.[3] Different groups were given different options if their stated willingness to pay exceeded costs, ranging from paying the amount stated to paying nothing at all. The result, in broad terms, is interesting in itself, for it was shown that different options designed to subject the individual to different degrees of incentive to reveal preferences made little difference to the responses of the different groups. 'Cheating' strategies did not appear to be widely used. However, consider the subterfuges that the Bohm experiment had to use to produce this result:

> The persons in each sub-group were placed in a room with two TV-sets and were, for *allegedly 'practical reasons'*, immediately given the fees promised them (in four ten-Crown bills, one five-Crown bill and small change to make Kr.50). The administrator gave an oral presentation of the test which involved a half-hour program by Hasse Alfredsson and Tage Danielsson, not yet shown to the public. The subjects *were given the impression* that there were many groups of the same size simultaneously being asked the same question in other rooms elsewhere in the broadcasting company. The responses given in writing by the persons in each sub-group were taken away and *said to be added* to the statements from other groups. In all relevant cases *they were told* that the aggregate sums of their stated amounts turned out to exceed the 'cost' of the closed circuit televising (presented as rental of a videotape machine and labor costs of operators). Hence the program was to be shown to them and the payments were actually collected when relevant. [Bohm, 1972, pp. 118–19; italics mine.]

I leave to your imagination how the results would have been affected in a repeat of the experiment if participants knew they had not been provided with all relevant information, though no doubt sufficient 'takers' would be found if their opportunity costs of participation were less than Kr.50!

Secondly, given the conventional list of goods that have the characteristic of 'publicness', and the list seems to grow, our VCT might have serious doubts whether he could stand the strain of continuous preference revelation. If the Bohm-type experiment is anything to go by, the opportunity costs of continuous participation might be high, remembering that taxpayers would presumably have to foot the bill for any financial inducements offered to improve the degree of participation. (What would your preferences reveal about your evaluation of schemes to maximise preference revelation?) Furthermore, experiments would have to be repeated frequently to pick up changes in preference systems, if anything approaching the sensitivity of the market system is to be sought after.

Accepting an individualistic view of welfare, the attractions of a mechanism for revealing preferences must be made manifest to the VCT as an alternative to other systems of public choice. As standard public choice theory makes clear, a system of voluntary agreement imposes bargaining costs on potential beneficiaries from public goods, which rise progressively with their number. The alternative system of representative government, while reducing bargaining costs, imposes costs of coercion inevitably associated with the continuum of decisions about public goods and their finance that have to be taken by periodically elected representatives. Superficially, the attractions of preference revelation lie in the avoidance of such bargaining costs and such costs of coercion. Our brief analysis indicates, however, that our vCT could justifiably regard this claim with scepticism. The fulfilment of the rigid requirements necessary to achieve preference revelation, including revelation of changing preference structures, imposes heavy direct or indirect costs on participants that are bound to be a positive function of the number of participants and the frequency of participation. Nor are coercion costs avoided if the *scope* of the public sector's activities is to be left to be decided by Superman simply on the basis of defining the characteristic of 'publicness' in goods, particularly when there is so much uncertainty surrounding the incidence of this characteristic. Nor need the vCT be led to believe that the scope of the public sector's activities *ought* to be defined by that characteristic and therefore that Superman should be left free to decide, for example how much allowance should be made for distributional considerations in setting pricing rules (cf. Rowley and Peacock, 1975).[4]

Probably the feature that will most strike our vCT is the context within which normative public goods theory is placed. He would find himself in an unfamiliar and possibly uncongenial position. He has to imagine himself in a 'state of nature' with no government and the prospect, in order to resolve the problem of market failure in the provision of public goods, of submitting to alternative systems of government reflecting the welfare criteria that public choice theorists would like him to accept or to have imposed upon him. He would be fully justified in arguing that this is the wrong starting point so far as he is concerned.

In Western-type democracies, at least, he already has assigned to him a political role. His welfare depends on how he exploits this role, either alone or in collaboration with others (e.g. within a political party or pressure group), in striking bargains with those who formalise, legalise and execute policies, subject to the rather flimsy check he may be able to exercise as a voter. A suitable digest of the work of Downs and his followers, Breton (1964), Breton and Scott (1978) and others will strike a sympathetic chord with our vCT and perhaps convince him that positive public choice theory is enlightening and possibly potentially useful to him. Positive public choice theory, notably recent attempts to develop a bargaining model in which vCTs, politicians and bureaucrats interact, may also help him to understand how the size and structure of the public sector has developed and, more particularly, why at present he is divested of a large proportion of his gross income for public sector use, causing him, perhaps, to ponder on the consequences for him of the wider issues that these changes have raised (cf. Noll and Fiorina, 1978; Peacock and Wiseman, 1979).

While I would argue that the point of entry by which one would want to enlighten our VCT about our analytical efforts is to be found in positive public choice theory, I am not suggesting that specialists in public finance should not be concerned with normative issues. However, what our VCT will seek from us in the presentation of schemes for improving his welfare and that of others is a description not simply of Nirvana but also of the *path* towards this blissful state and also the *time-scale* of reforms required to reach it. This is, of course, a counsel of perfection, and its pursuit may be unattractive to those who see their talents more usefully (and professionally more glamorously?) employed in 'designing magic castles rather than in solving the housing situation' (to paraphrase Umberto Ricci). Put in the most general terms, the great challenge to normative public finance and to political economy in general is how to overcome the 'isolation paradox' that besets the position of our VCT.

For example, there appears to be widespread support for a reduction in the rate of growth of public expenditure among taxpayers in Western-type democracies. At the same time, such an aim can be achieved in a whole variety of ways with very different effects on the time stream of real incomes of different income groups. Individual taxpayers attempting to maximise the present value of their expected utility, while offering support in principle for the aim, are faced with major uncertainties about how any political support they may offer for a 'cut-spending' programme will be reflected in the changed 'fiscal package' entering their own utility functions. A known place in the pale sun may be preferred to a leap into pitch-black darkness. Major fiscal changes, as we all know, can usually only be instituted after wholesale changes in the economic and political climate, but, with all the attractions of 'being able to begin again from scratch', who among us is advocating that we should devote our efforts to doing so? Interestingly enough, given his passion for building 'magic castles', Paul Samuelson argues 'if we address ourselves to the problem of optimal public finance for a society *far* into the future, there will be plenty of time to make changes without thwarting people's expectations or trampling on their legal rights (human and property)' (Samuelson, 1969, pp. 101–2).

VI

In conclusion I must emphasise that I fully realise that the general proposition of this paper – the necessity for promulgation – is contestable. I am not naive enough to believe that if promulgation is accepted as our responsibility we could arrive at a consensus about what is worth promulgating and that we are all equally good at the job. *Pace* John Stuart Mill, there are communication barriers between the professional economists and the public that are not all that easy to lower. Still, asking the question what aspects of public choice theory might engage the attention of non-specialists who could claim a right to know what we are doing, we may have to undergo a useful process of rigorous self-examination. I would like to hope that the result of that examination would be a favourable verdict from our VCT – unlike the Chinese writer Lin Yutang who observed 'I do not understand economics, but then economics does not understand me'.

NOTES

1. Closing address to the International Institute of Public Finance Congress, Hamburg, September 1978.
2. Curiously enough, the provision of lighthouse services, usually regarded as the public good par excellence, provides clear evidence of this. See Coase (1974) and chapter 9 of this volume.
3. It is, of course, contestable whether TV is a good example of a public good!
4. Accepting the confines of standard welfare theory, Roskamp (1970) states the dilemma very clearly: 'For the pricing rule to be chosen three criteria should be used, (1) it should induce preference revelation for public goods, (2) it should be effective with respect to adjustments in distribution and (3) it should be possible to approximate through political process.'

REFERENCES

Bohm, P. (1972) 'Estimating demand for public goods: An experiment' *European Economic Review* Vol. 3, No. 3.
Breton, A. (1974) *The Economic Theory of Representative Government* Macmillan, London.
Breton, A. and Scott, A. (1978) *The Economic Constitution of Federal States* University of Toronto Press, Toronto.
Buchanan, J. M. (1967) *Public Finance in Democratic Process* University of North Carolina Press, Chapel Hill, North Carolina.
Buchanan, J. M. and Bush, W. (1974) 'Political constraints on contractual redistribution' *American Economic Review* Vol. 64, May.
Coase, R. H. (1974) 'The lighthouse in economics' *Journal of Law and Economics* Vol. 17, October.
Edgeworth, F. Y. (1897) 'The pure theory of taxation' *Economic Journal*, reprinted in his *Papers relating to Political Economy* Macmillan, London, 1925.
Goldin, K. D. (1977) 'Equal access v. selective access: A critique of public goods theory' *Public Choice* Vol. 15, No. 1.
Mill, J. S. (1844) *Essays on Some Unsettled Questions in Political Economy* LSE Reprints of Scarce Works on Political Economy, No. 7.
Mirrlees, J. A. (1971) 'An exploration in the theory of optimal income taxation' *Review of Economic Studies* Vol. 38, April.
Mueller, D. C. (1976) 'Public choice: A survey' *Journal of Economic Literature* Vol. 14, March.
Musgrave, R. A. (1969) 'Provision for social goods' in J. Margolis and H. Guitton (eds) *Public Economics* Macmillan, London.

Noll, R. and Fiorina, M. (1978) 'Voters, bureaucrats and legislators' *Journal of Public Economics* Vol. 7, No. 2, pp. 239–54.

Peacock, A. T. and Wiseman, J. (1979) 'Approaches to the analysis of government expenditure growth' *Public Finance Quarterly* Vol. 7, No. 1.

Ricardo, D. (1823) Letter 548 in *The Works of David Ricardo Volume VII* (edited by P. Sraffa) Cambridge University Press, Cambridge, 1962.

Ricketts, M. (unpublished) 'A simple guide to the problems of utilitarian taxation'.

Roskamp, K. (1970) 'Optimal supply of a public good: A comment' *Review of Economics and Statistics* Vol. 52, August.

Rowley, C. K. and Peacock, A. T. (1975) *Welfare Economics, A Liberal Restatement* Martin Robertson, London.

Samuelson, P. A. (1969) 'Pure theory of public expenditure and taxation' in Margolis and Guitton *op. cit.*

Tideman, T. N. and Tullock, G. (forthcoming) 'A new and superior process for making social choices' Proceedings of the IIPF Congress, Hamburg, 1978.

PART IV

A Variety of Governmental Experience

INTRODUCTION

What Economists Do in Government

I. Preliminaries

From October 1973 – I arrived the weekend of the Yom Kippur War – until September 1976 I was seconded to the Department of Trade and Industry as Chief Economic Adviser and found myself jointly in charge of six mixed divisions of economists and statisticians each headed by an Under-Secretary, my fellow charge-hand being Laurie Berman, the Statistical Director. A piece of political surgery resulting in the setting up of a separate Department of Energy reduced the number of divisions to five, leaving us still with a staff of about 500. A further piece of surgery in February 1974 split the Department into three – Industry, Trade, Prices and Consumer Protection, each with its own Secretary of State. We continued however to manage economic and statistical advice for all three ministries. So in the course of only three years I served no fewer than seven Secretaries of State and six Permanent Secretaries.

I must avoid the temptation to expand on my personal experiences, which provide ample material for a novel or two. My purpose in mentioning these few facts is to justify the title of this part of the book – a variety of governmental experience.

My way of distilling this experience is to stick to my last, to employ economic analysis in explaining the workings of government in two areas – the giving of economic advice itself and the recasting of the economic theory of bureaucracy in the light of close observation of the bureaucratic process. These studies (chapters 16 and 17) can be approached directly without any prefatory words, but a description of 'the daily round, the common task' of economic advice-giving may provide useful background and be of interest in itself. Such descriptions have been provided before, though I believe it is possible to provide something more than a catalogue of duties (cf. Coats, 1978, p. 312) by a taxonomy of the kind of 'products' that economist 'managers' have to deliver and the problems of delivery in 'markets' where the usual price 'signals' are absent.

In the following sections of this Introduction I describe the supply of and demand for economic advice, the structure of the market in which advice is given, and, finally, offer some speculations on how efficient such advice is likely to be.

II. Supply of and Demand for Economic Advice within a Department

Sir Robert Giffen (1882) made the following observations about the approach to his task:[1]

> As regards political economy, it is quite certain that any study of that science in its applications is impossible without statistics. A theoretical teacher may trace out tendencies or forces on paper, but in the real world quantities must be dealt with. It is easy to prove theoretically, for instance, that a protectionist tariff does harm, but it is a different thing in the real world to give any notion of how much harm is done, and when the protection is slight in proportion to the whole business of the country to measure the effect at all. How to deal with these questions is the problem for the economist who is also a statistician, and they are much more difficult and complex than those belonging to theoretical or deductive political economy.

Giffen would no doubt have been delighted at the extent to which his advice has been followed within those departments that grew out of the former Board of Trade, but he would also have been struck by the immense variety and scope of the analytical and empirical work undertaken. This is indicated by the classification of these activities into four kinds of production.

(1) *'Regular orders'*. These orders consist of 'batch' production for administrators and ministers of periodic reports on the national, international and regional situation and prospects. Some of these reports will be 'own' production based on raw material collected by economic statisticians within the department concerned. Even where 'retailing' of the products of other 'producers' e.g., in the UK, periodic reports on the economic situation and prospects by such organisations as the Confederation of British Industries, National Institute of Economic and Social Research and even other government departments such as the Treasury is called for, some additional production in the form of interpretation and commentary is normally expected and provided.

(2) *'Bespoke trade'*. A very considerable proportion of business involving a major claim on resources clearly consists of *ad hoc* demands for information, analysis and advice, some of it generated from regular orders. The trade can vary from services fulfilled by a short telephone conversation, through Parliamentary Questions, to major exercises in which several economists are engaged in supplying complementary intermediate inputs to administrators

and other professional branches aimed at a final product of major policy input. Some of this demand is predictable because it is periodic (e.g. the input to the Budget exercise), though only in the broad sense that the aggregate demand for resources will peak at particular times of the year, but the exact input necessary is another matter.

(3) *'Speculative' production.* This form of production depends on the judgment that economists should anticipate the demands of 'buyers' and can cover anything from the devising of some new form of economic reporting of a specialised kind to offering solutions to major and sometimes controversial policy problems.

Two examples from my own experience may elucidate this point. The possibility that energy rationing might be necessary at the end of 1973, because of oil quotas which might have been imposed by oil producing countries, required economists to remind officials of the interdependency of the economy. Thus schemes to save energy by better insulation would have to take account of the energy input of alternative insulation materials. It is astonishing in my experience how often simple points of this kind may be overlooked even by intelligent administrators and politicians. A second example is to be found in trying to devise some form of control over aggregate demand by the fiscal system that does not produce the kind of 'backlash' in the form of generation of demand for higher real wages associated with increases in both income tax and taxes on expenditure. (I managed to have one scheme of this kind discussed at Cabinet level but it was much too radical for my masters and, consequently, was thrown out!)

(4) *'Prestige' production.* Subject to overriding commitments determined by immediate pressures generated by ministers and administrators, it is common for a modest amount of 'prestige' production to be undertaken by economists in government so as to maintain standing within the economics profession. Even senior economists in government see the necessity for disarming outside criticism of the professional standards inside government. In addition, 'worker alienation' may arise from having to direct all professional effort at dealing with the exigencies of the moment. Opportunities for economists to maintain and improve professional standing, even if it means diverting resources to research, is one way of reducing it. In any case, the results of this research may improve internal efficiency through the experience gained in developing and mastering new techniques and the professional contacts resulting from such work.

With isolated exceptions, the demand for the services of economists in government is a derived demand, the services being embodied in final output of officials and ministers, unfortunately not always in a form that would be recognisable. The structure and volume of this demand, as indicated in chapter 16, is a function of the increasing extent to which national objectives are believed to be best fulfilled by government intervention. It is also apparent from the 'matrix' in that chapter that there is a vast 'intragovernmental' trade, so that the intermediate input by economists in one department may become part of the final output in several other departments, though usually heavily 'orchestrated' on the way by professional confrères.

III. The Market Structure of Economic Advice

> Few men are presumptuous enough to dispute with the chemist or mechanician upon points connected with the studies and labours of his life; but almost any man who can read or write feels himself at liberty to form and maintain opinions of his own upon trade or money. [General Francis Amasa Walker quoted in J. N. Keynes *Scope and Method of Political Economy* 1890]

It is well known that economists, themselves often committed to widely differing views of policy aims and trade-offs, disagree about analysis and the interpretation of testing procedures. They can take consolation from the view of Max Planck who, according to Keynes, gave up study of economics because its subject matter was too intractable compared with the physical world. Government economists are no exception. The fact that economists do not close their ranks and promote some false orthodoxy is a healthy sign but it has the important consequence that there is fairly vigorous competition in the 'advice market'. Customers, in the form of ministers and officials, are well aware of this and, for a variety of motives (see chapter 16), understandably wish to compare the internal 'official' product with that of others.

Competition emanates from both 'outside' and 'inside'. From the 'outside' comes first of all the vast range of press and periodical reporting of economic ideas, advice and information corresponding roughly to 'batch production' activities. It has the important characteristic that most of it is virtually free, though the interpretation of results will not be costless. Administrators as customers are also pressurised by consulting firms to buy their wares and not infrequently commission *ad hoc* studies that might otherwise be conducted 'inside'. In contrast with batch production, such studies have an additional opportunity cost because they have to be paid for out of departmental funds in addition to being monitored and interpreted, usually by the 'inside' competitor. In Britain a unique position is occupied by the quasi-outside competitor, the National Economic Development Office (NEDO), which frequently canvasses for business from the Cabinet through its Director-General, often justifying its wares in preference to others on the grounds that these can and should be marketed to the public at large.

'Inside' competition displays interesting facets. Ministers may prefer to derive a varying part of their economic advice from personal advisers rather than from government economists. When I asked a senior minister what a personal adviser could do that his official advisers could not, he explained his 'transfer of custom' in these terms. He relied on officials for information and analysis and on his personal adviser for the translation of their work into policy action conforming with his party's mandate. It is worth a parenthetical note that things never seemed to work in this clear-cut way! Even the analytical product was frequently rejected by the minister and on at least one occasion analysis based on the work of his personal adviser that was communicated to the Press had outside complaints about it referred to us as its supposed originators! The most frequent and regular form of competition however, emanates from administrators and not always only at working level. Not by any means all of them are 'enthusiastic amateurs' acting like those who prefer self-medication to treatment by doctors. One must allow for the growing numbers of administrators possessing a degree in economics (or one with an economics component) who can handle data and appraise economic argument in the financial press and bank reviews. I could name one very senior official in this category who had a much better 'feel' for the immediate economic future than most professional economic forecasters.

It is easy to exaggerate the importance of 'outside' competition, at least up to policy formation level (but not to ministerial level). There are certain factors beyond the control of the government economists that support imperfection in the market. Government economists are specifically employed to produce economic advice for government and in general are not permitted to meet competition by exporting to the private sector. Nor is it permitted to comment publicly on the alternative products available from the private sector or to answer the constant stream of 'knocking copy', though an opportunity may present itself in the defence of policy and research back-up provided for senior administrators who appear before parliamentary committees.

IV. THE EFFICIENCY OF ADVICE-GIVING

In chapter 17 below a short account is given of the current economic analysis of bureaucracy and some criticisms are made of it in the light of experience. Proponents and critic at least agree that the absence of the market in the formulation and execution of policy by bureaucrats means that they can exercise discretionary behaviour in a manner similar to managers in monopolistic firms. The outcome of this degree of discretion is that there may be 'over-production' of bureau services and/or services are costlier than they might otherwise be assuming that these services could be contracted out in whole or in part to private suppliers.

Applying this analysis to the supply of economic services, I hazard the guess that there are more pressures on government economists to be efficient than on non-professional civil servants. I offer four reasons for this:

(i) As argued in section III above, there are alternative sources of economic advice, at the margin, for administrators and politicians. This means that the quality of our services is under constant critical scrutiny. This is perhaps a partial check on their X-inefficiency if not on that of others;
(ii) The income-elasticity of demand for economists' services may be high and unlikely to be influenced by the government economists' 'bargaining power' in the way that other civil service groups may be able to operate;
(iii) The monitoring of costs per government economist plus supporting staff are conceivably less, at least in the area of 'batch production';
(iv) Professional pride may be just as important an element in the objective function of 'managers', alongside leisure and 'power', particularly if economists wish to retain their mobility within the profession and not merely to look for advancement in the Government Economic Service. This suggests that there is some incentive to take an interest in 'process' and 'product' innovation. How far the benefits of this interest can be captured and transformed into an increase in output relative to inputs through lowering of costs or the shift in the demand curve(s) to the right is a moot point.

Such arguments should not preclude discussion of alternative organisation of economic advice in government and certainly do not do so. Once economic advice is observed to be useful, administrators begin to argue in favour of the destruction of arm's length provision of advice and therefore of backward integration to absorb economics divisions and branches into administrative divisions. Where this has been done it is claimed that communication difficulties are reduced, quicker adaptation of economics input to administrative output can be achieved and as a result the economics product itself can be improved. There are circumstances where backward integration may be efficient, but there are dangers, too. These presuppose a continual flow of work, no diseconomies associated with professional isolation of the economist that produce 'alienation', and lack of time for expert scrutiny of the advice being given. Some of these problems may be circumvented by limiting the period of assignment of economists and by a 'dual' reporting system to both administrative and economics branch or division chief. However, on the scale that administrators envisage it, i.e. with whole economics branches 'bedded out' in the administration, flexibility is bound to be reduced by the tendency of economists as 'factors of production' to become too specific and the advice itself may deteriorate as economists develop the schizophrenia induced by the strain of dual loyalties.

Finally, there is the question whether some if not all of the economic services to government could be more efficiently conducted by contracting out to private firms and institutions protected only by a time limit to their franchise. Given the present state in the economics industry, it is difficult to imagine, with freedom of entry into the advice industry, that the Government Economic Service could not beat off interlopers given their position on the relevant learning curves and the presumption that initial costs of negotiations with outside bodies would be high. However, the issue in the long run probably turns on the advantages that policy-makers see in confidentiality as well as speed in the provision of information and advice. For example, it is conceivable that there are better macroeconomic models of the economy for sale outside government, but the problem still remains of how to purchase and operate these models in such a way as to avoid leakage of information on policy simulations. To the ultimate consumers, the politicians in power, apart from the prestige associated with being served by a bevy of senior administrators and economic advisers, a contract of employment that forbids the disclosure of sensitive information to outsiders may seem preferable, always provided that the economist employees can be kept on their toes by bombarding them with requests to defend their advice against that freely offered from outside.

Views on the functional relationship between confidentiality and the quality of political decision-making are now changing rapidly and it is already fashionable to believe that more open government, including the revelation of policy simulations, will improve both the quality and speed of such decision-making. I am inclined to share the doubts of those who question whether the political masters, whoever they may be, will move much further towards open government. One reason for my doing so is the observation that they are not particularly willing to share their secrets even with one another. But one thing I have learnt from being in government is that predictions of administrative and political change are not improved simply by being close to the events on which these might be based. One can be certain of only one thing and that is that so long as we have big, highly centralised government, politicians will cry out for economic advice from somewhere even though, as is clearly the case with many ministers, they hate to have to do so.

NOTE

1. Sir Robert Giffen, whose name is particularly associated through Marshall's writings with the so-called Giffen Paradox, combined the present day functions of Chief Economic Adviser and Statistical Director to the Board of Trade from 1876 to 1893. His contract included a dispensation that allowed him to offer public comment on controversial economic questions. He exploited it to the full.

REFERENCES

Coats, A. W. (1978) 'Economists in government: a research field for the historian of economics' *History of Political Economy* Vol. 10, No. 2.

Giffen, Sir Robert (1882) in *Economic Enquiries and Studies 1869–1902* 2 vols, Bell, London, 1904, Vol. I.

CHAPTER 16

Giving Economic Advice in Difficult Times[1]

I

In his book on *The Treasury*, Henry Roseveare records Churchill's description of summoning R. G. Hawtrey, the well-known monetary economist, employed to give economic advice: 'the learned man should be released from the dungeon in which we were said to have immured him, have his chains struck off and the straw brushed from his hair and clothes to be admitted to the light and warmth of argument in the Treasury Boardroom' (1969, p. 27). That was in the late 1920s by which time only a handful of economists had served full-time in government in a professional capacity since cabinet government began.[2] Today the economists have penetrated the prestigious second floor of the Treasury Chambers and even that part of it known as the Rotunda to which many are called and only a few permanent secretaries and deputy secretaries are chosen. Yet it is important to note that nowadays most major government departments employ a Chief Economic Adviser (notable exceptions being the Ministry of Defence and the Home Office) with the minimum status of under-secretary. When vacancies occur in their ranks, the gossip columns of the financial press buzz with mild excitement. Economists may still be regarded in parts of Whitehall as *arrivistes* but it is not denied that they have arrived.

A number of economists who have flitted between government, academia and business have given their impressions of their advisory function.[3] In order to differentiate my product from theirs, I adopt a rather different approach which I hope reveals another dimension of giving economic advice – the dependence of its structure on the motivation of politicians and the problems which result from this. These problems are accentuated in what I have called 'difficult times' characterised by economic crises coupled with unusual political instability. I have come to explore this dimension after being struck by the paradox that professional economists inside and outside government who usually regard themselves as experts in appraising the efficiency of the workings of the market are largely immune from its immediate pressures. Their frequent reliance on introspection in developing their theories of economic behaviour suggests that they should be at least as interested in examining the problems of delivering services when market signals are absent, as is true of their own operations within government, and particularly in observing whether efficient delivery is taking place.

I shall develop my theme in the following way. I shall present what might be called the 'mechanistic' view of the economist of the policy process and what instructions it would offer on the structure of economic advice giving. I shall contrast this with what may be labelled the political economist's view of government derived from the recently developed economic theory of democracy, which seems to me to offer a better explanation of the place of economists in government. I shall endeavour to illustrate this latter view by reference to the economist's role in the development of the New Industrial Strategy. Some final remarks consider the wider question of the efficiency of economic advice giving.

II

In presenting the problems of economic policy confronting government, economists frequently make use of either a 'deterministic' or 'stochastic' control model, as they are known in the trade. The distinction can be simply explained by saying that the latter explicitly allows for uncertainty, usually by the use of propositions derived from the theory of probability, while the former does not. The distinction is not explored here but the constituents of the model are broadly similar.

The first thing the economist wants to know is how the aims of government can be expressed in terms of movements in important economic variables, the obvious ones being the rate of inflation, the level of employment, the rate of economic growth, and the distribution of income. He wishes further to explore the 'trade-off' between these variables, that is to say, he must have information about the relative importance of the policy objectives because the pursuit of, say, a more equal distribution of income could be at the cost of a lower rate of economic growth than might otherwise be possible.[4]

The second element in the model is a set of equations designed to explain the workings of the economy and particularly what influences will govern movements in the policy variables themselves. This model must be a computable one, meaning that we must have information not only on the direction of change but also on the magnitude of change in the policy variables based on econometric analysis. The Treasury short-term forecasting model, for example, contains 600 equations and requires elaborate computation facilities in order to assign values to the relevant variables.

If the computable model of the economy displays 'adverse' or 'undesirable' movements in the policy variables given the policy objectives, then the policy maker will want to know to what extent these movements can be corrected. Thus the third element in the model is to identify the policy instruments available to the government and their place in the model itself. For example, the model can include government expenditure on current goods and services as a variable and the economist can investigate how variations in government expenditure would affect the policy variables and with what speed. Many 'simulations' of this kind covering the whole range of instruments available to the government (but capable of identification in the model itself) can be carried out. The process of simulation may be qualified by building in political constraints which reflect, among other things, objectives which are not easily embodied in the 'trade-off' system.

This 'paradigm' of the process of economic policy formation is of necessity an over-simplification, though, as pointed out in chapter 1, it may be defended by the argument that Cabinet Ministers clearly find it useful to explain what they are doing, both to each other and to Parliament, by reference to policy targets and how these targets may be reached, subject to constraints, by employing a particular instrumental 'mix'. An examination of the annual Financial Statement (The Red Book) would easily confirm this. However, one should note the organisational implications of the 'paradigm'. The government is clearly assumed to be a 'unitary being' offering complete and unequivocal information on its policy objectives, the trade-offs between them, not only at a point in time but also through time, for objectives may not be attainable overnight and, in any case, the objectives and trade-offs may themselves change through time. It follows further that there is perfectly efficient co-ordination of policy instruments both 'horizontally', i.e. between the various branches of the executive working for the 'government', and 'vertically', i.e. between layers of government.

If such a paradigm bore any close relation to what happens in the real world, the organisation of economic advice would be very simple, and there would be a perfect and harmonious division of labour between politicians, administrators and economists. The Chief Economist would simply be presented with perfect information on policy objectives and trade-offs and his advice would not be sought or offered on this essentially political matter. He would be the technical head of a production plant producing a stream of information on the feasibility of 'maximising' the objectives. His job would be to keep the plant in good repair and to explore innovations and improvements which would enhance the quality of the forecasts and simulations. There might be a few economists employed in subordinate branches of government, humble 'cost–benefiteers' appraising and monitoring the efficiency of individual investment and other projects which policy implementation demanded, but the real action would be somewhere close to the Cabinet room, with only the computer and its slaves left in 'Hawtrey's dungeon'.

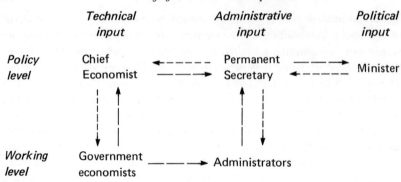

FIGURE 16.1

A highly simplified diagram (Figure 16.1) may help to illustrate the 'supply' of and 'demand' for economic advice. The hatched arrows show the demand for advice on a policy matter emanating from the 'Minister' in charge of economic affairs. His 'final demand' to his chief official will set up a 'derived' demand for information and analysis from economists and administrators. The supply of economic advice will be scrutinised and co-ordinated by the Chief Economist and the combination of this advice with the input of advice on administrative and executive matters connected with the proposed policy will be co-ordinated by the Permanent Secretary. (This does not necessarily preclude direct contact between the Chief Economist and the Minister, provided the Permanent Secretary knows what is going on.)

Some economists might prefer this world of technocratic bliss though others would want to combine their technical function with instructing the 'government' in the right policies to follow based on fashionable welfare economics. One need not take sides in this issue if the purpose is to investigate what actually conditions the role of the economist in government. One can concentrate as I propose to do on explaining why such a world does not exist.

III

It must be true in a tautological sense that policy actions by a government reflect *some* view of what it is best for that body to do. However, the 'paradigm' used in section II only displays the outcome of policy discussion and not the *process* by which policies are arrived at. It also implies that the 'objective function', i.e. the statement of policies and trade-offs, remains stable or at least any changes in it are predictable and can be fixed in time. A glance at the newspapers is sufficient to dispel the impression that policy decisions by government are so easily arrived at. A Cabinet is a body of powerful politicians whose members at any one time may have very different views about which policy variables should be included in the 'objective function' and which trade-offs they would prefer. They may also attach very different rates of time discount to the variables, e.g. the desired time-path to 'full employment' will differ markedly between different Ministers. Furthermore, individual Ministers have a tendency to change their minds rather suddenly, and in the course of a few years the turnover in Cabinet membership may be high. Thus the 'unitary being' has become an oligarchy with varying membership and in consequence its 'objective function' keeps undergoing a process of constant mutation.

If one wants to know how a government will organise its executive, including its economic services, it is important to discover what motivates the Cabinet in its choice of policy objectives and trade-offs rather than simply to assume that these are given. Following the theory of Anthony Downs (1957)[5] economists interested in the workings of government have fastened on the intuitively obvious proposition that governments in power want to stay in power – they wish to 'maximise their length of political life.' Policies are therefore only means for maximising the support of the voting public and the administration must be organised in such a way as to give as full information as possible on the vote-getting potentialities of policies and trade-offs. This sordid statement of political motivation reminds one of the *bon mot* attributed to Keynes in his description of a particular American senator: 'he had both ears so close to the ground that he could not hear what an upright man was saying'! However, policy variables which may be termed 'idealistic' and which are derived from the political philosophy of the party in power are not thereby precluded but their relevance to policy action will at least be subject to the overriding constraint of retaining power by vote-getting. Their relevance will vary according to the actual extent of political support at any one time and such important events as the timing of elections.[6]

Clearly the *type* of economic advice demanded by the Cabinet will depend on the policies chosen but I have produced no argument which would account for the devolution of economic advice mentioned at the beginning of this article, which requires the attachment of senior officials and considerable staffs to individual Ministries.[7] This requires me to develop the Downs type thesis somewhat further by taking account of the struggle within parties for political leadership.

A Cabinet usually comprises ambitious men and women who to a greater or lesser degree are concerned with their actual or potential status within that body. Clearly their views of policy objectives and trade-offs will reflect not only what will promote the chances of their party of retaining power but also their conception of what will maximise their own support within the party. Party popularity is not enough, however, and must be accompanied by a reputation for being able to control bureaucrats and to execute policy measures in at least an apparently efficient and business-like manner. This offers a strong incentive for politicians within sight of Cabinet rank to get their hands on major instruments of policy which enable them to make their mark with their party and particularly with its leading members.

There is one important recent development which has improved the opportunities for gaining the appropriate kind of experience and power. Competition between parties to retain power has forced them to differentiate their product by seeking to achieve more ambitious targets. Thus in the 1960s, employment policy had become a question no longer of minimising the percentage unemployed, subject to the constraints exercised by other objectives, but of minimising the dispersion of unemployment rates between regions. This has induced governments to utilise a whole range of selective measures outside the normal range associated with macro-economic policy (and therefore with instruments directly under the control of the Treasury) if for no other reason than that they must be seen to be acting vigorously within the appropriate regions. The hard knock administered to the British economy by the oil crisis and the ensuing economic depression may have lowered the level of aspiration of politicians but it has reinforced the political necessity for dramatic actions of a selective character designed to save firms and jobs, as well as for reinforcing macro-policy instruments, such as incomes and prices policy, again outside the traditional range of responsibility of the Treasury. Whatever view one takes of the desirability of increasing the scope of state intervention of this kind, it has increased the opportunities for extra-Treasury Ministers to dramatise their position as custodians of these instruments, and has thereby promoted a vested interest in their retention, provided that in the long run voters are not alienated by the results achieved.

The combination of the political objectives of the Cabinet coupled with the ambitions of its individual members has turned Departments of State previously wholly subordinate to the Treasury in matters of economic policy with, at most, executive and monitoring responsibilities into organisations with distinct control over a separate instrumental capability.[8] Their Ministers may not be as powerful as the Chancellor of the Exchequer but they will have an independent voice in Cabinet on matters of economic policy. If the Chancellor is to maintain his hold on overall economic policy matters he must at the very least demonstrate to the other Secretaries of State concerned with economic questions why their particular instrumental capability must be used in a way which promotes consistent action. He must provide them with economic information and analysis which they can assess and appraise with the help of separate advisers.

The administrative devolution of economic advice follows directly from the acceptance of the proliferation of 'new' policies and instruments. But there is more to it than simply calling upon senior administrators and economic advisers to brief a Minister on the Chancellor's views on the conduct of economic policy. As my analysis of political motivation indicates, a Secretary of State may wish to persuade the Cabinet that his particular set of objectives and trade-offs fulfils the government's programme best, in which case he may want to explore alternative economic 'scenarios' from those chosen by the Chancellor. He will expect administrative and technical resources to be devoted to the preparation of briefing material which will stand up to scrutiny by the Chancellor and his advisers. If, for example, he takes a different line from the Chancellor on the need to reduce a rise in unemployment, he will expect his advisers to show how the time-path of employment and its level will be affected by alternative policy measures and what the side effects will be on other policy variables. This implies either the development of an independent economic forecasting and analytical capability closely geared to his requirements or access to such facilities which will produce the answers he needs. His advisers will be made uncomfortably aware that economics and econometrics are not exact sciences and that, if the results they produce surprise and disappoint him, he will study them very closely and make comparisons between them and those which may be available to him from alternative sources of advice, e.g. his personal advisers who will normally share his political views, or the Think Tank. A situation could arise in which a Minister may be so committed to his own view of what policies are 'right' that he will instruct his officials to prepare for him a persuasive case whatever doubts there may be about the support these policies receive from economic analysis and the related empirical evidence.

The differences between the real situation and our 'paradigm' are clear, but what must be noted is the professional dilemma created by it. In order to maintain credibility, the Government Economic Service must be seen within Whitehall as giving broadly consistent economic advice based on a common analytical and statistical framework which can stand up to fire from outside professional critics of high repute whose views may well be known to such awkward Parliamentary watchdogs as the Expenditure Committee (see *Ninth Report*, 1974). To retain influence with Ministers, however, senior economists in individual Ministries may be under considerable pressure to produce economic argument and statistical back-up which supports their position on economic policy. Only in rare cases will a senior economist be influential enough to change a Minister's mind on a major issue of policy and even then he will be able to do so only with the firm backing of senior administrators, and particularly that of the Permanent Secretary.

In cases where Ministers in Cabinet have widely differing views on economic policy, the awkwardnesses associated with disagreement are legion. Professional cohesion of view calls for rapid and frequent consultation with opposite numbers in other Ministries. Ministers are well aware of this network activity. Individually they may dislike it, for it may undermine a strategy of presentation at Cabinet which relies on an element of surprise. Collectively, they may also dislike it, particularly if experienced senior officials from different Ministries, economists included, have reservations about the policy measures which Ministers may finally have agreed to institute.

Purchases \ Sales			Department 'A' Administrators: Policy level	Department 'A' Administrators: Working level	Department 'A' Economists: Chief economist	Department 'A' Economists: Working level	Department 'A' Economists: Special adviser	Department 'B' Administrators: Policy level	Department 'B' Administrators: Working level	Department 'B' Economists: Chief economist	Department 'B' Economists: Working level	Department 'B' Economists: Special adviser	Final buyers: Minister 'A'	Final buyers: Minister 'B'
Department 'A'	Adminis-trators	Policy level			(x_{13})			x_{16}					X_{11}	
		Working level	x_{21}		x_{23}	x_{24}			x_{27}					
	Economists	Chief economist	x_{31}				(x_{35})			x_{38}			(X_{31})	
		Working level	x_{41}	x_{42}	x_{43}		(x_{45})			(x_{48})	x_{49}			
		Special adviser											X_{51}	
Department 'B'	Adminis-trators	Policy level	x_{61}							(x_{68})				X_{62}
		Working level		x_{72}				x_{76}		x_{78}	x_{79}			
	Economists	Chief economist			x_{83}			x_{86}				$(x_{8\cdot 10})$		(X_{82})
		Working level			(x_{93})	x_{94}		x_{96}	x_{97}	x_{98}		$(x_{9\cdot 10})$		
		Special adviser												$X_{10\cdot 2}$

FIGURE 16.2

Figure 16.2 expands Figure 16.1 in the form of a kind of 'input–output' table showing the 'trade flows' generated between administrators, economists and politicians. Imagine a situation in which two Ministers have responsibility for presenting to the Cabinet their views on some important issue of economic policy, but who differ in their evaluation of the appropriate instruments to be used in resolving it. The Ministers are, as before, the 'final buyers' of advice and information and their 'purchases' (='officials' sales') are represented by a large 'X'. Behind these Ministerial 'purchases' will lie a vast network of official exchanges across departmental boundaries corresponding to 'intermediate' purchases and sales of information and advice. These exchanges are represented by a small 'x'. In both the large X and small x cases, the subscripts denote the row and column of the transactions, e.g. X_{11} denotes the first row and first column within the 'final buyer' sector (briefing provided by senior administrator(s) to Minister 'A'), whereas x_{83} denotes the eighth row and third column within the 'intermediate' sector (denoting perhaps a telephone call from the Chief Economist in Department 'B' to Department 'A'). The diagram displays only official contracting arrangements and the unofficial ministerial and administrative acts of exchange inside and outside the government machine can well be left to the imagination!

The entries are only illustrative and their position will vary from case to case, with bracketed items indicative of the possible 'spread' of exchanges. There are two features of Figure 16.2 which perhaps deserve comment. I have assumed that each Minister has a 'special economic adviser' but it will be noted that he/she 'sells' to the 'final buyer' (his Minister) but does not 'purchase' advice and information from officials. He/she may well do so to a limited extent but several have complained in public that they have been kept in the dark about the reasoning behind official briefing, particularly that based on economic forecasting. I, for one, have some sympathy with their point of view, granted their existence, but one may not always find that special advisers are always willing to support reciprocal trading arrangements. The second feature is the rather equivocal position in which a Chief Economist might find himself, as denoted by the bracketed (X_{31}) and (X_{82}). Whether there will be an entry or not will depend on the extent to which a Minister will consult his Chief Economist directly or through the policy level administrators, and his view of the different roles of the Chief Economist and his special adviser.

IV

The attempts to devise a new industrial strategy[9] offer a clear illustration of the problems encountered by economic advisers resulting from the understandable political aspirations of Ministers.

The first problem has been that of discerning a clear, consistent and operational set of objectives governing the attempt to improve the performance of manufacturing industry. Ministers might agree in principle that any such attempt represented a long-term aim which could only be fulfilled within a period extending far beyond the latest date of the next general election, but differ about whether the emphasis should be placed on preserving jobs through the building up of existing capacity in traditional industries or on promoting adaptability and change in the light of the demand for our goods abroad upon which manufacturing growth depends. The latter policy would only be compatible with job preservation if redeployment of labour on a considerable scale could be engineered. On the other hand, the time horizon of politicians being usually short, given their assessment of the ways in which voters' support might be maximised, an industrial strategy must appear to be offering immediate benefits to the community, and with unemployment dominating the short-term situation Ministers may be under strong pressure to seek out measures which will preserve jobs in the short term, subject to the binding constraints on using a reflationary policy which could have adverse effects on the rate of inflation and on the balance of payments. The number of simultaneous short- and long-term scenarios under constant and prolonged economic and statistical investigation suggested by these policy disagreements may therefore be considerable.

The second problem arises from the role which economic advice might be expected to play in attempting to meet any combination of objectives. Concentrating on the longer-run problem, what do economists know about the factors determining the size, structure and growth of the manufacturing sector and how that sector and its components might be influenced by policy measures? The answer is that they claim to know a good deal but there is a wide range of disagreement which is bound to penetrate the industrial strategy discussion. A particularly influential view which has itself gone through a complicated process of change is associated with Lord Kaldor.[10] The growth of manufacturing output is significantly dependent on the demand for exports. This demand for exports will depend on an 'income' effect, the growth in world trade for manufacturing output, and a 'substitution' effect, the ratio of domestic prices of our exports to those of our competitors. As export sales are highly sensitive to our competitiveness, the important factor in their promotion must be unit labour costs, which form such a major element in price. The crucial factor determining labour costs, according to Kaldor, is the rate of growth of output itself, for, it is claimed, the higher that rate of growth the higher the level of the average productivity of labour. This is the so-called 'Verdoorn's Law', a supposedly empirical relationship which has close kinship to the proposition that manufacturing activity is characterised by technical economies of scale. If some means can be found, e.g. a large increase in the proportion of investment to net value added in manufacturing industry, to produce a once and for all improvement in labour productivity, then exports will become competitive, and the resultant growth, through the operation of Verdoorn's Law, will become self-sustaining.

The apparent virtue of this view of the process of growth is that the remedies are administratively simple to introduce. However, there are strong doubts about its validity. There is little, if any, empirical evidence to support the operation of Verdoorn's Law at least in the strong form on which the thesis depends.[11] Even if the Law were to operate, the analysis assumes that, in the process of output expansion, unit wage costs do not rise faster than average productivity of labour, which rests on the strong assumption that in the course of expansion there are no labour shortages and no trade union pressures to raise money wages. But even if Verdoorn's Law did produce the desired effect, it is presumably also valid in other industrial countries undergoing similar expansion, so that our competitors' prices relative to our own may not rise, and the sought-for export-led growth would have to depend on factors other than price.

An alternative view of the growth process recognises that maintaining the ratio of manufacturing investment to net value added in the manufacturing sector may be a necessary but it is hardly a sufficient condition. There is ample evidence that labour productivity in the U.K., relative to that in our major competitors, has been declining, (see, for example, Jones, 1976; also Panic, 1976), suggesting that the problem of improving our relative growth performance lies in some attempt to improve the efficiency with which labour and capital inputs are used. However, in contrast to the previous view, which points towards general measures to stimulate investment, among other instruments, any remedies would have to be administered at the firm and even plant level. Indeed, such remedies, if they can be identified, may have to be designed to cancel out the barriers to efficient use of factor inputs produced by other government actions, such as the likely reduction in labour mobility resulting from subsidised housing coupled with rent control and security of tenure.

Faced with our present economic difficulties, politicians, being under pressure to act decisively and dramatically, will naturally be impatient with any manifestations of the philosophic doubts which plague economists, and will risk making strong assumptions about the efficacy of the policy instruments which have been assigned to their control.

At the same time, they have been quick to realise that the variability of industrial performance by sector revealed by productivity studies offers support in principle for selective measures. At the same time they have been understandably reluctant to admit that labour productivity is not mainly a function of investment in new capital equipment rather than a function of defects in the operation of the labour market.

It should come as no surprise to find that such a landmark as the White Paper, *An Approach to Industrial Strategy* (Cmnd. 6315, 1975), coupled with later pronouncements of the government through the NEDC and in Parliamentary speeches, offers few clues as to the precise economic policy model which is considered operational. The prime objective of 'a high output–high wage economy' is unexceptionable but no indication is given of the time-scale or of the degree of improvement in economic growth which is aimed at. There is an interesting change in emphasis in the background analysis of our industrial problems towards recognition of our poor productivity performance but a reluctance to commit anyone to a particular view of the causes of our relative economic decline. With no clear indication which objectives of policy are being maximised and a lack of commitment on the precise nature of the constraints on doing so, there can be no assessment of the relative merits of alternative courses of action to be taken. But what comes over very clearly is the major role to be played by selective measures, notably Planning Agreements and the National Enterprise Board, which were designed to bring about the desired changes in efficiency at the company level. Further, while the methods used to devise and institute a National Plan associated with the 1960s are rejected, an elaborate machinery for consultation with both sides of industry at national, sector and company level, co-ordinated by the NEDC, has been set up which highlights the role of economic Ministers outside the Treasury. Indeed, it is significant that the White Paper itself is a joint product of the Treasury and Department of Industry.

From the point of view of the economic adviser, the salutary lesson to be learnt from a document of this kind is the very limited nature of his influence. The role of the economist as the impartial, cautious technical observer always appealing to the evidence, cuts little ice with politicians and administrators thirsting for action. It is no use to them, so they would argue, to be told what will *not* work. If the economic policy model linking up industrial objectives to policy instruments offers no concrete indications of what action to take, other, say, than measures to restore competition in the product and factor markets (which neither labour nor capital like), then so much the worse for the model. In such circumstances the economist in government is faced with a situation rather like the political scientist friend of mine asked to lecture some years ago on Communism to high-ranking naval officers. As he was entering the lecture hall he was drawn aside by a four-ring captain who whispered to him: 'Of course we all hate Communism – and we have brought you here to tell us why.' The policies will be instituted despite the warnings of the economist about the strong assumptions on which they are based, but he will have to find ways of adapting his skills to further them if he is to be listened to.

V

The particular example of the problems facing senior economists involved in extra-Treasury policy initiatives is not meant to convey the impression that they are likely to be consigned once more to 'Hawtrey's dungeon'. They are too useful as organisers of economic intelligence services on a considerable scale, as monitors of the constant stream of outside economic advice (some of it pretty crazy) which flows in the direction of Ministers and senior administrators, as suppliers of the economic dimension to a whole range of policy scenarios which administrators may wish Ministers to consider, and sometimes even as policy innovators. If anything, the growing proportion of senior administrators with an economics training produces more and not less contact between economic services and administrative divisions, if only because of the growth in the general appreciation of the solid virtues of the dismal science.

An economist in government may be content to be judged by the preferences of politicians and senior administrators, but this may not satisfy members of his own profession. Professor Hayek has gone so far as to argue (*Daily Telegraph*, 26th August 1976) that the British economy would be in better shape without her government economists, adding that 'one sometimes feels that untaught commonsense would probably have done better'. Hayek's view is based on a misunderstanding of the role of the economist in government. As I have indicated (and here I am simply echoing the weighty judgment of Sir Alec Cairncross), it is a misconception to believe that a senior economist in government sits constantly by the side of his political master whispering continually in his ear like a powerful mediaeval courtier. Even if Hayek had in mind (though he is not clear on this matter) personal advisers, the image of power and influence is much exaggerated. Cabinet ministers are firmly convinced that economic policy is much too important to be left to economists, or administrators for that matter, just as the conduct of war is too important to be left to generals. A government economic adviser might agree with Hayek that protecting labour from the rigours of competition policy may have promoted the long-term relative decline of the British economy, but he knows that even the most sympathetic Minister is not going to risk his neck and that of his colleagues by promoting measures which would require the repeal of major acts of employment and labour legislation.

Of course, any adviser who feels that the constraints under which he works do not allow him to promote policies which will be regarded as sensible and which have some chance of acceptance can make a choice. He can undergo a test of patience and try to persuade his masters to alter these constraints. He may live in the hope that they will act as the Florentine statesman, Francesco Guicciardini, counselled the Medicis:

> Although we may act on the best advice, the future is so uncertain that the results are often contrary. Nevertheless, we must not surrender, like animals, a prey to fortune; rather we must follow reason like men. The truly wise man should be more content to have acted on good advice though it yielded bad results than to have had good results from bad advice. [1965]

The alternative choice is obvious. He can pack his bags and try to practise his skills elsewhere.

234   *A Variety of Governmental Experience*

NOTES

1. Reproduced with minor amendments from *Three Banks Review* Vol. 106, March 1977.
2. The development of economic intelligence in the Bank of England is associated with a similar scepticism of economists. See the amusing account in *Bank of England Quarterly Bulletin*, December 1976, pp. 436–7.
3. Notably Sir Alec Cairncross (1971).
4. For some simplified examples of economic models embodying 'traded-off' policy objectives see Peacock and Shaw (1976) Chapter 8.
5. For a useful critique of Downs, see Tullock (1976).
6. For evidence of the influence of the 'political cycle' on macro-economic policy, see Lindbeck (1976) and Frey (1978).
7. For example, the Department of Environment and the combined Departments of Trade, Industry, Prices and Consumer Protection (which operate a common service) each employ more economists than the Treasury.
8. The imagination boggles at the further complications of co-ordination of economic policy which would follow from political devolution to Scotland and Wales.
9. For an authoritative account of the evolution of the present industrial policy programme, see Lord (1977).
10. For an interesting exposition of Lord Kaldor's position which has his approval, see Dixon and Thirlwall (1975).
11. For criticisms of the empirical and analytical validity of the Kaldorian thesis, see particularly Rowthorn (1975a) with Lord Kaldor's reply and Mr Rowthorn's rejoinder (1975b). See also Vaciago (1975).

REFERENCES

Cairncross, Sir A. (1971) *Essays in Economic Management* Nos 10 & 11, Allen & Unwin, London.
Dixon, R. and Thirlwall, A. P. (1975) 'A model of regional growth rate differences on Kaldorian lines' *Oxford Economic Papers* July.
Downs, A. (1957) *The Economic Theory of Democracy* Harper & Row, New York.
Frey, B. (1978) 'The political business cycle: Theory and evidence' in Institute of Economic Affairs Readings 18 *The Economics of Politics* IEA, London.
Guicciardini, F. (1965) *Maxims and Reflections of a Renaissance Statesman* (translated by Mario Domandi) Torchbooks, New York.
Jones, D. T. (1976) 'Output, employment and labour productivity since 1975' *National Institute Economic Review* August.
Kaldor, Lord N. (1975) 'Reply' to Rowthorn (1975a) *Economic Journal* Vol. 85, December.
Lindbeck, A. (1976) 'Stabilisation policy in open economies with endogenous politicians' *American Economic Review* Vol. 66, May.
Lord, A. (1977) 'A Strategy for Industry' Sir Ellis Hunter Memorial Lecture No. 8, University of York.
Ninth Report from the Expenditure Committee: Public Expenditure, Inflation and the Balance of Payments (1974) House of Commons Papers, 328.
Panic, M. (ed.) (1976) *The UK and West German Manufacturing Industry 1954–72* National Economic Development Office monograph.
Peacock, A. T. and Shaw, G. K. (1976) *The Economic Theory of Fiscal Policy* revised edition, Allen & Unwin, London.
Roseveare, H. (1969) *The Treasury* Allen Lane, Penguin Press, London.
Rowthorn, R. T. (1975a) 'What remains of Kaldor's Law?' *Economic Journal* Vol. 85, March.
Rowthorn, R. T. (1975b) 'Rejoinder' to Lord Kaldor (1975) *Economic Journal* Vol. 85, December.
Tullock, G. (1976) *The Vote Motive* Hobart Paperback 9, Institute of Economic Affairs, London.
Vaciago, G. (1975) 'Increasing returns and growth in advanced economics: A re-evaluation' *Oxford Economic Papers* July.

CHAPTER 17

The Economics of Bureaucracy: An Inside View[1]

I. Introduction

The Institute of Economic Affairs has paved the way in this country for the study of the economics of bureaucracy by its publication of the work of William A. Niskanen (1973) and Gordon Tullock (1976).[2] My own experience,[3] for what it is worth, suggests that their analyses rest on rather strong assumptions, though I recognise that they have provided a useful point of departure for this contribution.

II. The Theoretical Framework

The essence of the Niskanen/Tullock (N/T) approach is that there is a close analogy between the theory of the firm and the theory of bureaucratic operation. Though trained and treated like an élite, bureaucrats are not cast in some god-like mould so that their thoughts and actions can be deemed superior to those of other persons. They maximise their utility, subject to constraints. They, too, sell their skills, by providing technical and administrative advice to producers of government policies, i.e., to politicians in power. It is true that they are precluded from maximising money profit, as does the archetypal entrepreneur, and they produce nothing for direct sale; but their sources of satisfaction are similar to those in other occupations. In Niskanen's words (which I shall recall later):

Among the several variables that may enter the bureaucrat's motives are: salary, perquisites of the office, public reputation, power, patronage, output of the bureau, ease of making changes, and ease of managing the bureau. *All except the last two* [italics mine] are a positive function of the total *budget* of the bureau during the bureaucrat's tenure. [1973, p. 22]

So, fortunately for the mathematics of the argument, the bureaucrat's 'maximand', the element he tries to maximise, can be reduced to a measurable quantity, for his motivation leads him to maximise the size of the bureau's budget.

The important proposition which N/T are anxious to establish about this kind of behaviour is that it leads to 'over-production' by the bureaucrat. The entrepreneur in a competitive market is induced to produce an amount which is optimal from the consumers' point of view, firstly, because he is forced to minimise costs in order to survive and, secondly, because, at the margin, the costs of production are equated with the price consumers are willing to pay. However, the bureaucrat is more in the position of a monopolist. He is the sole supplier of particular administrative and technical services; moreover, and no less important, he is the sole source of information about his costs of production. The entrepreneur in the competitive market can only extract the minimum sum consumers are willing to pay for his product, but the bureaucrat can extract the maximum sum which the purchasers of his services are willing to pay. As economists would put it, this allows him to equate total costs with total benefits instead of marginal costs with marginal benefits. However, as the bureaucrat is precluded from maximising profits, he 'captures' the total budget by pushing output *beyond* the competitive optimum to conform with his desire to enhance his prestige and power.

The conclusion of interest for government policy is that, if all bureaucrats act in the way described, there is a waste of resources in producing government services which can be avoided only by methods of improving bureaucratic efficiency. Niskanen (1973, Ch. IV) considers such methods as competition between bureaus, altering the reward system for bureaucrats (e.g. bonuses to 'top' officials) in order to encourage economy in resource use, turning over production to private firms (e.g. refuse collection), and facilitating investigation of government departments by 'watchdog' committees of the legislature.

Are Bureaucrats Dominant and Politicians 'Passive Adjusters'?

If Niskanen's argument has substance, it may be asked why politicians supplying public funds must really be assumed to act as passive adjusters to the actions of bureaucrats, for if all bureaus behave in this way somewhere along the line the suspicion of being 'taken for a ride' must occur to politicians. In seeking to answer this question, several economists have turned their attention to the motivation of those social and political groups who 'bargain' directly or indirectly with bureaucrats, for example Borcherding (1977) and also Peacock and Wiseman (1979). Indeed, their studies are designed to employ public choice theory in such a way as to explain the most important economic phenomenon about modern government, the growing proportion of annual resources to which it lays claim, with the bureaucrat playing a crucial role.

The argument can be summarised, rather baldly, in the following way. Voters do not pay directly for government services and their individual tax payments may bear little if any relationship to the benefits which they may derive from such services. They have every incentive to maximise their gains from government services and will vote for politicians who will facilitate access to them. Incumbent legislators, faced with potential and (at election time) actual competition from other political parties, can beat off challengers only by promoting the services which voters want at apparently no cost to them. Legislators are therefore strong supporters of bureaucratic organisations which supply these particular services, such as education and health. They will not inquire too closely into the possibility that there may be 'fat' in bureaucrats' budgets, particularly if bureaucrats help their constituents materially by giving them government jobs, by being generous in their interpretation of regulations governing the allocation of subsidies, and so on.

As the public sector expands in response to the short-term common interests of the groups active in the political market-place, a larger proportion of the working population acquire a vested interest in government employment, and form also a larger proportion of *voters*, thus re-inforcing the process of government expenditure. The process will be self-defeating in the sense that voters will be faced with growing tax burdens; but no group in isolation has any incentive to reduce its demands for supposedly free government services and therefore no brake is applied to stop the expansion of the public sector.

III. A Critique

The first problem I face in matching this analysis with personal experience is that of identifying the bureaucratic decision-maker. He is by definition in charge of a budget, authorised to bargain with a 'supplier' of funds, that is, over its amount and composition, and to be at least formally accountable for how the funds are used. If this is the case, then in the UK it would be entirely misleading to identify Niskanen's 'bureaucrat' with senior civil servants. The appropriate person is the Ministerial head of a Department of State who presents his annual estimates in the first and crucial instance to the Chancellor of the Exchequer for approval, but with right of appeal to the Cabinet, a body of which he is normally a member. What must now be investigated is whether a Minister will act differently from N/T Man and whether the limitations on his doing so are different.

Components of a Minister's Utility Function

If I had to guess at the components (or 'arguments', as the economics profession calls them) in a Minister's utility function, I would say that he 'trades off' political ambition within the Government against the perceived benefits to him of party loyalty. I have argued elsewhere (chapter 16 of this volume) that the first of these components leads Ministers to seek control of policy instruments which dramatise their actions. In all probability a Minister will regard maximising his budget certainly as a sufficient, but not a necessary, condition for achieving this end. Clearly, more expenditure enables him to extend the range of instruments which become associated with his Ministry and therefore with himself. Altering the composition rather than the amount of the budget may have too high an opportunity cost, e.g. the personal 'wear and tear' in arguing with officials and others with a vested interest in existing policies, particularly in a profession in which the future is discounted very heavily ('a week is a long time in politics', according to Harold Wilson). I have seen Ministers argue for hours in favour of budget adjustment to suit a change in the 'policy mix' but only under the threat of rigid 'cash limits' collectively agreed by the Cabinet and imposed by the Treasury Minister.

The second compartment in the Minister's scale of preferences places a brake on too singleminded a pursuit of budget maximisation. The costs to the party in power of granting an increased budget to an ambitious Education, Housing, Transport or other Minister are the alternative uses of tax receipts to promote party aims; it cannot always be assumed that all proposed increases in Departmental estimates can be covered simply by tax increases, particularly as such increases themselves may produce a 'backlash' effect which might weaken the long-run support for the party.

Incidental references I have made to the political environment in which politicians as bureau chiefs maximise their aims, point to further doubts about the applicability of the N/T analysis. Ministers as bureaucrats cannot act as discriminating monopolists, at least in the UK, even if they wanted to. They cannot afford to obstruct probing into their programmes by the Chancellor of the Exchequer through Treasury officials when they are in competition for funds. They may be the sole suppliers of particular services such as nuclear power, postal services, broadcasting, etc., and may find malleable officials who can exaggerate the costs of producing them, but, in terms of the ultimate aim of retaining power, few services are not substitutable at the margin for others.[4]

The second difficulty with the N/T analysis follows from the first. What does the bureaucrat (defined as a public official) maximise? In the UK, Administrative Class civil servants are normally appointed on the assumption that they will spend by far the major part of their working life in government and will obtain job security early in their career. (The position is similar in France and Germany.) They are relatively well paid and pensioned alongside those with comparable educational background, age and experience in the private sector, and a move into the private sector by a senior civil servant before retirement is news. This contrasts markedly with senior public officials in the USA. Few top officials have tenure, there is a high degree of mobility between the private and public sectors which is aided by the ability to trade a reputation for energy and 'go' in either sector.

In the kind of professional environment surrounding the British higher civil servant (say, Deputy-Secretary and above), one would be surprised if utility maximisation could be summed up in maximising the size of the bureau to the exclusion of other factors. Though the distinction cannot be tightly drawn, it is useful to distinguish between those who are primarily concerned with the *formulation* of policy for Ministerial consideration and those concerned with the *execution* of policy.

(i) *Policy formulation* Take policy formulation first. Though it frequently involves officials in quite junior posts (including technical staff, e.g. economists and lawyers), it is essentially the principal concern of those who have reached the top, the Permanent Secretaries. How do they achieve this exalted position? This is a complex question to answer, but as a cockshy I would suggest that they do so by maximising their reputation within their professional cadre. They are picked for the 'fast stream' at a relatively early age because they appear potentially able to combine two highly-prized qualities within their cadre: the clarity and persuasiveness of their drafting and their speed in designing and assembling the machinery for a policy 'exercise' and putting it into operation. Military terminology of this kind is only rivalled by cricketing analogies in civil service parlance. Briefs for Ministers are designed to help him bat on 'sticky' Parliamentary wickets, the deadline for their delivery usually being 'close of play' (circa 1800 hours). Indeed, one abiding impression I have is that designing and assembling the 'machinery' – often an elaborate *ad hoc* committee system sometimes spread across several Departments – is frequently considered as more important than what the machinery is supposed to produce.[5] In the words of the song popularised in the 1930s by that delicious US 'songbird', Alice Faye: 'It ain't what you do, it's the way that you do it. That's what gets results.'

Thus, while maximising one's reputation within the professional cadre is entirely compatible with a desire for prestige and power, and with more laudable motives such as a wish to serve the nation, maximising one's budget is neither a necessary nor a sufficient condition for achieving it. The most prestigious positions in the Civil Service are still in the Treasury, a Department of government principally concerned with the efficient use of resources, both public and private, and where officials do not make the obvious mistake of pursuing this aim by maximising the amount of 'fat' in their own budget.

(ii) *Policy execution* It is true that so far as heading up exercises in policy formulation, it is a case of many being called but few chosen. The job specification of a large proportion of senior civil servants is principally determined by the need to execute policies devised by superiors and approved by Ministers, though they may be responsible for offering 'feed back' on the effectiveness of the policy instrument which they must operate and consulted on possible improvements. It is difficult to believe that a significant number of them, who have been denied the power which goes with promotion to the highest echelons or who have forgone the chance of promotion having viewed with concern the incidence of heart attacks among their peers, do not maximise a very different utility function in order to enjoy the ease associated with long experience in working established routines. Certainly this impression would accord with the common man's view of the bureaucrat.[6,7]

'On-the-Job Leisure'

The kind of 'model' which I am in the process of developing out of my own casual empirical investigations would identify at least two aims in the bureaucrat's utility function, the bureaucrat being, say, the head of a Division, normally with Under-Secretary rank. He would certainly derive utility from the emoluments and the power and prestige going with the management of skilled administrators, but he would trade this off against the utility of what I shall call 'on-the-job leisure'. The larger the number of administrators he has to supervise, the more time spent on 'man management' and the less time available for such on-the-job leisure activities as 'eating for the Queen' (diplomatic lunches, dinners of professional societies) and attending prestigious national or international conferences (preferably only as an observer where formal attendance can be minimised). Where trade-offs are constrained by difficulties in adjusting the workload, then the appropriate instrument of the skilful 'satisficing' bureaucrat is delegation to carefully picked juniors. A senior member of the Foreign Office as a young man on his first overseas appointment tells the story that he reported to his Ambassador at 11 a.m. as ordered. The Ambassador informed him that he would be expected to be in his office by 11 and to stay at least until 3.30. The young diplomat inadvisedly remarked that this regimen seemed congenial. 'What?' said the Ambassador, 'I suppose you could put it that way, but you must agree that it does rather cut into one's day'!

Niskanen, as we have seen, specifically excludes 'ease of managing a bureau' from the factors which lead bureaucrats to maximise their budget. At the same time, there is nothing in the utility maximising behaviour of our bureaucrat which would lead him to make the size of his budget conform to something like the competitive optimum. His deviation from the optimum is unlikely to manifest itself in 'over-production'; it is more likely to take the form of 'producing' output at well above minimum cost. (Economists would call this 'X-inefficiency' as distinct from 'allocative inefficiency'.) This is because 'on-the-job leisure' normally requires complementary expenditure such as expense allowances and other perquisites of office. His 'desired' budget will certainly be higher than that which would be necessary to conform to the competitive optimum but his 'satisficing' behaviour will place a limit on the investment in time, energy and skill he would be willing to devote to maximising it. In short the N/T model, while employing strong assumptions about bureaucratic behaviour, lends itself to further development, along lines parallel to the development of the study of entrepreneurial behaviour which has grown out of the earlier literature in which profit was the sole element in the entrepreneur's structure of preferences.

IV. CONCLUSION

Finally, I must relate what I have said to the attempts, previously mentioned, to examine the role of bureaucracy in the political process. It follows from my analysis that I am not convinced that the senior civil servant plays the positive role assigned to him in promoting the growth of public expenditure as a means of helping his masters retain voter support. I have taken part in too many exercises where senior civil servants have tried to persuade Ministers of the incompatibility of their lavish extensions of spending programmes with longer-term, less vote-catching objectives to believe that. Indeed, it is worth remarking parenthetically that there is much to be said for the 'ganging up' of officials in the manner which aroused the wrath of Crossman – and arouses that of Benn – and for the associated intelligence network as being the only way in which officials can bring Ministers to the point of decision and to accept collective responsibility.

No Incentive to Reduce Public vis-à-vis *Private Sector*

On the other hand, my examination of the motivation of civil servants lends no support to the proposition that they should be fervent advocates of a reduction in the size of the public sector relative to the private sector. Doing a 'good professional job' requires only that Ministers can be persuaded to act consistently in relating their political aspirations to the resources available. It offers no incentive for bureaucrats to restrict the policy tools available by forgoing expansion of the public sector. Nor are promotion prospects enhanced by formulating schemes which drive close colleagues into early retirement, reduce the chances of advancement of younger colleagues, and risk confrontation with the major civil service unions. Anyone who took this line of action would be soon exposed as taking a strong political position offering him only the grim alternatives of retraction, resignation or removal to some departmental Siberia. A positive and influential action by bureaucrats to reduce public sector growth could follow only from mass resignation at the top. I see little prospect of that.

NOTES

1. Reproduced from Institute of Economic Affairs Readings 18 *The Economics of Politics* IEA, London, 1978.
2. Useful expositions of economic theory of bureaucracy by British authors are in Rowley (1977) and Hartley (1977) Chapter 11.
3. As Chief Economic Adviser, Department of Trade and Industry (later Departments of Trade, Industry, Prices and Consumer Protection) from 1973 to 1976. The Chief Economic Adviser in these Departments is a Deputy Secretary, jointly responsible for the management of five Divisions headed by a statistician or economist of Under-Secretary rank. In my time the total strength of these Divisions was about 500.
4. A well-known fallacy in economics is to suppose that the sole seller of separately identifiable produce or service necessarily has monopoly power. Studies of industrial concentration which base their findings on *types of product* rather than on market shares have to be interpreted very carefully. Monopoly can only be defined in terms of *market power*, i.e. the sensitivity of the quantity demanded of a product or service to a change in its price. For example, a visit to a concert is a substitute for a dinner in a restaurant as well as a substitute for another concert or a visit to the theatre. All these activities are competing ways of deriving satisfaction (utility) from an evening out.
5. After writing this I came across an intriguing statement by George Pottinger, the senior Scottish civil servant imprisoned for his part in the Poulson affair. Talking of Poulson he writes (*The Scotsman*, 22 April 1978): 'He found strange my assertion that civil servants had no politics and there was nothing a good civil servant liked more than a change in government and the chance to look at policies from the opposite point of view.' This is a clear indication of the intellectual attractions which go with policy formulation.
6. As epitomised in the splendid line in Louis Macniece's cynical poem, *Bagpipe Music*: 'sit on your arse for fifty years and hang your hat on a pension'.
7. In his *Bureaucracy* (1944), which is surprisingly sympathetic to his subject matter, Ludwig von Mises regards the pursuit of ease as the essential difference between European and US bureaucrats: 'In a properly arranged civil service system the promotion to higher ranks depends principally on seniority. The heads of the bureaus are for the most part old men who know that after a few years they will be retired. Having spent the greater part of their lives in subordinate positions, they have lost vigour and initiative. They shun innovations and improvements. They look on every project for reform as a disturbance of their quiet. Their rigid conservatism frustrates all endeavours of a cabinet minister to adjust the service to changed conditions. They look down upon the cabinet minister as an inexperienced layman. In all countries with settled bureaucracy people used to say: "The cabinets come and go, but the bureaus remain".' (p. 70) He adds the intriguing suggestion that able intellectuals might still be attracted by a bureaucratic career if only because of the leisure it would allow to pursue their talents as writers or artists!

REFERENCES

Borcherding, T. E. (ed.) (1977) *Budgets and Bureaucrats: The Sources of Government Growth* Duke University Press, Durham, North Carolina.
Hartley, K. (1977) *Problems of Economic Policy* Allen & Unwin, London.
von Mises, L. (1944) *Bureaucracy* Yale University Press, New Haven, Conn.
Niskanen, W. A. (1973) *Bureaucracy: Servant or Master?* Hobart Paperback 5, Institute of Economic Affairs, London.
Peacock, A. T. and Wiseman, J. (1979) 'Approaches to the analysis of government expenditure growth' *Public Finance Quarterly* Vol. 7, No. 1.
Rowley, C. K. (1977) 'Efficiency in the public sector' in C. Bowe (ed.) *Industrial Efficiency and the Role of Government* HMSO, London.
Tullock, G. (1976) *The Vote Motive* Hobart Paperback 9, Institute of Economic Affairs, London.

Index of Names